10—

Delighted to meet you!

The Future of Islam

The Future of Islam

John L. Esposito

OXFORD
UNIVERSITY PRESS

2010

OXFORD
UNIVERSITY PRESS

Oxford University Press, Inc., publishes works that further
Oxford University's objective of excellence
in research, scholarship, and education.

Oxford New York
Auckland Cape Town Dar es Salaam Hong Kong Karachi
Kuala Lumpur Madrid Melbourne Mexico City Nairobi
New Delhi Shanghai Taipei Toronto

With offices in
Argentina Austria Brazil Chile Czech Republic France Greece
Guatemala Hungary Italy Japan Poland Portugal Singapore
South Korea Switzerland Thailand Turkey Ukraine Vietnam

Published by Oxford University Press, Inc.
198 Madison Avenue, New York, NY 10016

www.oup.com

Oxford is a registered trademark of Oxford University Press

Library of Congress Cataloging-in-Publication Data
Esposito, John L.
The future of Islam / John L. Esposito.
p. cm.
Includes index.
ISBN 978-0-19-516521-0
1. Islam—21st century. 2. Islam—Relations.
3. Islamic countries—Relations—United States.
4. United States—Relations—Islamic countries. I. Title.
BP161.3.E867 2010
297.09'051—dc22 2009018732

1 3 5 7 9 8 6 4 2
Printed in the United States of America
on acid-free paper

For Jean
Past, Present, and Future

Contents

Foreword

This is an important book. Those of us who have been on the front line of the effort, since the atrocities of September 11, 2001, to explain Islam in the Western world soon became aware not simply of the widespread ignorance of Muslim religion in both Europe and the United States but also of an entrenched reluctance to see Islam in a more favorable light. People often look balked and vaguely mutinous when, for example, you explain that the Qur'an does not in fact advocate the indiscriminate slaughter of the infidel or the propagation of the faith by the sword, and that even though there is still much to be done to promote gender equality in Muslim countries, the message of the Qur'an was initially friendly to the emancipation of women.

One of the most frequently asked questions is: "Why has Islam not had a reformation?" The query betrays an ignorance of both Islamic and Western history. It assumes that there was something special and unique about the reform movement initiated by Martin Luther (1483–1556) and John Calvin (1509–64) that points to the inherent superiority and progressive nature of our Western culture. In fact, Luther's was a typical premodern reformation, similar to many of the movements of *islah* ("reform") and *tajdid* ("renewal") that have regularly punctuated Muslim history. They all, Muslim or Christian, follow a similar agenda: they attempt to return to the wellsprings of tradition and cast aside the piety of the immediate past. Thus Luther and Calvin sought to return to the "pure" Christianity of the Bible and the Fathers of the Church, in exactly the same way as Ahmed ibn Taymiyyah of Damascus (1263–1328) advocated a return to the Qur'an and the *sunnah* ("customal practice") of the Prophet Muhammad. In his desire to get back to basics, Ibn Taymiyyah also overturned much revered medieval jurisprudence and philosophy, just as Luther and Calvin attacked the medieval scholastic theologians; like any Muslim reformation, therefore, their movement was both reactionary and revolutionary.

Reform movements usually occur during a period of cultural change or in the wake of a great political disaster, when the old answers no longer suffice and reformers seek to bring the tradition up to date so that it can meet the contemporary challenge. The Protestant Reformation took place during the profound societal changes of the early modern period, when people found that they could no longer practice their faith in the same way as their medieval ancestors. It was, therefore, the product rather than a cause of modernization, and instead of being regarded as the instigator of change, Luther should rather be seen as the spokesman of a current trend. A similar process is now under way in the Muslim world, where the modernization process has been even more problematic than that of sixteenth-century Europe, because it has been complicated by the colonial disruption and continued Western influence in the internal affairs of the former colonies.

Again, Western people are often skeptical about the ability of Islam to reform itself and doubt the presence and effectiveness of Muslim reformers, in part because these creative thinkers get little coverage in the Western press. Thanks to this much-needed book, there is no longer any excuse for such ignorance. Professor Esposito has given a clear and informative introduction to the work of such reformers as Tariq Ramadan, Amr Khalid, Shaykh Ali Goma'a, Mustafa Ceric, Tim Winter, and Heba Raouf. Like Luther, these individuals articulate an important trend in Muslim thinking that challenges the common Western view of Islam. This trend clearly does not regard a literal interpretation of scripture as normative; it is well aware that laws and customs have been conditioned by the historical circumstances in which they developed and must be interpreted in the light of this understanding; it regards self-criticism as creative, necessary, and a religious imperative; it abhors terrorism and violence; and it is anxious to initiate a "gender *jihad.*"

Most important, Professor Esposito makes it clear that Western people simply cannot afford to remain uninformed about these developments in the Muslim world. He shows how the failure of Western foreign policy has been one of the causes of the current malaise in the region and that, for example, ignorance about the Sunni/Shia rift in Iraq made it impossible for the United States to identify friends and foes. We now live in one world and share a common predicament. What happens in Gaza or Afghanistan today is likely to have repercussions tomorrow in London or Washington, D.C. To persist in the belief that all Muslims support terrorism, oppose democracy, and are atavistically opposed to freedom is not only counterproductive to Western interests but, as we see in these pages, flies in the face of the evidence, such as that provided in the recent Gallup Poll. Westerners cannot expect Muslims to adopt a more positive view of their cultural values if they themselves persist in cultivating a stereotypical view of Islam that in some significant respects dates back to the Middle Ages. Unless we can learn to live together in a more just and rational way, we are unlikely to have a viable world to hand on to the next generation.

One comes away from this book convinced that the future of Islam does not simply depend on the effectiveness of a few Muslim reformers but that the United States and Europe also have a major role to play. If short-sighted Western policies have helped to create the current impasse, they will, if not corrected, continue to have a negative effect upon the region, will weaken the cause of reform, and play into the hands of extremists. In the Qur'an, God calls all men and women to appreciate the unity and equality of the human race: "O people! Behold, We have created you all out of a male and a female, and have made you into nations and tribes so that you might come to know one another" (49:13). One of the major tasks of our generation is to build a global community, where people of all persuasions can live together in harmony and mutual respect. In writing this book, which will help many Western readers to achieve a more balanced, informed, and nuanced appreciation of the Muslim world, Professor Esposito has made a major contribution.

Karen Armstrong

Acknowledgments

There are so many people to whom I am indebted. I will only mention a few and know others will understand given limitations of space. John Voll, with whom I have collaborated closely and co-authored many times over the years, is always a gold mine of information and advice. Tamara Sonn and I have worked on more academic projects than I can remember, and she can always be counted on for a quick response and close read. Dalia Mogahed and the Gallup World Polls, which provide the most comprehensive and systematic polling of the Muslim world, have enabled us to listen to the voices of Muslims globally on critical issues. Dalia and I, in my capacity as a Gallup Senior Scientist, co-authored *Who Speaks for Islam? What a Billion Muslims Really Think* and have collaborated on other projects involving Gallup World Poll data, which has been a rich resource. Like my other colleagues, Natana DeLong-Bas, Jonathan Brown, and Shamil Idriss were always ready to read, comment, and contribute their suggestions and insights on a moment's notice.

I have been fortunate to have a wonderful group of Georgetown graduate students as researchers at different stages of this project. Melanie Trexler, Abdullah Al-Arian, and Hadia Mubarak provided extensive research that was augmented by Rebecca Skreslet, Fuad Naeem, and Adrien Paul Zakar.

Oxford University Press has a special place in my scholarly life. From 1981, when I nervously drove from Worcester, Massachusetts, to New York to hand-deliver my first Oxford book, until today, I have been privileged to work with so many first-class professionals: presidents like Ed Barry, book and reference editors, and marketing specialists. None has been more important than Cynthia Read, executive editor, who, as a young assistant to the then religion editor, took delivery of my manuscript. While it is customary for an author to thank his/her editor, Cynthia Read has truly been a very special and remarkable editor as well as a good friend, with whom I have worked for more than twenty-five years. She never ceased to be a source of encouragement and critical feedback and is a major reason why I have been an Oxford author all these years. I am fortunate to again have two consummate professionals, India Cooper as copy editor and Joellyn Ausanka as production editor, who as in the past are a pleasure to work with.

Georgetown University and the Center for Muslim-Christian Understanding (now the Prince Alwaleed bin Talal Center for Muslim-Christian Understanding), which I helped create and direct, have been my academic home since 1993. The creation of our Center, as well as support for much of its first decade of existence, was due initially to the generosity of Hasib Sabbagh and his Arab Christian and Muslim colleagues. Our current and future existence and the work of Prince Alwaleed Center are now assured by a generous endowment from Prince Alwaleed bin Talal's Kingdom Foundation. Critical to our existence have been Georgetown presidents Leo O'Donovan, S.J., who made the decision to create the Center and his successor John J. Degioia, Georgetown's current president, consistent in his support for the Center and its mission and my own professional development. I am especially grateful to an extraordinary administrative team that enables the Center and me "to run often and on time"! Alexa Poletto, associate director, Denisse Bonilla Chaoui, executive assistant, and Adam Holmes, program coordinator, are outstanding professionals and friends. They are a seamless team without whom I and my colleagues could not function, let alone be as active, visible, and effective.

Whatever I may have accomplished or achieved in life is due in large part to the presence and influence of my family. My parents, John and Mary Esposito, provided the most loving and supportive environment, in which they motivated and inspired "their boys" to care about family, society, and education and to value values. My brothers, Lou and Rick, have each in their own ways carried on their legacy. Jean Esposito, wife and life partner, has always managed to balance her life, career, and me and made the past forty-five years richer and more meaningful than I could have ever imagined. My best editor and critic, she is the reason I am not still a graduate student with five "incomplete" grades! Mandy, our sheltie, has quite literally always been at my desk-side throughout the writing of this book, the first to go to my office and the last to leave.

Finally, I end at the beginning. Ismail Ragi al-Faruqi took a reluctant Temple University graduate student, who insisted he would only take one course on Islam, and opened up a world that set me on a journey that has now spanned four decades of discovery and experiences. That journey has been both my profession and vocation; my experiences with so many Muslims across the world have enriched my life immeasurably.

Washington, D.C.
August 2009

The Future of Islam

Introduction

The lives and expectations of many were shattered by the 9/11 terrorist attacks against the World Trade Center and the Pentagon. Within hours a handful of terrorists had transformed the twenty-first century into a world dominated by an American-led war against global terrorism and strengthened the image of Islam and Muslims as a religion and a people to be feared and fought. Some spoke of a clash of civilizations. Others asked, "What went wrong?" or "Why do they hate us?"

America's expansive war on terror, continued acts of violence and terrorism by Muslim extremists, widespread anti-Americanism across the Muslim world (and much of the non-Muslim world), and the spread of Islamophobia have raised many questions about the future of Islam and of Muslims. For many, the war on global terrorism has come to be seen as a war against Islam and the Muslim world. America is seen as engaged in a neo-colonial attempt to redraw the map of the Middle East in light of American political and economic interests. The detention without trial and the abuse of Muslim prisoners, charges of the desecration of the Quran, the denigration of Islam and torture of prisoners at Abu Ghraib and Guantanamo, and the erosion of the civil liberties of Muslims through the use of secret evidence and the provisions of the Patriot Act undermined the claims of President George W. Bush's administration to be promoting democracy and human rights.

The Future of Islam seeks to understand the struggle for reform in Islam, sometimes described as a struggle for the soul of Islam, to explore the religious, cultural, and political diversity of Muslims facing daunting challenges in Muslim countries and in the West, to clarify the debate and dynamics of Islamic reform, to examine the attempt to combat religious extremism and terrorism, and to look into the future of Muslim-West relations.

This book is the culmination of my work on Islam and Muslim politics. I have drawn on my work and experiences over several decades, begun at a time when Islam was relatively invisible on our cognitive and demographic map in the West. Today, it is hard for many of us to appreciate that only a few short decades ago, this book would have been unthinkable. Neither Islam nor Muslim politics was particularly visible or seemed to be relevant to affairs in the West. This lack of knowledge and interest in government, academia, and the media was also reflected in a dearth of publishing on Islam, as a review of publications and library holdings prior to the 1970s will demonstrate. In many ways my professional career chronicles and reflects the sea change that has occurred in just a few short decades, as Islam and Muslim politics have moved from offstage to center stage, and we have witnessed an explosion of interest in and coverage of them.

Today, Islam is among the fastest-growing religions in Africa, Asia, Europe, and America. More than 1.5 billion Muslims live within some fifty-seven Muslim-majority countries and constitute significant minorities in Europe (where some twenty million Muslims make Islam the second-largest religion) and America (whose six to eight million Muslims make it the third-largest and fastest-growing religion there). Islam is more dispersed around the globe and interactive with other faiths and societies than at any other time in history. Its capitals and major cities cover a global expanse from Cairo to Jakarta in the Muslim world and from New York, Detroit, and Los Angeles to Paris, London, and Berlin in the West. For Americans and Europeans, understanding Islam and Muslims is both a domestic imperative (to know one's fellow citizens and neighbors) and a foreign policy priority.

It is important at the outset to remember that the topic of Islam and of Muslims is political as well as religious. Islam today is not only a faith that inspires personal piety and provides meaning and guidance for this life and the next. It is also an ideology and worldview that informs Muslim politics and society. Muslim governments and opposition movements, religious leaders and laity, appeal to and use religion to legitimate their beliefs, policies, and actions. Rulers in Saudi Arabia, Sudan, Iran, and elsewhere appeal to Islam for legitimacy, as do political and social movements, mainstream and extremist. Muslim societies now are often polarized between secular and more religiously oriented sectors.

Because of the impact of Islam on foreign affairs and international relations, Islam, specifically political Islam, has been and continues to be a concern for policymakers, political analysts, and commentators. As such, Islamic political and social activism is a highly contentious topic. It is fraught with contending and conflicting interpretations, often broadly divided into two camps sometimes characterized as the confrontational and the accommodationist. Members of the former believe that all Islamic activists are a threat, whereas adherents of the latter, the school of thought to which I belong, distinguish between moderate or nonviolent activists who function in mainstream society and a dangerous minority of violent extremists and terrorists.[1]

The Future of Islam is about all of our futures. Islam and Muslims today are integral players in global history. They are part of the mosaic of American and European societies. In a world in which we too often succumb to the dichotomy between "us" and "them," we are challenged to transcend (though not deny) our differences, affirm our common humanity, and realize that "we," whether we like it or not, are interconnected and co-dependent, the co-creators of our societies and our world.

The most important lesson I have learned from my years as an academic and as a student of Islam and Muslim societies is obvious and yet elusive. If you want to know what people believe, if you want to grasp the reality of their everyday lives, you have to look, to use the current academic jargon, at both "text and context." Understanding the faith of others requires not only knowledge of the sacred sources of a religion (scriptures, creeds, dogmas, and laws) but also knowledge of what people actually believe and do. Appreciation of the essentials of a religion cannot exclude awareness of the diversity of its forms and expressions. However important the Hebrew Bible (or Old Testament) and the New Testament, understanding Judaism and Christianity also requires that you observe what Jews and Christians believe and practice in specific historical, cultural, and social contexts. Judaism is Torah and Talmud. Judaism in Ethiopia, Israel, and New York may have an underlying similarity, but in fact its cultural expressions differ enormously. Similarly, beyond their shared identification with Jesus Christ, Western Christians and their Eastern counterparts have rich theologies and practices that are conditioned by their unique historical and cultural experiences. Although many tend to see Islam and Muslims through images drawn from Saudi Arabia or Iran, Muslim practice varies widely from Africa and Asia to America and Europe.

All too often we succumb to a common temptation, comparing "our ideal" to "others' realities." When discussing their faith, believers often present its ideals and distinguish it from the faith of others by emphasizing the negative realities, beliefs, and actions of certain others, however unrepresentative they may be. In a Judeo-Christian culture, we have become sensitized to respect for the other, or at least feel a need to act publicly in a politically correct manner. We have only begun to realize that Muslims, the other Children of Abraham, and Hindus, Buddhists, and Sikhs are entitled to the same respect. If a group of Jews or Christians had been responsible for the bombing of the World Trade Center, few would have attributed it to the beliefs of mainstream Judaism or Christianity. The assassination of Prime Minister Yitzak Rabin by a Jewish fundamentalist was not attributed to something in mainstream Judaism; nor was the clergy sex abuse scandal attributed to the heart of Catholicism. The most heinous crimes committed by Jewish or Christian extremists are not tagged as reflections of militant or radical Christianity or Judaism. The individuals who commit such crimes are often dismissed as fanatics, extremists, or madmen rather than labeled Christian or Jewish fundamentalists. By contrast, too often the statements and acts of Muslim extremists and terrorists are portrayed as integral to mainstream Islam. I am not denying that Muslims commit outrageous acts of violence and terrorism but rather questioning the way these are identified and equated with the faith of Muslim majorities.

The brushstroking of Islam and the majority of Muslims with the acts of a minority of terrorists and the need, as President Barack Obama and others have stated, to rebuild relations with the Muslim world have been major motivations for writing *The Future of Islam*. I want to tell the story about how we got to where we are and what we need to understand and do to create what President Obama calls "a new way forward."

I address key questions and issues in a series of chapters that, although interrelated, can also stand on their own. Among the many questions explored are: Is the future of Islam to be one of reformation or revolution? Are Islam and modernity compatible? How representative and widespread is Islamic fundamentalism? Is it a threat to Muslim societies and the West? Is Islam compatible with modern notions of democracy, rule of law, gender equality, and human rights? Can Muslim minority communities be loyal citizens in America and Europe?

Chapter 1, "The Many Faces of Islam and Muslims," provides a brief introduction to Islam and Muslims, to Islam *in* the West, and to Islam *and* the West. Critical to understanding the future of Islam is its diversity, religious, cultural, and political. Who and where are Muslims? What do Muslims believe, and why? What is the difference between Sunni and Shia Muslims, and does it matter?

Regrettably the impact of global terrorism has created a climate of fear and distrust of Islam and mainstream Muslims. It is important to address the questions: Why haven't Muslims spoken out? Is there a danger that Islam will sweep across Europe and transform it into what some have called "Eurabia"? Responding to these concerns requires a hard look at Muslims in the West. What experiences and challenges do American and European Muslims face? Have they adapted? If not, why not? If so, then how? And given attacks in the United States and England, Spain, and Scotland, what is the nature and extent of the threat of Muslim terrorism?

A common refrain in recent years has been that Islam and the West are involved in a centuries-long and inevitable clash because of an unbridgeable divide in our principles and values and that this is the source of anti-Americanism and terrorism. So, what do Muslims today really think and want? What are their concerns, fears, and hopes? Part of the problem policymakers and the public have in understanding the diverse world of Islam and Muslims is that they are faced with contending and often diametrically opposed opinions of experts and pseudo-experts and the outspoken threats of the extremist or terrorist minority. The missing link has been the voices of the mainstream Muslim majority. Today, we do have direct access to mainstream Muslim views on a broad spectrum of topics. At many points, we will look at data from major polls, in particular those of the Gallup Organization, whose World Poll is the largest and most comprehensive and systematic poll of Muslim countries and societies globally.

In 1979–80 the world looked on stunned as an aged ayatollah, living in exile in a suburb of Paris, led a revolution that overthrew one of the most powerful rulers in the Middle East. For many, Iran's Islamic revolution was the first sign of an Islamic resurgence that had in fact begun a decade earlier. The extent to which this reassertion of religion occurred in Muslim politics and society and in some of the more modernizing Muslim countries challenged many of the beliefs and expectations of experts on modernization and development and was seen as a threat to Western allies and interests. Chapter 2, "God in Politics," provides the background and context for understanding political Islam, the role of religion in politics and society, and its impact on Muslim societies and the West. What are the major events that have shaped Muslim politics and our perceptions of Islam and the Muslim world? Why and how did religion emerge in Muslim politics? Are Islamic political and social movements a monolithic threat now and in the future?

What were and are the root causes of global terrorism, and what role does religion play? Why and how did national opposition and extremist movements give rise to a global jihad? Who were its ideologues and leaders? What events and actions influenced Osama bin Laden and the formation of al-Qaeda and its role in the spread of global terrorism? We will also discuss the significance and influence of Wahhabi/Salafi Islam, the role of Muslim authoritarian governments, the impact of Sunni-Shii sectarianism, and the influence of American foreign policy.

Critical to the future of Islam and Muslims and countering global terrorism in the twenty-first century is the issue of Islamic reform. Chapter 3, "Islam Needs a Reformation," will address critical questions and issues in Islamic reform. Who are some of the major reformers, the major religious thinkers and televangelists of Islam? What do they identify as and say about key issues in Islam and in relations between Muslims and the West in the twenty-first century?

Since the late nineteenth century, Islamic reformers have grappled with the relationship of Islam to the changing realities of modern life. This chapter will look at the roots of reform and the extent to which it continues today from Egypt to Indonesia as a broad array of Muslim religious leaders and intellectuals, men and women, traditionalists and more modern-oriented reformists, discuss and debate in a dynamic process of reinterpretation and reform. As our discussion will demonstrate, a lively debate exists on issues as diverse as the extent and limits of reform, the role of tradition and its relationship to change, women's empowerment, legitimate and illegitimate forms of resistance and violence, suicide bombing and martyrdom, the dangers of fundamentalism, the question of Islam's compatibility with democracy and religious pluralism, and the role of Muslims in the West. The reformers debunk entrenched perceptions: that Islam is medieval, static, and incapable of change; that Islam is a violent religion that also degrades women; that Islam and democracy are incompatible; that Muslims do not speak out against religious extremism and terrorism; that they reject religious pluralism and interfaith dialogue, and they certainly cannot be loyal citizens of non-Muslim countries.

At the same time, a new breed of popular Muslim televangelists blend appeals to Islam with motivational speaking to mobilize young men and women, middle class and poor, urging them to combine faith and action to improve their lives. Like Christian theologians and preachers who have become religious media stars, Muslim televangelists reach millions, sometimes hundreds of millions, filling huge auditoriums and sports stadiums and spreading their message on DVDs, video and audio tapes, satellite television and radio, and the Internet.

Televangelists and their organizations provide a religious alternative to traditional clerics, mosques, muftis, and fatwas. Prominent ulama may call for a greater centralization of religious authority, but these popular alternative outlets enable Muslim televangelism, like Christian televangelism, to move in the opposite direction, toward a decentralization of religious authority. Most preach a direct, down-to-earth message, dispensing advice on everyday problems, promoting a practical, concrete Islamic spirituality of empowerment and success in this life as well as the next. Their audiences are drawn not so much by their religious or scholarly credentials as by their personalities, preaching styles, and distinctive messages.

Finally, where do we go from here? What are the critical issues and obstacles that face Muslims and that affect America's and Europe's relationship with the Muslim world? In his inaugural address, President Obama distanced himself from the Bush administration's failed policies and expressed the desire that America reemerge as a global and principled leader, one that did not sacrifice "our legacy," our principles and values, in the name of fighting a war on terrorism. Acknowledging the seriousness of the fracture in our relationship, he expressed a desire for the restoration of "the same respect and partnership that America had with the Muslim world as recently as twenty or thirty years ago." Obama spoke directly to the peoples of the Muslim world: "To the Muslim world, we seek a new way forward, based on mutual interest and mutual respect."

Chapter 4, "America and the Muslim World: Building a New Way Forward," looks at the challenges of Islamophobia, failed American foreign and domestic policies, the roles of militant Christian Zionists and the media, and the continued threat posed by religious extremism and terrorism. Is there a need for a new paradigm in Muslim-West relations? How can the Obama administration rebuild America's image, role, and influence in the Muslim world?

What would an agenda for reform look like?

However different in orientation, a broad spectrum of religious leaders and Muslim intellectuals, as we shall see, have come together and drafted major statements and undertaken projects to both address the threat of religious extremism and establish a stronger basis for better relations between Islam and Christianity, as well as Muslims and the West. At the same time, international organizations, including the United Nations and the World Economic Forum, as well as major religious organizations, have brought together groups of religious, political, corporate, media, and nongovernmental organizations in efforts to improve and strengthen Muslim-West relations and build a global culture of pluralism through international dialogue and jointly sponsored activities and projects.

Finally, chapter 4 looks at the role of public diplomacy in a new paradigm to rebuild America's image and role in the Muslim world. How best can the United States reach out to its target audience, the moderate mainstream, and respond effectively to the fears and concerns of potential radicals? What would a new approach to both America's authoritarian allies and Islamist groups look like?

Chapter One

The Many Faces of Islam and Muslims

For many, understanding Islam and Muslims can be confusing. Muslim leaders speak of Islam as a religion of peace and justice; Osama bin Laden and other Muslim terrorists slaughter non-Muslims and Muslims globally. President George W. Bush referred to Islam as a religion of peace; the evangelist Franklin Graham called Islam an evil religion; Samuel Huntington, prominent Harvard professor and author of *The Clash of Civilizations,* wrote, "Islam has bloody borders . . . and innards." But, as President Barack Obama has pointed out, "Islam has demonstrated through words and deeds the possibilities of religious tolerance and racial equality. . . . Partnership between America and Islam must be based on what Islam is, not what it isn't."

Muslims and non-Muslims alike face new challenges in the twenty-first century. The forces of globalization have made us interdependent politically, economically, and environmentally: mass migrations of Muslims in the twentieth century created new immigrant communities in America and Europe that have enriched societies but also resulted in social unrest. However, whatever the hopes and fears of Muslims and non-Muslims, 9/11 and "the war on global terrorism" signaled a major transformation in global history and relations between the Muslim world and the West.

The 9/11 terrorist attacks against the World Trade Center and the Pentagon and subsequent acts of terrorism in Europe shattered the lives of many, in what some characterized as an Islamic threat that was now both domestic and foreign. The impact of the attacks in New York and Washington, as well as in Madrid and London, has raised fresh questions about the religion of Islam and the loyalty of Muslims.

In the twenty-first century, the growth of global terrorism and an exponential increase in anti-Americanism and anti-Westernism in general have been accompanied in America and some European countries by right-wing politicians, political commentators, media personalities, and religious leaders who have conflated mainstream Islam with terrorism. They have fed an increase in discrimination against Islam and Muslims ("Islamophobia"), resulting in widespread suspicion of mainstream Muslims, hate crimes, and the belief that Islam, not just Muslim extremism, is a threat.

9/11 has been characterized as the result of a clash of civilizations whose peoples have diametrically opposed principles, values, and interests. Some have seen this as a battle between global terrorists and the West, but many others have cast it as a conflict between a traditional, religious, authoritarian, anti-Western Islamic tradition and a modern, democratic, capitalist, Western secular worldview. Critics charge that Islam is incompatible with democracy, pluralism, and human rights, that it is the underlying cause for the fact that many Muslim countries are authoritarian, limit free speech, and have weak civil societies. At the same time, many Muslims believe that preserving their Islamic traditions and values is essential to any success they will have in strengthening their societies and fostering democratization and development. Is Islam the root cause of the problem or part of the solution?

Islam or Islams?

While we commonly speak of "Islam," in fact many Islams or interpretations of Islam exist. The images and realities of Islam and of Muslims are multiple and diverse: religiously, culturally, economically, and politically. Muslims are the majority in some fifty-seven countries, and they represent many nationalities, languages, ethnic and tribal groups, and customs.

Most of the world's 1.5 billion Muslims are not Arab but Asian or African. Only about one in five of the world's Muslims are Arabs (and there are also Arab Christians in many Arab countries, and have been since the time of Jesus). The largest Muslim communities live in Indonesia, Bangladesh, Pakistan, India, and Nigeria rather than Saudi Arabia, Egypt, or Iran. Millions of Muslims also live in Europe and North America, where they now represent the second- and third-largest religion, respectively. As a result, major Muslim communities today are not only in Dakar, Khartoum, Cairo, Damascus, Riyadh, Tehran, Islamabad, and Kuala Lumpur but also in London, Paris, Rome, Berlin, New York, and Washington, D.C. Muslim languages include not only Arabic but Persian, Turkish, Urdu, Swahili, Bahasa Indonesian, and Chinese, as well as English, French, German, Danish, and Spanish.

Like all powerful and compelling religions and ideologies, Islam has a history in all of these diverse cultures that reveals both a transcendent and a dark side. Like other religions, Islam affirms the existence of a supreme, ultimate reality. For Muslims, Allah (Arabic for "the God") is the one, true God—all-powerful, compassionate, and merciful God, creator and Lord of the universe, and judge on the Last Day of humankind. He calls upon and enables human beings to transcend their limitations, follow his righteous path, lead morally responsible lives, and work to create a just society. At the same time, Islam, like other faiths, has historically been a source not only of compassion, morality, and virtue but also of terror, injustice, and oppression.

Experiencing the Dark Side

Few cared to know about the Muslim world prior to the Iranian revolution of 1979. Islam and Muslims were not seen as particularly consequential or relevant. Today, Islam and Muslims generally are equated by some with the vitriolic statements of Muslim preachers of hate, Osama bin Laden and al-Qaeda, Sunni-Shii clashes, suicide bombings, beheadings, the destruction of mosques and slaughter of innocent men, women, and children in Iraq, Pakistan, India, and Afghanistan, and, closer to home, terrorist attacks in Europe. Christian televangelists, political commentators, and politicians dismiss Islam as an evil and violent religion and mock the Prophet Muhammad as a pedophile. The net result is that an increasing number of Americans see Islam, not just Muslim extremism, as *the* problem facing the world today:

A *Washington Post*/ABC News poll in 2006 "found that nearly half of Americans—46%—have a negative view of Islam, seven percentage points higher than a few months after Sept. 11, 2001."[1]

In Europe, Islam was overwhelmingly singled out as the religion most prone to violence, with percentages of those who agreed with this ranging from 63 percent in Britain to 87 percent in France and 88 percent in the Netherlands.[2] Is it any wonder that Islam and Muslims, not just an extremist minority, are the focus of Islamophobia and victims of Muslim bashing?

"Islamophobia" is a new term for a now widespread phenomenon. We are all very familiar with "anti-Semitism" or "racism," but there was no comparable term to describe the hostility, prejudice, and discrimination directed toward Islam and the 1.5 billion Muslims in the world. In 1997, an independent think tank on ethnicity and cultural diversity, the Runnymede Trust, coined the term "Islamophobia" to describe what they saw as a prejudice rooted in the "different" physical appearance of Muslims as well as an intolerance of their religious and cultural beliefs. Like other forms of group prejudice, it thrives on ignorance and fear of the unknown, which is spreading throughout much of the non-Muslim world. At a 2004 UN conference, "Confronting Islamophobia: Education for Tolerance and Understanding," Kofi Annan addressed the international scope of this problem:

> When the world is compelled to coin a new term to take account of increasingly widespread bigotry—that is a sad and troubling development. Such is the case with "Islamophobia." . . . There is a need to unlearn the stereotypes that have become so entrenched in so many minds and so much of the media. Islam is often seen as a monolith . . . [and] Muslims as opposed to the West. . . . The pressures of living together with people of different cultures and different beliefs from one's own are real. . . . But that cannot justify demonization, or the deliberate use of fear for political purposes. That only deepens the spiral of suspicion and alienation.[3]

But what do we know about Muslims who are citizens in America? Many of the facts may surprise you.

Making It in America

Islam in America has a broad spectrum of believers representing one of the most diverse communities in the world. Dalia Mogahed, executive director of the Gallup Center for Muslim Studies, says Muslims "are in every way a cross-section of the nation . . . the only religious community without a majority race."[4] Muslims are Americans who came here from sixty-eight different countries as well as indigenous African Americans and converts from a variety of ethnic backgrounds. According to Gallup's 2009 report *Muslim Americans: A National Portrait*, 28 percent of American Muslims identify themselves as "white"; 18 percent say they are Asian, and a surprising 18 percent classify themselves as "other," perhaps reflecting identification with more than one group. One percent say they are Hispanic. Those who identify themselves as African American Muslims make up 35 percent.

This spectrum of Muslims in America, some who came to pursue political and religious freedom, economic prosperity, or education, others who were the descendants of slaves shaped by the civil rights struggle and issues of economic and social justice, represents one of our most diverse religious groups, economically, racially, and politically. As Tayyibah Taylor, founding editor in chief of *Azizah* magazine, has observed, Muslim diversity "gives us access to an amazing array of ideas and . . . solutions. Superimposing the cultural elasticity of Islam on the cultural elasticity of the United States, we cannot only respect . . . diversity . . . but leverage it to mine our various talents."[5]

Muslims in America are a very young group. The sample size of Muslims sixty-five and older in the Gallup study was too small to report, but of the major faith groups they have the highest number of young adults ages eighteen to twenty-nine (36 percent versus 18 percent in the general U.S. population) and also the highest percentage of people ages thirty to forty-four (37 percent versus 26 percent for Americans overall). Jihad Saleh Williams, program and outreach coordinator for the Congressional Muslim Staffers Association, believes that when Muslims invest in their youth, "they cultivate the next generation of American leadership to expand the traditions of pluralism democracy [*sic*]. America's global standing as a land of opportunity depends . . . on the successful unfolding of this process."[6]

Education is a priority for many Muslims, who, after Jews, are the most educated religious community surveyed in the United States. Forty percent of Muslims say they have a college degree or more, compared to 29 percent of Americans overall.[7] Muslim women in America, unlike their Jewish counterparts, are statistically as likely as Muslim men to hold college or postgraduate degrees. Muslim women also report monthly household incomes more nearly equal to men's, compared with women and men in other faith groups.[8]

Muslims reflect the socioeconomic diversity seen in the general U.S. population. Asian and white Muslims are the most educated racial groups both in the general U.S. population and among Muslims. African American Muslims, also resembling their racial peers, are less likely than Asian, white, or "other" race American Muslims to report having at least a college degree. Like the general population, Muslims in America also reflect income disparities along racial lines. Muslim Asian Americans are among the most likely and Muslim African Americans are the least likely to report high incomes.[9]

Over the past few decades, the vast majority of American Muslims have become economically and increasingly politically integrated into mainstream American society. Muslims resemble the rest of the U.S. population in terms of work. They represent men and women spanning the socioeconomic spectrum: professionals (doctors, lawyers, engineers, and educators), corporate executives, small business owners, or blue-collar workers and laborers. In fact, 70 percent of Muslim Americans report that they have a job (paid or unpaid) compared to 64 percent of Americans overall. However, a higher proportion (24 percent) are self-employed. Most significantly, among nonworking American Muslims, 31 percent are full-time students as compared to 10 percent in the general population.[10]

A look at Muslims globally illustrates the advantages enjoyed by American Muslims, who are much more able to find work. In contrast to the 70 percent of American Muslims who report having a job, the figures for Muslims in Europe show a radically different picture: 38 percent in the U.K., 45 percent in France, and 53 percent in Germany. Across the predominantly Muslim countries surveyed in the Gallup study, "being engaged in some kind of labor activity ranges from a low of 31% in Pakistan to a high of 59% in Indonesia."[11] American Muslims' better employment position is reflected in the fact that a majority of American Muslims, 71 percent, agree that most people who want to get ahead in America can succeed if they are willing to work hard. This is a higher proportion than in the American public as a whole. African American Muslims, affected by racial discrimination and poorer economic conditions, however, are more disillusioned than the Muslim immigrant majority.[12]

The advantageous position of Muslims in America when compared to Muslims globally is also reflected in their satisfaction with their lives: 41 percent report that they are thriving, which is similar to Americans overall and much higher than Muslims in all other Western and Muslim countries except Germany and Saudi Arabia. On the other hand, 56 percent report that they are "struggling," versus 50 percent of Americans overall.[13] While Muslims have made significant progress in America, since the 9/11 attacks many have found themselves under intense scrutiny from airport profiling and questioning, wiretapping, and mosque and home surveillance. More than half of those surveyed by the Pew Research Center say it is more difficult to be a Muslim since that date; they believe that they are singled out by the government for extra surveillance.[14]

Several indicators of Muslims' feelings reflect a sense of discomfort. As a group Muslim Americans report feeling less well rested and less respected than those in most other religious groups; they are least likely to experience happiness or enjoyment and more likely than respondents in most other groups to experience worry and anger. Signs of social alienation, such as more pessimism than other groups about the future of their communities, lower volunteerism than most other groups, and lower percentages registered to vote, especially among the youth, surface in the Gallup poll. Sixty-four percent are registered to vote, which is the lowest percentage among religious groups, and among youths the percentage (51 percent) is even lower. "There is still a sense among American Muslims of being excluded from the mainstream," said Ahmed Younis, a senior analyst at Gallup, "and among young people that's more acute."[15] Lack of political engagement and a political presence has fed a feeling of exclusion, but there are some indications that this is slowly changing. Today, Muslims have become more visible in American political life: two Muslims now serve in the U.S. Congress, with others increasingly active in local politics. Muslim organizations have also become more visible in lobbying Congress.

The diversity of Muslim Americans is clearly reflected in their political views. They are the religious group that is the most evenly spread out along the political spectrum. Thirty-eight percent claim to be moderate, and others are equally divided on either side (29 percent liberal or very liberal and 25 percent conservative or very conservative). They resemble Jews' political ideology the most and Mormons' the least.

Despite their political diversity and the fact that fewer than half of American Muslims indicate they are Democrats, Muslims overwhelmingly (eight to one, including both men and women) favored Obama over McCain in the 2008 presidential race, the highest percentage of all religious groups surveyed.[16]

In a Project MAPS/Zogby International American Muslim Poll, 87 percent said Muslims should financially support worthy non-Muslim political candidates. Contrary to the conventional wisdom, 44 percent of Muslims cited domestic policy as a more important factor in influencing their votes versus 34 percent who cited foreign policy.[17]

The Many Challenges of "Making It in America"

Peering into a crystal ball of the twenty-first century, the future of Muslims in America looks very positive, given their youth, educational and employment profiles, and growing population, which make them a potential political force. But this optimism is tempered by the realization, as we will now see and throughout this volume discuss, that when asked in a 2005 Gallup poll what they admired about Islam, 57 percent of Americans responded "nothing" or "I don't know." Understandably, many negative attitudes have been influenced by the attacks of 9/11 and the threat of global terrorism. But the gaps in our knowledge of Islam and Muslims, in a post-9/11 world, have also been filled with one-sided, often sensational information, leading us to fear and ostracize these "strangers."

Media are driven not by all the news that is fit to print but all the news that will spike sales and profits. Their bottom-line approach privileges explosive headline events and disproportionately emphasizes conflict and violence. Neo-conservative voices, which were so predominant during the George W. Bush administration, saw the war against global terrorism as an opportunity to implement their belief that America's destiny as "the" global leader was to create a New American Century, one whose agenda often dovetailed with that of hard-line Christian Zionists, a policy to transform the Middle East. The net result has been a tendency to see Islam and the 1.5 billion Muslims in the world, as well as the six to eight million Muslims in America, through the lens of religious extremism and terrorism, allowing the venomous rhetoric and threats of a minority of terrorists to brushstroke and obscure our understanding of the mainstream Muslim majority.

Therefore, any discussion of the future of Islam must look squarely at the multitude of negative voices that should not be taken at face value, voices that need to be examined. Where do popular stereotypes of Islam come from? What have many political pundits, policymakers, and Christian Right preachers said? How have the pictures of Muslims and Islam that they have painted made a difference, and why are these pictures wrong-headed and counterproductive?

ISLAM AND THE PRESIDENTIAL ELECTIONS OF 2008

Muslim alienation could be clearly understood as we witness the many Islamophobic comments made during the 2008 American presidential campaign. "I am not a Muslim." "I am not a Muslim." "I am not a Muslim." It is difficult to count the number of times Barack Obama or his campaign believed it necessary to reassure the American electorate that the Democratic candidate for president was not a Muslim. Although Barack Obama is a self-proclaimed Christian, a practicing Christian, his Muslim name (from his nonpracticing African Muslim father) and the fact that he lived in Indonesia and attended a Muslim school fed intense speculation that Obama was a Muslim. The report originated from the ironically named *Insight* magazine, owned by the same company as the *Washington Times*. Obama had noted in his two books, *Dreams from My Father* and *The Audacity of Hope*, that he spent two years in a Muslim school and another two years in a Catholic school while living in Indonesia from age six to age ten. However, despite his personal assurances and his campaign's charges that the story was "appallingly irresponsible," the rumors and charges persisted.[18]

The Obama campaign's sensitivity, even hypersensitivity, on this issue was clear. Their responses sounded like modern-day versions of denials during the Communist Cold War: "I am not now nor have I ever been a Muslim." Some Muslim observers, understanding the political sensitivities, nevertheless wondered why Obama never said: "I am not a Muslim. But, on the other hand, what's wrong with being a Muslim?"

Candidate Obama was careful not to visit a mosque or be photographed with Muslims. In Dearborn, zealous campaign workers were careful to remove two Muslim women wearing hijabs from a photo op with the Democratic candidate. Despite the facts and all the supportive data, 12 percent of Americans, fed by both Islamophobic Web sites and anti-Obama blogs, doggedly clung to the belief that he was hiding his real identity. Critics continued to scrutinize his family background, arguing that whether his "absent" Kenyan father was a practicing Muslim or not, Obama was "technically" a Muslim, and calling his boyhood primary school an Indonesian madrasa with a deliberate connotation of radicalism.

The issue continued throughout the campaign. Colin Powell in his endorsement of Barack Obama spoke forcefully to his concern about senior members of his own (Republican) party:

> I'm also troubled by, not what Senator McCain says, but what members of the party say. And it is permitted to be said such things as, "Well, you know that Mr. Obama is a Muslim." Well, the correct answer is, he is not a Muslim, he's a Christian. He's always been a Christian. But the really right answer is, what if he is? Is there something wrong with being a Muslim in this country? The answer's no, that's not America. Is there something wrong with some seven-year-old Muslim-American kid believing that he or she could be president? Yet, I have heard senior members of my own party drop the suggestion, "He's a Muslim and he might be associated [with] terrorists." This is not the way we should be doing it in America.[19]

SILENCING THE MUSLIM MAJORITY

Reasons for the Obama campaign's extreme cautiousness and sensitivity about the political consequences of any association with Muslims were illustrated at the Democratic convention. Dr. Ingrid Mattson, a Canadian convert to Islam and a prominent scholar at Hartford Seminary in

Connecticut, was invited to represent the Muslim community at the first-ever interfaith prayer service at the Democratic nominating convention. Dr. Mattson is also president of the Islamic Society of North America (ISNA), a large, mainstream Muslim American organization that has existed for several decades, engaged in community organizing, education, and outreach to Muslims, Christians, and Jews. ISNA leaders and Dr. Mattson have met with government officials such as Defense Deputy Secretary Gordon England and Undersecretaries of State Nick Burns and Karen Hughes, who have all praised the association's work.

Yet Frank Gaffney, an outspoken critic of Muslim leaders and organizations, whose editorial track record in the *Washington Times* is long on accusation and short on supportive evidence, asserted with no substantiation or proof that ISNA was "created by the radical, Saudi-financed Muslim Students Association" and is "a Muslim Brotherhood front organization."[20] Neither of these organizations has been indicted for any alleged crimes or support for terrorism, nor has any proof been given to link them with any act of terrorism.

In wondering why the Obama campaign would "allow itself to be put in such company," Gaffney exploited legitimate fears about terrorism and national security, using false accusations to label and condemn moderate professional Muslims and organizations.

Recalling the witch hunts of the McCarthy era, some Muslims in America see it as professional suicide if they have any association with major Muslim leaders or organizations (in contrast to American Jews who are associated with major Jewish organizations like the Zionist Organization of America, the American Jewish Committee, or the pro-Israel lobby AIPAC, the American Israel Public Affairs Committee), or if they oppose questionable or illegal Israeli policies or actions in Israel/Palestine. A coterie of neo-conservative media (the *Weekly Standard* and the *New York Sun* as well as the *Washington Times*) and interrelated Web sites (Campus Watch, Jihad Watch, and *FrontPage*) have coordinated their efforts to demonize Dr. Mattson and ISNA. They repeat unsubstantiated charges and claims, and take quotes out of context to create "facts on the ground." They support and enhance each other's accusations by recycling the same charges, themes, and articles to make it look like masses of people and groups are constantly uncovering new threats. Not only Muslims but also non-Muslim academics, journalists, and policymakers who speak out against their bigotry and disinformation are targeted and attacked as unpatriotic, anti-Semitic apologists for Islam or supporters of suicide bombers.

The goal of these anti-Muslim individuals and organizations is to discredit Muslim organizations and keep them weak and disenfranchised and to marginalize Muslim representation in politics, government, and major American organizations. To illustrate, we need only look at the case of the Obama campaign's first Muslim coordinator, Mazen Asbahi, who, after barely one week on the job, resigned because he was attacked for serving on a board associated with NAIT (the North American Islamic Trust). Gaffney, followed by others, characterized the organization, again offering no proof, as "a powerful instrument in the Islamists' campaign to dominate and radicalize the Muslim community in America."[21] The tactics used to discredit Muslims are a threat not only to American and European individuals but to the very principles and values we cherish, in particular pluralism, tolerance, and civil liberties.

Conservative columnists, some of them best-selling authors or prominent radio and television talk show hosts with large audiences, have regularly employed hate speech and dangerous invective aimed not just at extremists but at Islam and Muslims in general. Ann Coulter advised, "We should invade their countries, kill their leaders and convert them to Christianity."[22]

Will Cummins (a pseudonym) observed, "It is the black heart of Islam, not its black face, to which millions object."[23] According to Michael Savage, "These people [Arabs and Muslims] need to be forcibly converted to Christianity. . . . It's the only thing that can probably turn them into human beings."[24] Several years later, in the October 29, 2007, broadcast of his widely syndicated show featured on some three hundred stations, Savage ranted:

> I'm not gonna put my wife in a hijab. And I'm not gonna put my daughter in a burqa. . . . *And I'm not gettin on my all-fours and praying to Mecca. . . . What kind of religion is this? . . . a book of hate. . . . You can take C-A-I-R and throw 'em out of my country. . . . Without due process. You can take your due process and shove it.*[25]

Savage subsequently brought a suit against CAIR (the Council on American-Islamic Relations), a Muslim civil rights organization. The suit charged that CAIR had misused audio clips of his show (CAIR had rebroadcast just over four minutes from his radio show on its Web site to illustrate his use of anti-Muslim rhetoric) as part of a boycott campaign against his three-hour daily program. The suit was amended to include charges that the group "has consistently sought to silence opponents of violent terror through economic blackmail, frivolous but costly lawsuits, threats of lawsuits and abuses of the legal system." The amended lawsuit also called CAIR a "'political vehicle of international terrorism' and even link[ed] the group with support of al-Qaida."[26] The Northern District of California "dismissed the suit, agreeing that CAIR's use of the material for commentary and criticism was a classic example of fair use."[27]

JOHN MCCAIN AND THE HARD-LINE CHRISTIAN ZIONISTS

Among the most hardcore Islamophobes are American Christian Zionist leaders. In the 2008 presidential campaign, Republican candidate John McCain's desire to credential himself with the Christian Right, whose votes he aggressively sought, led him to embrace pastors of megachurches and televangelists with highly divisive views.

McCain received endorsements from Rod Parsley and John Hagee, prominent Christian Zionists. They believe that the establishment of the State of Israel in 1948 and the return or "restoration" of the Jews to the Holy Land are prerequisites for the Second Coming of Jesus Christ, rooted in biblical prophecies like "Those who curse you [Israel] will be cursed, and those who bless you will be blessed" (Genesis 27:29). Parsley and Hagee, like Jerry Falwell and Pat Robertson, leaders of the Christian Right in the 1980s and 1990s, take a hard-line Zionist position, welcomed by Israeli leaders from Menachem Begin to Ariel Sharon and Benjamin Netanyahu.

Rod Parsley, leader of a twelve-thousand-member megachurch and hailed as John McCain's spiritual adviser and his strong supporter in the Ohio primary, devoted an entire chapter in his 2005 book *Silent No More* to warning of a "war between Islam and Christian civilization." Parsley decries the "spiritual desperation" of America's civil libertarians who advocate the separation of church and state, and he identifies Islam as an "anti-Christ religion" predicated on "deception." Muhammad, he writes, "received revelations from demons and not from the true God." Parsley says, "The fact is that America was founded, in part, with the intention of seeing this false religion destroyed, and I believe September 11, 2001, was a generational call to arms that we can no longer ignore." He warns us, "We find now we have no choice. The time has come. . . . We may already be losing the battle."[28]

For Parsley there is no distinction between violent Muslim extremists and mainstream Muslims. Islam, he believes, "inspired" the 9/11 attacks on an America that "has historically understood herself as a bastion against Islam," and he urges us to believe that Islam is a "faith that fully intends to conquer the world."[29]

The Rev. John Hagee, a strong supporter of McCain, is a major Christian televangelist and Christian Zionist who broadcasts on television and radio in over 190 nations around the globe. In February 2006, he and four hundred Christian and Jewish leaders formed Christians United for Israel (CUFI), an organization that addresses Congress regarding the biblical justification for defense of Israel. Hagee warned his followers:

> Jihad has come to America. If we lose the war to Islamic fascism, it will change the world as we know it. . . . It's here. . . . They are waiting to respond as terrorist cells against this nation. It is a war between the culture of death and the culture of life, liberty and the pursuit of happiness. . . . Radical sects, which include about 200 million Islamics, believe they have a command from God to kill Christians and Jews. . . . Our crisis is that half of America doesn't know the war has started. . . . This is a religious war.[30]

When informed of Hagee's extreme statements about Islam, McCain initially refused to disassociate himself from this pastor. It was only after the revelation of Hagee's past anti-Catholic comments, in which he had argued that Adolf Hitler merely built on the work of the "Roman Church," which he called "the Great Whore of Babylon," that McCain finally severed his ties, although McCain's very close adviser Senator Joseph Lieberman did not.[31]

Many in the Republican Party seemed undisturbed by the offensive campaigns against Obama's "Muslim" name and the use of rumors that he was in fact a Muslim to discredit him. One prominent and outspoken exception, Colin Powell, observed this at the time of his endorsement of Obama and was critical of some senior members of the party who had suggested that Obama was a Muslim and might be associated with terrorists.

The most compelling portion of Powell's remarks came from the story he told, one that illustrates the humanity of American Muslims not often seen in the media:

> I feel strongly about this particular point because of a picture I saw in a magazine. It was a photo essay about troops who are serving in Iraq and Afghanistan. And one picture at the tail end of this photo essay was of a mother in Arlington Cemetery, and she had her head on the headstone of her son's grave. And as the picture focused in, you could see the writing on the headstone. And it gave his awards—Purple Heart, Bronze Star—showed that he died in Iraq, gave his date of birth, date of death. He was 20 years old. And then, at the very top of the headstone, it didn't have a Christian cross, it didn't have the Star of David, it had [a] crescent and a star of the Islamic faith. And his

> name was Kareem Rashad Sultan Khan, and he was an American. He was born in New Jersey. He was 14 years old at the time of 9/11, and he waited until he [could] go serve his country, and he gave his life. Now, we have got to stop polarizing ourself in this way. And John McCain is as nondiscriminatory as anyone I know. But I'm troubled about the fact that, within the party, we have these kinds of expressions.[32]

"Who Am I?"—Muslim Identity in the West

The taint of "foreignness" and terrorism continues to brushstroke Muslims as "the other." As Hadia Mubarak, the first female elected president of the National Muslim Students Association, has said, "Islam is still equated with a foreign culture. . . . How do we demonstrate our commitment to Islam is integral to our American identity? How do Muslims demonstrate that acts of worship—wearing headscarves, taking off at work at noon on Friday to attend congregational prayers, building mosques, etc.—do not undermine our patriotism or pride in being American?"[33] Those who struggle to "make it" in American or European cultural and political environments often feel like strangers in their Western societies and believe that they must give up their identity to be accepted. This can encourage some to resist assimilation, lest they become so "Westernized" that they lose their distinctiveness as a unique culture and religious faith. Not only Westerners but also Muslims are led to question whether they are Muslims in America or American Muslims, Muslims who happen to live in Europe or European Muslims.

For the foreseeable future Muslims will face the challenge of retaining their faith and identity while integrating into sometimes hostile American and European societies. Western countries offer many freedoms not available in much of the Muslim world, but the pluralism the West values so highly is being tested as never before. What are the limits of this Western pluralism? Whom does it include or exclude? Is it staunchly secular or permanently Judeo-Christian? Can American and European societies fully accept Muslims (as well as Hindus, Sikhs, Buddhists, and others) not as "foreigners" to be tolerated but as respected fellow citizens and neighbors with equal political and religious rights?

The identity of Muslim immigrants has been shaped by their religious, ethnic, and cultural backgrounds as well as their experiences in the West. Living as a minority in a dominant culture that is often ignorant of or hostile to Islam, many Muslims find themselves in environments that, like Norway, Denmark, and Sweden, remain overwhelmingly homogeneous or, like

Britain, France, and Germany, cling to a bygone romanticized nationalist identity. While in America Christianity is regarded by many as integral to national identity, values, and culture, many Europeans, faced with growing Muslim minority communities, insist that European identity is inseparable from a secular national ethos and Judeo-Christian culture. Those Muslims in Europe and America who unfavorably compare their Christian or secular "national culture" with Islamic values further complicate and impede the efforts of their fellow Muslims to integrate and assimilate.

Two broad Muslim responses to Muslim identity in the West have coexisted. First, some Muslim leaders discourage integration and advocate creating separate religious/cultural communities within Western societies. Like ethnic Catholics and Jews in America, who initially looked to their countries of origin for many of their priests and rabbis, Western Muslims have relied on connections to the Muslim world for religious leadership and support. In the recent past especially, international organizations and agencies funded by Libya, Saudi Arabia, Iran, and other Gulf States have provided substantial funding to build mosques and schools and to hire imams (mosque leaders), teach Arabic and Islam, distribute religious literature, and support visits from popular religious leaders.

While this kind of support can initially strengthen Islamic institutions, it can also negatively affect communities in the long run. Dependence on foreign sources like Saudi Arabia with its Wahhabi brand of Islam or other Muslim countries can impede Muslim integration. Muslim communities that are too dependent on foreign-born and -trained religious leaders who often have little desire to acculturate tend to cling to a more traditionalist worldview. Leaders who are ill equipped to respond rather than react to the challenges of life in the West only reinforce a "cultural ghetto mentality," living, acting, and teaching as if they were back in Cairo, Mecca, or Islamabad rather than in New York, Detroit, London, Manchester, Marseilles, or Berlin. They may not only advocate isolation and reject Western political systems but encourage desire for Islamization of the West. As Hadia Mubarak commented, "In the past eight years, Muslim Americans have come to realize they cannot afford to live their lives in isolation without regard for the welfare of their society or the public image of Islam. While they face the same concerns as all Americans, . . . paying their mortgages and sending their children to college, they face the added responsibility of confronting increasing anti-Muslim sentiment."[34]

The second response, "We are American Muslims or Muslim Americans," represents the majority of Muslims in America, who have become increasingly integrated into their new mosaic society. Like other religious and ethnic groups before them, they see themselves as part of the fabric of America and have a strong desire for coexistence with their fellow citizens based on common civic, religious, and social values and interests. Luis Lugo, director of the Pew Forum on Religion and Public Life, concludes, "Muslim Americans are very much like the rest of the country.... They do not see a conflict between being a devout Muslim and living in a modern society."[35]

Altaf Husain at Howard University encourages Muslims to put "unrelenting focus on civic engagement ... to contribute to the betterment of American society through our strong emphasis on family and hard work, on protecting the environment, on establishing justice, struggling against injustice and oppression and on serving and taking care of the most vulnerable in society. Even as a minority of our cohorts in near and distant parts of the world carry out acts of terror in the name of Islam, we must be undeterred in making ourselves worthy in word and deed of American support."[36]

TO BE OR NOT TO BE?—THE QUESTION IN EUROPE

Muslim integration into society in Europe is more difficult than in America. In contrast to immigrant American Muslims, many of whom came with education and skills, Muslims came to Europe under very different circumstances, primarily as laborers and blue-collar workers when Europe had a great need for foreign workers. As a result, many had limited education, skills, and social mobility. Many Muslims in, for example, Britain, France, Germany, and Holland are trapped in social ghettos, plagued by poverty, crime, and gangs. Gallup polling of life evaluations provided by Muslims living in Europe reveals their problems. Sixty-nine percent of Muslims living in France and 72 percent in the United Kingdom consider themselves "struggling," while 23 percent of French Muslims and only 7 percent of Muslims in the U.K. say they are "thriving."[37]

In Europe, many news stories depict a vanishing Christianity endangered by Islam, the fastest-growing religion. The Muslim population on the Continent has grown from twelve to twenty million in a decade, and the number of mosques in countries like Britain, Germany, France, and Italy has grown exponentially. The transformation of empty European churches into mosques and the replacement of church bells by the call to prayer embody for some the "threat" from changing demographics. Seeing shrinking "indigenous" populations being overtaken by high immigrant, especially Muslim, birth rates has led many Catholic and Protestant church leaders to decry secularization and modernity, loss of faith, and moral breakdown; some warn that Christian Europe is increasingly powerless against the rise of "radical Islam."

Modern-day prophets of doom predict that Europe will be overrun by Islam, transformed by the end of the century into "Eurabia." The media, political leaders, and commentators on the right warn of a "soft terrorism" plot to take over America and Europe. Bernard Lewis, a Middle East historian and adviser to the Bush administration on its failed Iraq policy, received widespread coverage when he chided Europeans for losing their loyalties, self-confidence, and respect for their own culture, charging that they have "surrendered" to Islam in a mood of "self-abasement," "political correctness," and "multi-culturalism."[38]

Bat Ye'or (the pen name of an Egyptian-born Jewish writer who now lives in Europe) echoes Lewis's charge. In her provocative book *Eurabia*, Ye'or warns that Europe will reap what it has sown during thirty years of appeasement, accommodation, and cultural abdication, and she links Europe's vulnerability to its leaders' alleged pro-Arab, anti-Israel policies, their "paranoiac obsession with Israel," and their stress on the centrality of the Palestinian cause for world peace.[39] Melanie Phillips, a British Jewish journalist and author of *Londonistan*, who also subscribes to the threat of Muslims overrunning Europe, follows suit: "If you read the mainstream media, watch or listen to the BBC, go onto campus, or attend dinner parties, you come up against . . . breathtaking assertions about how the international Jewish conspiracy has hijacked U.S. foreign policy, which would have been simply unthinkable a few years ago."[40]

The threat of Eurabia has also been taken up by Bishop Tadeusz Ploski, head of Poland's Catholic military diocese: "The military defense against Islamic terrorism is being led today by the United States, which is playing a very similar role . . . to that (role) played centuries ago by Poland, when it was the rampart of Christianity." He urged Christians to prevent Europe from being turned into "Euro-Arabia."[41] In Germany, Peter Frisch, head of the Bundesamt fur Verfassungsschutz (Federal Office for the Protection of the Constitution), has repeatedly asserted, "Muslims want to rule the world." Warnings like this are regularly broadcast in national newspapers in Germany and elsewhere.

The anti-immigrant drumbeat about the impending demise of Europe's religious and cultural identity in the face of the Islamic threat has been aided by media coverage that lumps diverse identity, and demographic, economic, and social conflicts and issues together under the umbrella of religion. Rioting in French ghetto areas inhabited by North African Arabs is portrayed as "Muslim" rather than as protests against poverty and hopelessness. Muslim boycotts in London protesting Danish cartoons that depicted Muhammad as a terrorist with a bomb in his turban and conflicts over the hijab in France, Turkey, and Denmark are seen exclusively as "religious issues" rather than also as issues of civil rights and freedoms such as women's right to dress as they choose. Because European Muslims are defined simply in terms of their faith, these problems and issues are incorrectly seen as "Muslim issues" when in fact, given their nature and primary causes, they require social, not religious, solutions or policies.

The Danish cartoons and their subsequent publication and controversy in other European countries provided an occasion for right-wing anti-immigrant/anti-Muslim factions, who see an inherent clash between Islam and modern Western secular society and values, to challenge Muslims to demonstrate that they can be "proper Europeans." For Muslims, opposition to the cartoons was a matter of respect for their Prophet and religion. They see the cartoons as Islamophobic and racist, intended to humiliate rather than extend the same respect that Jews and Christians enjoy.

The victims of discrimination and hate crimes are not Muslim extremists but the mainstream moderate majority of Muslims in Europe and America. Counterstatements by Muslim government, religious, and intellectual leaders against extremism or violence did not receive equal time. The result, as noted by Dr. Jeremy Henzell-Thomas, chairman of the Forum Against Islamophobia and Racism (FAIR), is

> clichés which stigmatise the whole of Islam as fundamentalist, ideological, monolithic, static, unidimensional, implacably opposed to modernity, incapable of integration or assimilation, impervious to new ideas, retrogressive, retrograde, backward, archaic, primeval, medieval, uncivilized, hostile, violent, terrorist, alien, fanatical, barbaric, militant, oppressive, harsh, threatening, confrontational, extremist, authoritarian, totalitarian, patriarchal, misogynist, negatively exotic, and bent on imposing on the whole world a rigid theocratic system of government which would radically overturn every principle of freedom and liberal democracy cherished by the Western world. I have to say that I don't know a single Muslim who embodies even one of these characteristics, and I have Muslim friends and colleagues in all walks of life and from many cultures all over the globe.[42]

Given the proliferation of Islamophobic voices, is it surprising that Americans and Europeans, reeling from terrorist attacks in New York and

Washington and subsequent attacks in Europe committed in the name of Islam, feared the presence of "an enemy within"?

While European countries have provided a land of opportunity for some, many others find themselves in depressed areas with high unemployment and little access to education or job-skill development. These conditions feed a sense of second-class citizenship, social exclusion, marginalization, and alienation and contribute to problems with drugs and crime.

European Muslims struggle more intensely with their identity. Because of class structure and cultural attitudes, first- and second-generation European Muslims as well as recent immigrants feel that they will never be accepted as fully and equally British, French, or German. Despite being citizens, they have at best moved from being "guests" to being "foreigners." Often younger generations in Britain, France, and Germany become alienated both from their European identity and from the traditional national and religious identities of their parents.

While some Muslim youth become more vulnerable to militant interpretations of Islam, many conflicts and clashes are rooted in deep-seated political and socioeconomic problems as well. Alienation and radicalization occur among both religiously observant and nonobservant Muslims, and among well-educated and employed Muslim youth from stable economic and social backgrounds as well as the poor and oppressed. They are often influenced by what they see as a double standard in some European countries' foreign policies, including selective espousal of democracy and human rights in the Muslim world and support for authoritarian and repressive regimes. Their grievances have included the impact of sanctions on Iraqi Muslims in Saddam Hussein's Iraq, the U.S.-led invasion and occupation of Iraq, the Palestinian-Israeli conflict, Indian "occupation" in Kashmir, and Russian "occupation and rule" in Chechnya.

Finally, while the majority of European Muslims are mainstream and moderate, radicalization has also been fed by a minority of foreign militants, imams and political activists, who have infiltrated illegally or immigrated from Muslim lands and found asylum in Europe. Taking advantage of the openness of European society with its freedoms of speech and assembly, men like Abdullah el-Faisal, Abu Qatada, Omar Bakri Mohammed, and Abu Hamza al-Masri infiltrated mosques or started their own and found other public platforms from which to appeal to those who felt alienated or marginalized. They spew their theologies of hate, condemning the very countries and societies they live in, and calling for violence and warfare at home and in Muslim countries.

Abu Hamza al-Masri, an Egyptian-born Muslim, is a noteworthy example. Hamza insinuated himself into a position of influence and control of London's Finsbury Park Mosque from 1997 to 2003. Preaching a message of hatred and retaliation, Hamza described British society as a "toilet" unfit for prayer and said, "The main source of income in this country is actually what? . . . Usury, prostitution, alcohol, taxation, plotting against Third World countries, booties."[43] Hamza creates an unbridgeable divide between Muslims and non-Muslims, as well as between true and false Muslims (those who did not accept his message). Besieged by a proximate and pervasive threat to Islam, the struggle between believers and *kafirs* (unbelievers) requires violent jihad: "You must know the cause of Allah and you must help that cause in fighting, . . . you don't fight just to negotiate or to show off or to make videos or to make audios, fight to kill not fight to tape." Since he views Muslims as under siege, he maintains that "killing a Kafir for any reason, you can say it, it is OK—even if there is no reason for it."[44] Explaining how British Muslims could establish a caliphate, he said:

> Every court is a target, every brothel is a target and everybody who's endorsing that is a target. . . . You have to bleed the enemy whether you work alone or work with a group or you work with your family. . . . Then after you have done that, obviously you will be on the run.[45]

Attacks in London (July 7, 2005), Glasgow (June 30, 2007), and Madrid (March 11, 2008) and arrests in cities across Europe have underscored the dangers of domestic terrorism.

"Why Haven't Muslims Condemned Terrorism?"

Since 9/11, I have spoken across the United States and Europe to a broad cross-section of government officials, media, religious leaders, academics, and the public. Inevitably the same question is raised by members of the Senate, university alumni groups, and the media, not as an open-ended issue but as a definitive charge: Why haven't Muslim leaders condemned 9/11 and Islamic terrorism?

The fears and conflicting emotions among mainstream Muslims in America and overseas, reeling from the impact of 9/11, torn between defensiveness and self-criticism, are difficult to overestimate. Many in the Arab and Muslim world retreated to a state of denial, claiming that the Bush administration failed to provide hard evidence or proof that Muslims were responsible for the attacks. Some continue to grasp desperately at any and every other explanation: Israeli intelligence (Mossad) was behind the attacks, so Jews using World Trade Center offices were warned not to go to work on 9/11, or at the very least there was a cover-up that blames Arabs and Muslims for the tragedy. The level of disbelief among Muslims was and is astonishing—families of the hijackers in Saudi Arabia reportedly stating that their children were in fact still alive and Arabs insisting that no Arab could learn how to fly planes into the Twin Towers.

Media have contributed both indirectly and directly to linking Muslims to negative images. Guided by a principle Deborah Tannen, linguistics professor and author of *The Argument Culture,* has called "no fight, no story," the goal is not to balance coverage and adjudicate fact from exaggeration or misinformation but rather to focus on confrontation and conflict, violence and terrorism, crises and tragedy.[46] A small but vocal minority that celebrated the attacks as "payback time" for failed American foreign policies in the Middle East enjoyed widespread media coverage. Some Palestinians celebrating in the streets were featured over and over again on major stations.

Overshadowed were the shock and concern of many mainstream Muslims. The Gallup World Poll found that 91 percent of Muslims interviewed believed the attacks were morally unjustified. Eclipsed also was the fact that some 358 Muslim employees died in the World Trade Center; the number of Muslims working there was so large that the WTC had created a Muslim prayer room on the second floor. One of the most moving experiences I had was speaking at a memorial for a young married Muslim couple from Bangladesh; both were Muslim professionals who worked and perished in the Towers. Few media outlets, then as now, covered the statements of Muslim leaders and organizations that did speak out, quickly issuing public statements, denouncing the terrorist attacks and expressing their condolences. Why were these voices not heard?

The statements and positions of the mainstream Muslim majority are not headline news, often not even regarded as newsworthy. Preachers of peace or conflict resolution might, if lucky, get a little coverage buried somewhere in the back pages. Nowhere is the result of this more evident than in the persistent belief that Muslims have not spoken out against violence and terrorism.

The lack of coverage of Muslims' public pronouncements and major statements condemning religious extremism and terrorism has allowed the persistence of the question "Why don't more Muslims speak out?" Thus the actions of a dangerous minority of Muslim extremists and terrorists become the distorting prism through which all Muslims and their religion are seen and understood. As Franklin Graham expressed it: "The silence of the clerics around the world is frightening to me.... How come they haven't apologized to the American people, ... haven't reassured the American people that this is not true Islam and that these people are not acting in the name of Allah, they're not acting in the name of Islam?"[47]

The media's failure to provide balanced coverage, thus compounding the problem, included even informed political commentators like Thomas Friedman, currently foreign affairs columnist for the *New York Times*, who for six years had covered the Middle East. Astonishingly, the day after the London bombings, in his column "If It's a Muslim Problem, It Needs a Muslim Solution," Friedman charged: "To this day—to this day—no major Muslim cleric or religious body has ever issued a fatwa condemning Osama bin Laden."[48]

My initial shock that Friedman, who ought to know better, would make such a statement made me think of my father's exasperated response in heated discussions with his well-educated sons: "You're too bright to be that stupid." Friedman's assertion seemed all the more ironic since his own newspaper had published on October 17, 2001, a full-page ad from the Becket Fund for Religious Liberty proclaiming, "Osama bin Laden hijacked four airplanes and a religion," with published statements by some of the world's most prominent Muslim leaders condemning the attacks. Among those who signed were Sheikh Abdulaziz al-Shaikh (Grand Mufti of Saudi Arabia and chairman of the Senior Ulama), Zaki Badawi (principal of the Muslim College in London), Mufti Nizamuddin Shamzai of Pakistan, King Abdullah II of Jordan, and the Organisation of the Islamic Conference.

This published declaration was only the tip of the iceberg. As early as September 14, 2001, the BBC reported condemnations of the 9/11 attacks as acts of terrorism by a significant, influential, and diverse group of religious leaders, ranging from Sheikh Muhammad Sayyid Tantawi, the Grand Sheikh of Cairo's al-Azhar University and Grand Imam of the al-Azhar Mosque (viewed by many as one of the highest authorities in Sunni Islam) to Ayatollah Kashani in Iran.[49] Mustafa Mashhur (General Guide, Muslim Brotherhood, Egypt), Qazi Hussain Ahmed (Ameer, Jamaat-e-Islami Pakistan, Pakistan), Muti Rahman Nizami (Ameer, Jamaat-e-Islami Bangladesh, Bangladesh), Sheikh Ahmad Yassin (founder, Islamic Resistance Movement [Hamas], Palestine), Rashid Ghannoushi (president, Nahda Renaissance Movement, Tunisia), Fazil Nour (president, PAS—Parti Islam SeMalaysia, Malaysia), and forty other Muslim scholars and politicians were equally strong in their condemnations:

> The undersigned, leaders of Islamic movements, are horrified by the events of Tuesday 11 September 2001 in the United States which

resulted in massive killing, destruction and attack on innocent lives. We express our deepest sympathies and sorrow. We condemn, in the strongest terms, the incidents, which are against all human and Islamic norms. This is grounded in the Noble Laws of Islam which forbid all forms of attacks on innocents. God Almighty says in the Holy Qur'an: "No bearer of burdens can bear the burden of another" (Surah al-Isra 17:15).[50]

Moreover, on September 27, 2001, Sheikh Yusuf al-Qaradawi (chairman of the Sunna and Sira Council, Qatar), and Sheikh Taha Jabir al-Alwani (chairman of the North America Fiqh Council) issued a joint fatwa, signed by American Muslim leaders and internationally prominent Islamic scholars. The fatwa condemned bin Ladin's actions of 9/11 and sanctioned Muslim participation in the United States' military response in Afghanistan. The fatwa clearly stated that every Muslim had a duty to work to apprehend and bring to justice anyone who planned, participated in, or financed such attacks. Responding to the question of whether Muslim Americans could fight in the U.S. Army against fellow Muslims in Afghanistan or elsewhere, knowing that innocent Muslims would likely also be killed in such a massive campaign, the fatwa sanctioned Muslim participation in the U.S. military campaign.[51]

One of the clearest denunciations of terrorism and mindless anti-Westernism appeared in the *Arab News*, a leading Saudi newspaper, shortly after bombings that had targeted Americans in Saudi Arabia in May 2003:

> Words are inadequate to express the shock, the revulsion, the outrage at the suicide bombings in Riyadh. Are expatriates working here an army of occupation, to be slaughtered and terrorized into leaving? . . . We cannot say that suicide bombings in Israel and Russia are acceptable but not in Saudi Arabia. The cult of suicide bombings has to stop. So too has the chattering, malicious, vindictive hate propaganda. It has provided a fertile ground for ignorance and hatred to grow.
>
> There is much in US policy to condemn; there are many aspects of Western society that offend—and where necessary, Arab governments condemn. But anti-Americanism and anti-Westernism for their own sake are crude, ignorant and destructive. They create hate. They must end. Otherwise there will be more barbarities.[52]

Many major Muslim leaders and organizations continued to respond to every major terrorist attack. Thus, for example, after the terrorist attacks in London in 2005, in Glasgow in 2007, and in Mumbai in 2008, Muslim leaders and organizations globally issued statements condemning the terrorists and their actions.

More than five hundred British Muslim religious leaders and scholars issued a fatwa in response to the London bombings expressing condolences to the families of the victims, wishing the injured a speedy recovery, and stating that Islam condemns violence and destruction of innocent lives and that suicide bombings are "vehemently prohibited."[53] Al-Azhar's Tantawi also spoke out against the London attacks, saying they were the work of "criminals who do not represent Islam or even truly understand (its message)." Ayatollah Mohammad Hussein Fadlallah, a prominent Shiite scholar, asserted, "These crimes are not accepted by any religion. It is a barbarism wholly rejected by Islam." Surprisingly for some, even Hamas ("Targeting civilians in their transport means and lives is denounced and rejected," said Moussa Abu Marzouk, political bureau deputy chief) and Hizbollah (on "humanitarian, moral and religious grounds") joined the condemnations.[54]

Yet the conventional wisdom that Muslims do not condemn terrorism dies hard. To this day, American audiences still raise this charge despite the fact that Muslim scholars' and organizations' extensive condemnations (including fatwas) of the 9/11 attacks and subsequent acts of terrorism, issued in countries from Saudi Arabia to Malaysia to the United States, can be readily found in the international press and on the Internet.[55]

After 9/11, stunned Muslims in North America and Europe shared fears that Islamophobia among their communities, neighbors, and co-workers would grow, along with hate crimes, discrimination, and more erosion of civil liberties. Their fears have been realized. All Western Muslims have been forced to live in increasingly suspicious and hostile American and European environments. Yet this experience did compel Western Muslims to simultaneously reassess their identity and reexamine their understanding of Islam. Among the positive outcomes have been acceleration of internal discussion and debate among Muslims over what it means to be a Muslim in America or Europe, greater outreach on the part of Muslims to their non-Muslim communities, and more Muslim involvement in electoral politics and public affairs.

Becoming American and European Muslims

Muslims have recognized that making it in their adopted countries requires institution-building and reform. Both in America and in Europe, the last few decades have seen a great expansion in the number of mosques, Islamic centers, schools, professional and social associations, and advocacy groups. Because looking to former homelands and oil-rich countries like Saudi Arabia for financial support and imams can tend to strengthen theological (Wahhabi and Salafi brands of Islam) and political influences, there is a new emphasis on developing indigenous seminaries to train local religious leaders and scholars.

Muslims have created institutions to improve knowledge of Islam in the West and safeguard their rights. Educational associations monitor textbooks and the teaching of Islam to ensure accuracy and objectivity. Public affairs organizations monitor and educate the media, legislators, and the general public. Islamic information services develop and distribute publications, films, and videos on Islam and Muslims. In some communities, Islamic schools (primary and secondary) have been established, and teaching materials and syllabi on Islam and Muslim life have been created for children and adults at mosques and schools.

Western freedoms have enabled Muslim religious leaders, intellectuals, and activists to become major voices for religious, social, and political change. Their writings and sermons emphasize reinterpretation and reform, with respect to the role and rights of women, religious pluralism and tolerance, religious extremism, becoming an American or European Muslim, and preserving Muslim civil rights and liberties. As Ingrid Mattson points out, while scholars cannot provide all the solutions to challenges, they can "support practitioners by offering more realistic assessments of Islamic history . . . acknowledging the flaws as well as triumphs . . . [to] keep our youth from falling mindlessly behind charismatic individuals who might lead them to destruction."[56]

Today, both American and European Muslim leaders, sometimes with advice from prominent Islamic legal experts around the world, formulate fresh legal opinions to guide the Muslim community. Their fatwas range from matters of prayer and fasting to decisions about marriage, divorce, abortion, and stem cell research. They advise the community about Islamic banking as well as voting in a non-Muslim society, for non-Muslim candidates, and give guidance on the important issues of democratization, pluralism, and tolerance.

Although great headway has been made, the resources, numbers, and impact of such projects remain relatively small. Whether Muslim communities in America and Europe will be able to supply the financial and human resources necessary to build a strong self-sustaining community in the twenty-first century remains an important and unanswered question.

Muslims face challenges beyond finding resources to build their communities. Some non-Muslims in the West welcome the integration and institutionalization of Islam and Muslims, but others do not. As we have seen in quotes above, from Christian Right ministers linked with George W. Bush to Barack Obama's concern about being identified as Muslim, from anti-immigrant political parties and politicians to Zionist professors, Muslim organizations and individuals draw more than their share of criticism and often unsubstantiated condemnation. With a higher political profile for Muslim public institutions and political action groups have come accusations that they are fronts for radicals who support extremist activities abroad. As Muslim professionals seek to join governing boards, participate in politics, or apply for professional positions, they can be labeled as militants or terrorists. Nihad Awad, executive director of CAIR, encourages Muslims to confront the "anti-Muslim fear industry" by repudiating "hatemongers with the same determination that won American women the right to vote, challenged McCarthyism, and ended racial segregation."[57]

Does the spectrum of negative views about Islam represent informed opinion? How Islam-literate are most Americans? Despite many American concerns post 9/11 and the fact that Muslims are a permanent part of the American mosaic, nearly two-thirds of Americans confess that they don't have even a basic understanding of Islam. This lack of understanding has stubbornly persisted. Little change occurred from 2002 to 2007 in the large number of Americans who said they knew nothing at all (24 percent) or very little (41 percent) about Islam. From 2007 to 2009, only a slight decrease occurred, from a total of 65 percent to 59 percent, still an astonishing number. Similarly, the significant number of Americans who said they had an unfavorable opinion of Islam dropped only slightly, from 59 percent in 2007 to 54 percent in 2009.[58]

Manifestations of the dark side, of a "negative Islam," in Muslim countries are real and many. Muslim preachers, like Christian preachers such as John Hagee, Rod Parsley, or Pat Robertson, deliver intolerant sermons based on exclusivist religious worldviews of "I'm right, you're wrong; I'm going to heaven and you're going to hell." A Muslim student once described this ultraconservative, intransigent, self-righteous mentality and message as "No, No Islam": don't do this, don't do that; this is *haram* (forbidden) and will send you to hell. Those who are not personally acquainted with Muslims often struggle with two mindsets when they think about Muslim "strangers"—a feeling of superiority on the one hand and a feeling of fear on the other. Yet, as many polls have demonstrated, Americans who claim to be more familiar with Islam and Muslims are often more likely to have favorable opinions of them.

In the twenty-first-century West, moving beyond seeing our neighbors as the inferiors or the frightening "others" is a no-brainer, considering the growing visibility and presence of Muslims in Europe and America and demographics predicting that Islam may soon become the second-largest religion in America.

What Do Muslims Believe and Why Does It Matter?

On January 16, 2005, the Sunday *New York Times* had a headline: "A Reading List for Assignment to Iraq" developed by Lt. Gen. John R. Vines, American ground commander in Iraq, who assigned these books to his top staff members. Five of the eight books he recommended covered various aspects of Islam. The list included two books I wrote after 9/11, *What Everyone Needs to Know About Islam*, a Q&A on Islam, and *Unholy War: Terror in the Name of Islam*, a study of the origins and development of Osama bin Laden's influence and the spread of global terrorism. Both books were written in response to an endless flow of questions about hot button issues that seem never to be clarified.

I often say that I have the best/easiest job in the world because even after thirty years in the field and the increased interest and coverage of Islam and the Muslim world since the Iranian revolution of 1979, and again post 9/11, people keep asking the same basic questions: Is Islam a violent religion? What does the Quran say about terrorism? Is Islam compatible with modernity and democracy? Government agencies in Europe and America (State and Defense Departments, the Pentagon, CIA and NSA, the FBI), think tanks, world affairs councils, and the media ask not only about "political Islam," religious extremism, and terrorism but also about the religion of Islam itself. Why? Because, like it or not, in the twenty-first century, questions about the influence of religion and culture will be inextricably linked to discussions of emerging societies, politics, violence and terrorism, and all international affairs.

For many Muslims, Islam is the spiritual path that gives meaning and purpose—it's worshipping a God who is compassionate, merciful, and just, a God who brings peace and social justice. Although 65 percent of Americans acknowledge the importance of religion in their lives, Muslim Americans in even greater numbers (80 percent) cite the importance of faith. Among the major faith groups surveyed in America, only Mormon Americans

(85 percent) are more likely than Muslims (80 percent) to say religion plays an important role; while Jewish Americans are the group least likely (39 percent) to say religion is important.[59] Interestingly, across most religious communities surveyed, women are statistically more likely than men to say religion is an important part of their lives, but this is not true of American Muslims, among whom men are as likely as women to consider religion important.

Internationally Islam is seen as a key source of guidance, consolation, and hope and as a marker for the global Muslim community. This is not just a theological statement or an academic observation but what overwhelming numbers of Muslims globally consistently affirm. For example, in Gallup polls in 2001 and 2005–7, majorities of respondents in countries with substantial or predominantly Muslim populations report that religion is an integral part of their daily lives, several in the 90 percent range: in Egypt (100 percent), Indonesia (99 percent), Bangladesh (99 percent), and Morocco (98 percent). Significant percentages of Muslims rate "having an enriched religious/spiritual life" as an aspect of life that is essential, which one cannot live without. Moreover, when asked what they admire most about the Islamic world, the number-one response from Muslim populations as diverse as Turkey, Saudi Arabia, and Indonesia is "people's sincere adherence to Islam." Similarly, many European Muslims also respond affirmatively in significant numbers when asked whether religion is an important part of daily life: 82 percent in Germany, 70 percent in Britain, and 69 percent in France.[60]

Thus to understand this important source of meaning and influence in the world, we need to give as much attention to the faith of the mainstream majorities of Muslims as we do to the theologies of hate from the terrorist minority.

WHO ARE THE CHILDREN OF ABRAHAM?

I, like many of my generation, was raised in a "Christian America," or so we were taught and thought. Religious pluralism meant Protestants, Catholics, and more marginally Jews. Religion was taught in religiously affiliated schools and universities; Catholicism at Catholic colleges and universities, Protestantism at Protestant, and Judaism at Jewish institutions. After World War II, the connection between Christianity and Judaism was more popularly formalized in a new notion of a Judeo-Christian tradition: one that said, despite distinctive differences and a history of persecution of Jews, Christians and Jews shared a common belief in the One God and in his prophets and revelation (the Old Testament or Hebrew Bible). But where was Islam, the other monotheistic religion that began in the Middle East and that also recognized the same God, the biblical prophets, and revelations to Moses and Jesus?

Unity and Diversity: One God, Many Revelations

Over the years, especially when I first decided to study Islam, many asked, "Why? Why are you studying Islam after spending years in a Capuchin Franciscan monastery, after earning a graduate degree and a college teaching position in Catholic theology?" To respond adequately would take more space than is warranted here. Briefly, I had gone to Temple University to earn a Ph.D. in religion, majoring in Catholic studies. However, after shifting to concentrating on Hinduism and Buddhism, I was strongly urged, one might say strong-armed, to take a course on Islam with a new Muslim professor, Ismail al-Faruqi. To my surprise, I made the amazing discovery of how much Islam resembled Judaism and Christianity. At a time when Judaism and Christianity were linked in what had come to be called the Judeo-Christian tradition and Islam was grouped with all the other world religions such as Hinduism and Buddhism, I suddenly realized that, despite significant differences between these religions, there is a Judeo-Christian-Islamic tradition.

Muslims share with Jews and Christians a common belief in God, his prophets and revelation, moral responsibility and accountability, and the value of peace and social justice. All three faiths believe they have a divine covenant and are God's stewards, commanded to realize God's will, to preserve, protect, and improve the world for future generations. All three have claimed to be religions of peace.

Why do Muslims emphasize that Islam is a religion of peace? The very word "Islam" means "peace and submission to God." Just as Jews use the greeting *Shalom* (peace), and Christians greet each other with the sign of peace, Muslims say *Assalam wa alaykum* (peace be upon you) whenever they meet someone or say good-bye.

It is astonishing and disheartening for many Muslims to hear Christians or Jews refer to Allah as a personal name for a totally different God! Since Allah is Arabic for "god," everyone who speaks Arabic, including Christian Arabs, refers to God as Allah. Muslims believe that their God is everyone's one true God, the Creator, Sustainer, and Judge of the universe who sent his revelation to Jews, Christians, and Muslims.

Muslims are raised from an early age to associate compassion and mercy with God and their faith. Reading or reciting the Quran and prayer recitations reinforce these attributes of God in their everyday lives. The chapters of the Muslim scripture, the Quran, begin with the words "In the name of God the Merciful and Compassionate." Muslims recite this phrase before giving a public speech, before eating a meal or starting a car, and it is written at the top of all letters and legal documents.

A JUDEO-CHRISTIAN-ISLAMIC TRADITION?

Muslims do not see Islam as a new religion with a new scripture. Like Christians who believe that Christianity superseded Judaism, Muslims believe that God sent down his revelation one final time to Muhammad to correct the human errors that had made their way into the scriptures and belief systems of Judaism and Christianity.

Far from agreeing that theirs is the youngest of the great monotheistic religions, Muslims see their scripture, the Quran, as the original as well as the final revelation of the God of Moses, Jesus, and Muhammad. The Quran affirms God's earlier revelations to Moses in the Torah and to Jesus as it is told in the Gospels:

> We sent Jesus the son of Mary, confirming the Torah that had come before him: We sent him the Gospel in which is guidance and light, and confirmation of the Torah that had come before him, a guidance and an admonition to those who fear God. (Quran 5:46)

And again,

> He established for Noah, that which We have sent to you as inspiration through Abraham, Moses, and Jesus, namely that you should remain steadfast in religion and make no divisions within it. (Quran 42:13)

Muslims see themselves as Children of Abraham who, with Jews and Christians ("People of the Book" who received God's revelations), represent different branches of the same religious family. Both the Quran and the Hebrew Bible or Old Testament tell the story of Abraham, his wife Sarah, and Hagar, Sarah's Egyptian servant. While Jews and Christians see themselves as descended from Abraham and Sarah through their son Isaac, Muslims trace their religious roots back to Abraham through Ismail, his firstborn son by Hagar.

Common Muslim names such as Ibrahim (Abraham), Musa (Moses), Daoud (David), Sulayman (Solomon), Issa (Jesus), and Maryam (Mary) testify to the significance of biblical figures for Muslims. Christians are often surprised to discover that Jesus is mentioned by name in the Quran more than Muhammad and that Mary is mentioned more times in the Quran than in the New Testament. Both Jesus and Mary play important roles not only in the Quran but also in Muslim piety and spirituality. In fact, one of my Muslim colleagues, frustrated about the portrayal of the Prophet Muhammad as a terrorist in the Danish cartoons, commented, "Ironically, we can't do the same to Jewish and Christian prophets because they are also ours; we respect and love them too!"

Muslim children learn many of the same scriptural stories about Adam and Eve, Noah's Ark, the Ten Commandments, David and Solomon, and Mary and Jesus that are studied by Jewish and Christian children, sometimes with the same and sometimes with differing interpretations. For example, in the Quran, Eve is not portrayed as a temptress; Adam and Eve both disobey God, and both are equally responsible for their actions. However, their disobedience does not result in an "original sin" inherited by future generations. In another example, the Quran (37:99–113) designates Abraham's oldest son, Ismail, rather than Isaac, as the son that God commanded Abraham to sacrifice (Genesis 22:1–2).

Being a Muslim gives one a community identity and responsibility. Muslims of every sex, race, and ethnic or national background are members of a transnational, worldwide community of believers (*ummah*), responsible for creating a just society on earth. Thus the critical questions in Islam, as in many other faiths, are: "How do I know God's will and how do I follow it? What does God want me to do?" The articulation of what the Quran calls the "Straight Path" of Islam resulted in the development of Shariah (path), or Islamic law.

SHARIAH: MORAL COMPASS OR SOURCE OF OPPRESSION?

Islamic law (Shariah) is often portrayed as a medieval legal system used by religious zealots to oppress women and deny human rights for Muslims and non-Muslims alike. There are good reasons for this perception. Islamic law in countries like Saudi Arabia, Iran, Sudan, and the Taliban's Afghanistan has been used to restrict women's rights and to mandate stoning of women charged with adultery, amputating the limbs of thieves, and prosecuting any Muslim who tries to convert to another religion for apostasy.

But why, then, do many Muslims regard Shariah so positively, as central to their faith? Looking more deeply, we discover that Shariah has many meanings. For many centuries, across the Muslim world, Shariah has functioned as a positive source of guidance, a law whose principles and values have provided a moral compass for individuals and society. This is clearly reflected in the Gallup World Polls in 2006 and 2007, which found that large majorities of Muslims, both women and men, in many and diverse Muslim countries from Egypt to Malaysia, want Shariah as "a" source of law.

Debates surrounding the drafting of new constitutions in Afghanistan and Iraq also reflect the desire for Shariah as a source of law. Fear of Shariah as uncompromising, punishing, and oppressive was deeply ingrained in the views of the Bush administration and some Iraqi secularists who staunchly oppose it. Ambassador Paul Bremer, viewing Shariah as a synonym for religious rule, oppressed women, and no human rights, stood firm in 2004 against any role for Shariah in Iraq's new interim constitution. He declared, "Our position is clear. It can't be law until I sign it."[61] Donald Rumsfeld, then secretary of defense, confusing the idea of including the Shariah in Iraq's new constitution with creating clerical rule, warned that the United States would not allow Iraq to become a theocracy like Iran.[62]

The desire for Shariah is also easier to understand if we realize that across the world many Muslims, like conservative Christians (both Protestant and Roman Catholic), share deep concerns about how modern secularism has challenged faith and family values. They see secularism as undermining personal and public morality, weakening marriage as an institution, and leading to rampant divorce, sexual promiscuity, dysfunctional families, and alcohol and drug abuse. We don't have to look far from home to find Americans whose attitudes resemble those of many Muslims when it comes to religion's role in law and society. A majority of Americans want the Bible as a source of legislation: 44 percent say the Bible should be "a" source, and 9 percent believe it should be the "only" source of legislation. Perhaps even more surprising, 42 percent of Americans want religious leaders to have a direct role in the writing of a constitution.[63] Likewise, many Muslims want their democracy to incorporate Shariah, not a democracy that is solely dependent on Western values.

Islamic law provides a reservoir of principles and values, created to answer the question "What should a good Muslim be doing?" Like the great theologians of Christianity and rabbis of Judaism, the ulama were the interpreters, teachers, and guardians of the faiths who devoted their lives to studying, debating, and developing God's law for Muslim societies. Islamic law is especially important to Muslims, as Jewish law is to Jews, because like

Judaism and in contrast to Christianity, Islam has no central religious authority or "church," no pope to determine what people are to do or believe. Another reason is that Judaism and Islam tend to emphasize law while Christianity relies on doctrines and dogmas.

Islamic law was developed to serve as the blueprint for an ideal Muslim society. It regulates a Muslim's religious duties to God such as prayer, fasting, and almsgiving, social obligations as well as social transactions such as marriage, divorce, and inheritance, business contracts, and political issues including war and peace.

Central to a Muslim's moral compass are the Five Pillars of Islam, which are fundamental religious requirements or observances for all, Sunni and Shia alike. Amidst the national, ethnic, cultural, and racial diversity of Muslims, they provide a basic unity or core of belief and practice and an important foundation for Muslim-Christian-Jewish understanding.

THERE IS NO GOD BUT GOD (ALLAH): PROFESSION OF FAITH

As a Catholic who had to struggle as a child to memorize the Nicene Creed, it came as a great surprise for me to discover that one could become a Muslim by simply professing a brief statement: *There is no god but God {Allah}, and Muhammad is the messenger of God*. This statement, called the *shahada* (witness, testimony), is the fundamental Muslim statement of belief. Repeated many times each day in the call to prayer, the shahada represents the two preeminent fundamentals of Islam: first, an absolute monotheism, a belief in the one true God. Nothing except God deserves to be "worshipped"—not money, ambition, or ego. If a Muslim values any person or thing more than God, he or she is committing idolatry (*shirk*), the one unforgivable sin. Islam's uncompromising belief in the oneness, or unity, of God (*tawhid*) is reflected in the development of Islamic art, especially in the Arab world. Associating anything else with God is idolatry. To avoid such a sin resulting from the depiction of human form, for example, Islamic religious art tends to use calligraphy, geometric forms, and arabesque designs and is thus often abstract rather than representational.

The second great fundamental of Islam centers on the crucial importance of Muhammad, God's final messenger/prophet, the ideal model for Muslim life. Muhammad is one of the great figures of world history. Few have had more of a global religious and political impact; yet no prophet has been more vilified throughout history. The intolerant and vicious (yes, un-Christian) statements by some Christian Right leaders are nothing new. They are part of a more than thousand-year tradition during which Christians, threatened by the challenge of Islam's spread theologically and its expansion politically, dismissed the Prophet's prophetic character, calling him an imposter, a lecher, a rapist, and a drunkard. He has been labeled a renegade Catholic cardinal and portrayed as the anti-Christ and, in the words of Martin Luther, as "the devil's son." Critics in the past and today contrast Muhammad, the "Warrior-Prophet," with Jesus, the "Prince of Peace." In their rush to judgment, they myopically overlook those in their own tradition who had comparable roles: biblical warrior-prophets like David, Saul, and Solomon (an integral part of Christianity as well as Judaism) as well as the many Christian popes and emperors who exercised or legitimated military might, holy wars, in the name of God.

This vilification of Muhammad by some stands in stark contrast with the reverence for Muhammad's piety, integrity, and leadership that billions of Muslims throughout history have maintained. Like Jesus for Christians, Muhammad is the central role model for Muslims, but unlike Jesus, he is believed to be solely human, not divine. His life, as an ideal husband, father, and friend, provides guidance; he is also the ideal political and military leader, diplomat, and judge. Volumes of narrative stories, called *hadith* (tradition), record what the Prophet is reported to have said and done: how he dealt with friends and enemies, how he behaved with heads of state and with servants, how he treated his spouse or child, and how he conducted himself in battle.

In his lifetime, throughout Muslim history, and today, the Prophet Muhammad is seen as the "living Quran," the embodiment of God's will in his behavior and words. Sunni Muslims (85 percent of the world's Muslims) take their name from *sunnah*, meaning those who follow the example of the Prophet. Muslim veneration of Muhammad explains why so many Muslims have been given the name Muhammad or names derived from it (Ahmad, Mahmud, and Amin).

Understanding Muhammad's special role and status helps us appreciate the widespread frustration, sense of humiliation, and anger of many mainstream Muslims, not just extremists, at the denigration of Muhammad and Islam.

PRAYER (*SALAT*)

The practice of prayer or worship at fixed times of the day is found in many faiths. In early Judaism, prayers and sacrifices occurred in certain hours of the day and night; Psalm 119:164 says, "Seven times a day I praise you for your righteous laws." Christianity developed the canonical hours, or Divine Office. The ringing of bells not only called Catholics to mass but also signaled the recitation of the Prayers of Hours, which were recited or chanted seven or eight fixed times of the day and night.

Muslims are called to pray five times each day, at sunrise, noon, midafternoon, sunset, and evening. Like many other visitors to Muslim countries, when I first lived in the Middle East, I was struck by the public as well as private observance of prayer. I would look out my window from our home in a Lebanese village at a farmer prostrating in the field, or glance from my car window to witness drivers parking their trucks and cars on the side of the road to answer the call to prayer. This reminder is chanted by muezzins, whose voices, aided by a megaphone on the top of mosque minarets, echo throughout the cities and countrysides: "*Allahu Akbar* (God is Great). . . . There is no God but God. . . . Muhammad is the Messenger of God . . . Come to prayer. . . . "

More recently, my memories of prayer times were refracted for the modern day when young Muslim professionals who were driving me to lecture halls in England stopped at a McDonald's to find a quiet space to pray, or when passengers in London's Heathrow and Washington's Dulles airports left our conversation to go to the airport Prayer Room or excused themselves to find a place to pray unobtrusively in a quiet corner of the airport. Today, Muslims often rely on more modern reminders of prayer times, which are printed in virtually every Muslim newspaper or on the Internet. Special wristwatches and clocks can also be set to ring at prayer time. The Japanese were among the first to corner the market with creative ideas like a small mosque-shaped clock with an audiotape that begins with birds chirping and the sound of running water, symbolizing ablution (cleansing to prepare for prayer), and continues with the muezzin's call to prayer. Hotel rooms in the Muslim world routinely provide believers with small prayer rugs, a Quran, and a *qibla* indicator, an arrow painted on a desk or nightstand that points toward the holiest city in Islam, Mecca in Saudi Arabia, which Muslims always face when they pray.

Not surprisingly, like many other religious believers, Muslims hold prayer to be an important, central part of their lives. Overwhelming numbers of Muslim respondents around the world report that they pray not only because it is a religious obligation but also because it makes them feel closer to God and is a source of consolation. More than two-thirds in countries as diverse as Morocco (83 percent), Pakistan (79 percent), Kuwait (74 percent), Indonesia (69 percent), Lebanon (68 percent), and Iran (68 percent) said prayer helps them a great deal in soothing their personal worries.[64]

Forgetting the history of the prayer times throughout the day in Judaism or the Prayer of Hours in Catholicism, many Americans express surprise at what they see as the excessive and time-consuming frequency of Muslim prayer. "Five times a day seems like a lot," an American businessman admitted frankly at a workshop about doing business in Muslim countries. In response, an American management consultant who is also a practicing Muslim explained:

> How many times do people in our comfortable society eat? Dietitians recommend three meals and two snacks, but if you are a teenage male, it's more like five meals and ten snacks. Well, Islam views the human being as not only a physical being, but a spiritual being as well, and just as our physical dimension requires regular nourishment throughout the day, so does our spiritual dimension. I pray my morning prayer at dawn before I go to work. I pray my noon and afternoon prayer at work in my office during my lunch break and as a ten-minute break in the afternoon. My other two prayers are in the evening when I get home; one in the early evening and one before I go to bed—five small meals for the soul. I honestly cannot imagine keeping up with my hectic work and family life without this constant connection with God.[65]

THE FAST OF RAMADAN

If prayer five times a day strikes some as demanding, how about no food, no drink, no smoking, no sex, not losing your temper—from dawn to dusk for a whole month! Inspiring, awesome, extreme, or crazy? In our secular, materialistic world, some see such abstinence as extreme or even harmful. Yet we live in a society where rigorous dieting and exercise for health, to stay in shape, to get a "to die for" body, support a multibillion-dollar industry. Grueling marathons and triathlons or twelve- to eighteen-hour professional workdays are often lauded with our modern mantra of "No pain, no gain."

For Muslims, the month of Ramadan is a time for physical and spiritual discipline: controlling desires, performing good works for the poor and less fortunate, and devoting more time and attention to prayer and reflection on human frailty and dependence on God. Surprisingly, even many Muslims who are not particularly religiously observant during the rest of the year choose to observe this communal fast.

Ramadan is a family and community activity. Family and friends come together to break their fast by sharing a "breakfast" at dusk. Those who can, often go home to be with family during the month of Ramadan. In the evening, many meet at a nearby mosque to participate in the discipline of reciting the Quran, read in its entirety during this special month. Traveling in the Muslim world, one sees scrolls and wall hangings showing the entire Quran divided into thirty sections. These are aids to the Ramadan practice of reciting a different Quranic section each night. Quranic recitation (*Quran* translated means "the recitation") is meant to transform the person reciting—just as it transformed Muhammad from a Meccan businessman to the Prophet of a major world faith. As the Quran says, "This Quran has been sent down by the Lord of the Worlds: The trusted Spirit brought it down upon your heart" (26:194).

Ramadan ends with one of the two major Islamic feasts (Eids), the Festival of Breaking the Fast, Eid al-Fitr. The celebration resembles Christmas in its religious joyfulness, special celebrations, and gift-giving. Family members often come from far and wide to visit and celebrate together for several days or even weeks. Muslims in the West (like Jews in the past) have faced major challenges in celebrating and preserving their religious observances when many schools and workplaces do not recognize their special holy days. However, this situation is changing.

ALMSGIVING (*ZAKAT*)

The pillar that, as the popular saying goes, gains Muslims entrance to heaven is *zakat*, or almsgiving. Social justice, in particular a concern for the poor, orphans, and widows and for family members, is a major Quranic theme. The Quran specifically condemns those who say people are meant to be poor and should be left to their own fate because God wills it. Like tithing in Christianity, Islam requires its followers to help less fortunate members of the community. Unlike tithing, however, zakat in Sunni Islam is a wealth tax, requiring the believer to give 2.5 percent of all liquid assets each year, not simply a percentage of income. (Shii calculate zakat differently.) Zakat is not viewed as voluntary or as charity—it is required to purify one's wealth (*zakat* comes from the root of the Arabic word for purification). Since the true owners of things are not men and women but God, zakat is a required sharing of the wealth that Muslims as God's stewards have received as a trust from God. A prominent Muslim scholar commenting on the many times the Quran links "salat and zakat" together notes:

> "Salãt" represents God's rights upon us and "zakãt" represents the rights of other people that God has placed upon us. By combining

"zakāt" with "salāt," we are being constantly reminded that Islam is not a religion that only gives importance to fulfill the rights that God has upon us, it also gives importance to the rights that other human beings have upon us.[66]

PILGRIMAGE TO MECCA (*HAJJ*)

It is difficult to overestimate the great desire that Muslims have to make the *hajj*, or pilgrimage to Mecca. Despite the tremendous cultural diversity of Muslim countries worldwide and substantial Muslim minority populations in Europe, North America, and across the world, certain practices unify the Islamic ummah. Just as all Muslims unite five times each day as they face Mecca, the birthplace of Muhammad, to pray, so too each year more than two million believers travel from all over the world to this same holy city to perform the fifth pillar.

On hajj, men and women participate in rituals together. There is no sexual segregation in this holiest of places. Wearing simple coverings to symbolize purity, unity, and equality, they reenact key religious events. Crowds circle around the Kaaba, a cube-shaped structure known as the House of God, seen as the most sacred place in the world. Like prayer, this walk symbolizes spiritual contact with God. In another ritual, they reenact Hagar's frantic search for water for her son Ismail when they were lost in the desert, calling to mind humankind's struggle through life; toward the end of the pilgrimage, they assemble at Mount Arafat to commemorate Muhammad's final pilgrimage and farewell sermon to his people.

Those who have made the hajj describe the incredible experience of two million pilgrims praying together as equals, entering into the divine presence, connecting them to something greater than themselves. Many see this as a symbolic experience preparing them for death, when all humans will eventually come together to meet their creator on the Day of Judgment.

The hajj had a transforming effect on the black American activist Malcolm X, whose time on pilgrimage led to a spiritual transformation and a new understanding of human brotherhood. As he explains:

> There were tens of thousands of pilgrims, from all over the world. They were of all colors, from blue-eyed blonds to black-skinned Africans. But we were all participating in the same ritual, displaying a spirit of unity and brotherhood that my experiences in America had led me to believe never could exist between the white and nonwhite.[67]

At the end of the five-day hajj, Muslims throughout the world celebrate the Festival of Sacrifice (Eid al-Adha), commemorating the occasion when God sent a ram as a substitute for Abraham's son Ismail, whom God had commanded him to sacrifice. In this time of grand celebration, Muslim families, like Jews and Christians in their celebrations of Hanukkah and Christmas, come together to visit and exchange gifts.

JIHAD: THE STRUGGLE FOR GOD

Jihad is sometimes referred to as the sixth pillar of Islam, though it has no such official status. The importance of jihad is rooted in the Quran's command to struggle (the literal meaning of the word *jihad*) in the path of God and in the example of the Prophet Muhammad and his early Companions. In its most general meaning, jihad refers to the obligation incumbent on all Muslims, individuals and the community, to follow and realize God's will: to lead a virtuous life and to extend the Islamic community through preaching, education, example, writing, etc. Depending on the circumstances in which one lives, it also can mean fighting injustice and oppression, spreading and defending Islam, and creating a just society through preaching, teaching, and, if necessary, armed struggle to defend Islam and the community from aggression. Throughout history, the call to jihad has rallied Muslims to the defense of Islam.

The two broad meanings of jihad, nonviolent and violent, are contrasted in a well-known Prophetic tradition. Muslim tradition reports that, when Muhammad returned from battle, he told his followers, "We return from the lesser jihad to the greater jihad." The greater jihad is the more difficult and more important struggle against one's ego, selfishness, greed, and evil.

Jihad is a concept with multiple meanings, used and abused throughout Islamic history. Although it is not associated or equated with the words "holy war" anywhere in the Quran, Muslim rulers, with the support of religious scholars and officials, have historically used armed jihad to legitimate wars of imperial expansion. Early extremist groups also appealed to Islam to legitimate rebellion, assassination, and attempts to overthrow Muslim rulers. In recent years religious extremists and terrorists have maintained that jihad is a universal religious obligation and that all true Muslims must join the jihad to promote a global Islamic revolution.

The earliest Quranic verses dealing with the right to engage in a "defensive" jihad, or struggle, were revealed shortly after the *hijra* (emigration) of Muhammad and his followers from Mecca to Medina as they escaped from persecution. At a time when they were forced to fight for their lives, Muhammad was told: "Leave is given to those who fight because they were wronged—surely God is able to help them—who were expelled from their homes wrongfully for saying, 'Our Lord is God' " (22:39–40). The Quran's emphasis on the defensive nature of jihad is clearly emphasized in 2:190, "And fight in the way of God with those who fight you, but aggress not: God loves not the aggressors." At critical points throughout the years, Muhammad received additional revelations from God that provided guidelines for the jihad.

As the Muslim community grew, questions quickly emerged about proper behavior during times of war. The Quran provided detailed guidelines and regulations regarding the conduct of war: who is to fight and who is exempted (48:17, 9:91), when hostilities must cease (2:192), and how prisoners should be treated (47:4). Most important, verses such as 2:194 emphasized that warfare and the response to violence and aggression must be proportional: "Whoever transgresses against you, respond in kind."

According to Islamic law, for a war to be morally justifiable it must be fought in defense of the faith. Other strict rules also apply: the war cannot be waged primarily for material gain and possession; the rights of non-combatants, their safety, freedom, and property, must be respected; women, children, old people, and invalids cannot be harmed; prisoners of war must not be tortured; places of worship cannot be demolished, and religious leaders or priests cannot be killed.

Quranic verses also underscore that peace, not violence and warfare, is the norm. Permission to fight the enemy is balanced by a strong mandate to make peace: "If your enemy inclines toward peace, then you too should seek peace and put your trust in God" (8:61) and "Had Allah wished, He would have made them dominate you, and so if they leave you alone and do not fight you and offer you peace, then Allah allows you no way against them" (4:90).

Much has been made of the "sword verses," Quranic verses such as "When the sacred months have passed, slay the idolaters wherever you find them, and take them, and confine them, and lie in wait for them at every place of ambush" (9:5). This is one of a number of Quranic verses critics cite to demonstrate the inherently violent nature of Islam and its scripture. These same verses have also been selectively used (or abused) by Muslim extremists to develop a "theology of hate" and intolerance and to legitimate unconditional warfare against unbelievers.

During the period of expansion and conquest, many of the religious scholars (ulama) who enjoyed royal patronage repaid their patrons by providing them with a rationale for pursuing their imperial dreams and extending the boundaries of their empires. The ulama rationalized that the "sword verses" abrogated or overrode the earlier Quranic verses that had limited jihad to defensive war. In fact, however, the full meaning and intent of the above-quoted passage from Quran 9:5 is distorted when applied simply to unbelievers or non-Muslims and quoted in isolation. The verse refers specifically to a particular group, Meccan "idolaters," accused of oath-breaking and warfare against Muslims. Moreover, in the same verse it is directly followed and qualified by "But if they repent and fulfill their devotional obligations and pay the *zakat* [the charitable tax on Muslims], then let them go their way, for God is forgiving and kind" (9:5).

Sunni-Shia: One Faith, Multiple Branches

Islam, like other faiths, has multiple branches or sects. Religious differences can have important political and economic as well as theological implications. Ignorance of such religious issues can have life-and-death consequences. Our ability to anticipate and plan an effective strategy after the invasion of Iraq, to limit and contain sectarian violence and warfare, to effectively assist in the development of democracy, and to control what has become a trillion-dollar debt has been dependent upon our awareness and understanding of powerful social and religious forces. Sunni-Shii rivalry in Iraq has devastated lives and threatened to break the country into rival states; it has exacerbated relations between Shiite Iran and Saudi Arabia and other Gulf Sunni states. Yet years after the invasion and occupation of Iraq, key American officials remained ignorant of basic facts.

In 2007, congressional leaders responsible for counterterrorism, some on key congressional committees that oversaw U.S. foreign policy, were interviewed and asked about the difference between Sunni and Shii Islam. Astonishingly few were able to distinguish between the two religious groups—and this occurred several years after the American occupation of Iraq with its sectarian political rivalry, militias, and violence.

CAN YOU TELL A SUNNI FROM A SHII?

Jeff Stein, the national security editor at the Congressional Quarterly in Washington, had been surprised in 2005 when Jon Stewart and other television comedians joked about depositions taken in a whistleblower case that revealed top FBI officials unable to answer basic questions about Islam. Not only did they admit their ignorance but, even worse, they at first dismissed their need to know.

In 2006 Stein asked similar questions in extensive interviews with U.S. counterterrorism officials and members of Congress: "Do you know the difference between a Sunni and a Shiite?" When he asked officials whether they knew "who's on what side today, and what does each want," what did he discover? "Most American officials I've interviewed," said Stein, "don't have a clue. That includes not only intelligence and law-enforcement officials, but also members of Congress who have important roles overseeing U.S. spy agencies."

Willie Hulon, then chief of the FBI's new National Security Branch, indicated the importance of knowing the difference between Sunnis and Shiites, "to know who your targets are," but wasn't able to say whether Iraq was Sunni or Shii. Asked whether Iran and Hizbollah were Sunni or Shii, Hulon wrongly responded, "Sunni." Congressional leaders did no better. When Representative Terry Everett, Republican of Alabama, then vice chairman of the House intelligence subcommittee on technical and tactical intelligence, was asked, "Do you know the difference between a Sunni and a Shiite?" Everett responded: "One's in one location, another's in another location . . . No, to be honest with you, I don't know." Informed of some of the differences, he replied: "Now that you've explained it to me . . . what occurs to me is that it makes what we're doing over there extremely difficult, not only in Iraq but that whole area."

Representative Jo Ann Davis, Republican of Virginia, who headed a House intelligence subcommittee overseeing the CIA's performance in recruiting spies and analyzing information, had similar problems distinguishing between Sunnis and Shii. When asked if she knew the difference, she said: "You know, I should." Her response? "The Sunni are more radical than the Shia. Or vice versa. But I think it's the Sunnis who're more radical than the Shia."

Stein's interview experiences underscore the magnitude of the problem: "Some agency officials and members of Congress have easily handled my 'gotcha' question. But as I keep asking it, I get more and more blank stares. Too many counterterrorism officials simply don't care to learn much, if anything, about the enemy America is fighting."[68]

Knowing the origins of Sunni and Shii Muslims, and the differences and sources of conflict between the two groups, helps us to understand religious and political events throughout history, from the first days of the Muslim community to multiple modern tensions and conflicts around the globe. In addition to Sunni-Shii conflicts in Iraq and Pakistan, sectarian conflicts and fighting have flared multiple times in Lebanon, Pakistan, Afghanistan, Yemen, Kuwait, Bahrain, and Saudi Arabia. Examining the roots of deep divisions and animosity between Sunni and Shia is essential in understanding the sources of sectarian strife today.

Islam has two major branches: a Sunni majority (85 percent) and a Shia minority (15 percent). Differences in their beliefs, views of history, and reactions to contemporary events originate with the death of the Prophet Muhammad in seventh-century Arabia. Muhammad's death in 632 was a traumatic event for the early Muslim community, marking the end of direct guidance from the Prophet as well as direct revelation from God. The burning question for the new community was "Who will succeed Muhammad?"

Some of the Prophet's followers claimed that the mantle of leadership should pass down within the Prophet's family to his cousin and son-in-law Ali, and they argued that Muhammad himself had made this designation. This group became known as the Shiat Ali (the Party of Ali), or the Shia. Most Muslims, however, opposed this position. They preferred to rely on tradition that gave tribal elders the right to choose a leader (caliph) who had the most prestige or family power in the tribal system. These became the Sunni, those who follow the path of Muhammad, those who follow tradition, or Sunna.

Shii history, past and present, is that of a minority whose rights have been denied by the Sunni majority. Abu Bakr, Muhammad's close companion and trusted adviser, was selected as the first caliph. Ali was passed over for the position three times. He finally became caliph after thirty-five years, only to be assassinated a few years later. To make matters worse, Ali's charismatic son Hussein, who led a rebellion in order to take over from the caliph Yazid, was massacred along with his band of followers at Karbala (a city in modern Iraq).

The failures of the Shii in their efforts to lead, their ongoing status as an oppressed minority under the Sunnis, and the symbolic memory of Hussein's "martyrdom" at Karbala have produced a worldview of injustice and the need to protest against it. The realization of a just social order became the dream for which Shii struggled throughout the centuries. It provided meaning, inspiration, and mobilization to the Shii community in the twentieth century when the Shii in Lebanon struggled for social and economic opportunity in the 1970s and 1980s, and during Iran's "Islamic" revolution of 1979, in which the shah was equated with Yazid and the Ayatollah Khomeini and his followers with Hussein.

Although united in their common confession of faith in God, the Quran, and the Prophet Muhammad, the histories of Sunni and Shii produced different notions of leadership. In Sunni Islam, the caliph serves as the selected or elected successor of Muhammad. He functions as the political and military leader of the community, but not as their prophet. In Shii Islam, the Imam (leader), selected from among the members of the community, must be a direct descendant of the Prophet's family. The Shii Imam is not only the political but also the religious leader of the community. Though not a prophet, he is considered the divinely inspired, sinless, infallible, final authoritative interpreter of God's will as formulated in Islamic law.

Sunni and Shia also have differing interpretations of history. For Sunni, the success and power of Sunni caliphs in Islamic history were signs of God's guidance, rewards for their faith, and historic validation of Sunni claims to rule. In contrast, the Shia saw these same events as the illegitimate usurpation of power by Sunni rulers. Despite Shia opposition and rebellions, with few exceptions, the Sunni rulers prevailed over the Islamic community for much of Islamic history. For the Shia, history became a theater for the struggle of a righteous, oppressed, and disinherited minority community, who must continue to fight to restore God's rule on earth under his divinely appointed Imam.

Because of disagreements about how many legitimate successors (Imams) of the Prophet and Ali should be acknowledged, the Shia split into three major subdivisions: Zaydi (Fivers), Ismaili (Seveners, who are led today by the Agha Khan), and Twelvers (Ithna Ashari), the most populous group today, who represent a majority in Iran, Iraq, and Bahrain. The Twelvers, whose twelfth imam disappeared, developed a doctrine of the Hidden Imam, a messianic figure who will return at the end of time to restore a perfect Islamic society of justice and truth. Twelver Shii Islam, in contrast to Sunni Islam, developed a clerical hierarchy of religious leaders, called ayatollahs (signs of God) because of their reputations for learning and piety. In Iran, the Ayatollah Khomeini claimed the authority to reinterpret Shii Islam. Khomeini maintained that in the absence of the Imam, the clergy (ulama), who are interpreters of Islamic law, had the right to govern.

Past history and tradition are important for understanding where we are today. The continued importance and influence of Shii Islam can be seen in many charged political events: the powerful role of the clergy in Iran; Iran's regional influence in Iraq and Afghanistan; the political presence and power of AMAL and Hizbollah in the Lebanese parliament and cabinet; Hizbollah's role as an armed militia in its struggle with Israel; sectarian politics and conflicts in Iraq and Pakistan. Sunni Gulf countries like the United Arab Emirates, Qatar, Kuwait, and Bahrain continue to fear Shii Iran's influence and expansion of power in the Gulf. At the same time, Saudi Wahhabi ulama and some Salafi leaders spark conflicts by condemning Shii as heretics and even calling for their death.

Many Muslims have expressed frustration with their own countries' inability to get along and cooperate. When asked what they like least about their countries, they tend to mention "closed-mindedness." To understand Islam and Muslims today, we need to go beyond history and texts to find out what Muslims actually believe about themselves, their world, and global affairs.

What Do Muslims Today Want?

When asked what they admired about Islam, 57 percent of Americans responded "nothing" or "I don't know."[69] Why is that the case? Most of us interact with neighbors, friends, and colleagues who are Christians or Jews; some are religiously observant, others are not. But for many, knowledge of Muslims comes not from direct experience but from media images of explosive headline news, 9/11 and other global terrorist attacks. For many of us, the religion of Islam and the vast majority of Muslims remain "strangers." A well-meaning physician I met recently casually remarked that "Muslims need to reform their religion so their leaders can tell people the Quran doesn't command Muslims to kill us." He, and many others, remain "hostage" to the statements and acts of extremists and lack the knowledge base needed to see the human face of Islam. As a result, "nearly one quarter of Americans, 22%, say they would not like to have a Muslim as a neighbor."[70]

Hearing directly what Muslims around the world say about the West, and about themselves and their world, can work to dispel stereotypes and baseless fears. Are Muslims optimistic about the future? How do Muslim attitudes compare to those of other Americans and Europeans? Surprising similarities and differences emerge from polls. On the one hand, 94 percent of Americans say their lives have an important purpose, compared to only 68 percent of the French and 69 percent of the Dutch. On the other hand, 96 percent of Indonesians give the same answer as most Americans, as do 91 percent of Saudi Arabians.

A similar pattern emerged when respondents were asked if they feel enthusiastic about their future: 86 percent of Americans answer affirmatively compared with only 69 percent of French citizens and a surprisingly low 36 percent of Poles. In contrast, 89 percent of Saudis and 84 percent of Jordanians were closer to Americans in their optimism, versus 67 percent of Turks.[71]

Muslims' answers in the Gallup World Poll with respect to their top priorities demonstrate that we think a lot in common. The hopes and fears of a billion Muslims transcend differences in religions and cultures and reveal our common attitudes and values. Top priorities for majorities of Muslims polled are to:

- improve their economic conditions, employment opportunities, and living standards for a better future;
- strengthen law and order, promoting democratic ideals, eliminating civil tensions and war, and enhancing respect and independence for their countries;
- eradicate illiteracy and ignorance, and achieve gender equality, social justice, and religious freedom.[72]

Obviously, these priorities reflect a desire for massive social, economic, and political change in the Muslim world But will the religion that is so important to Muslims get in the way?

No discussion of the future changes in Muslim countries and in relations between the Muslim world and the West can overlook the multiple and sometimes conflicting roles of religion in politics and society. Rulers appeal to religion for legitimacy when opposition parties seek to challenge their authoritarian regimes. Islamic reform movements reinterpret their faith to better respond to the world today while many hardcore conservatives stubbornly cling to the past. Muslim freedom fighters resist and fight against occupation while extremists wage their wars of terror both in the Muslim world and against the West.

We now turn to examine the reassertion of Islam in Muslim politics and society, looking at its impact and global implications, seeking to answer questions like: Why has so much of the Muslim world rejected a secular path to modernization and development? What is political Islam, or Islamic fundamentalism? When and why did Islamic radicalism emerge in the twentieth century? Are all Islamic movements a threat?

Chapter Two

God in Politics

We face a twenty-first century in which relations between the Muslim world and the United States are at an all-time low. The Bush administration's war against global terrorism made the world less safe; global terrorists and anti-Americanism have grown exponentially; the war against global terrorism has come to be seen by many Muslims (friends and foes alike) across the world as a war against Islam and Muslims, and America is viewed as a major part of the problem, not of the solution.

How did we get here, and what lessons need to be learned? What are the major events that have shaped Muslim politics and our perceptions of Islam and the Muslim world? Why and how did religion emerge in Muslim politics? Are Islamic political and social movements a monolithic threat now and in the future? What are the primary causes of terrorism? What role does religion play? What does the transformation from a local to a global jihad mean for future generations? How has American foreign policy affected the perception of America and future relations with the Muslim world?

The Problem

We are all too familiar with the dark side of Muslim politics and events: the Iranian revolution and American hostages, Osama bin Laden and al-Qaeda, the attacks in New York and Washington on 9/11 and in London on 7/7, suicide bombings, barbaric beheadings, Sunni-Shii conflicts destroying mosques and slaughtering men, women, and children. When President George W. Bush called for a war against global terrorism, his words conjured up images of fighting masked militants, saving innocent victims, and preventing destruction that inspired many in the West. On the other hand, across the world

Muslims see themselves as the primary victims of this terrorism, and they despair over our efforts to fix the problem. Many in the Muslim world also see America using the global terrorism threat as a pretext to extend its neo-imperial ambitions, to create a new world order by redrawing the map of the Middle East to exploit the resources in the Muslim world. Anti-Americanism has grown tremendously not only among the minority of extremists but also among a majority of mainstream Muslims, the so-called moderate Muslims whose very existence it is so fashionable to question.

A NEW EVIL EMPIRE?

We were confronted at the dawn of the twenty-first century with a highly polarized, black-and-white world awash with slogans like "a clash of civilizations," "a war between the civilized world and terrorists," or "a war against fundamentalists who hate democracy, capitalism, and freedom."[1] President Bush's penchant for using the term "evil," characterizing the war on global terrorism as a cosmic war between good and evil and as a struggle against an axis of evil countries, mirrored bin Laden's call for a holy war that pits the forces of God against Satan.[2] The 9/11 attacks, followed by terrorist strikes from Morocco, Spain, and England to Saudi Arabia, Pakistan, Indonesia, and the Philippines, seemed to some to have confirmed post–Cold War warnings of a global Islamic threat.

For many today, it seems self-evident that the religion of Islam, not just Muslim extremism, is evil, the source of terrorism and suicide bombings. Comparing the reactions to Islam in the 1980s, in the aftermath of Iran's "Islamic" revolution, to reactions today might lead some to conclude: "It's déjà vu all over again!" "We were right all along. The threat is real and growing." But a closer look will show that such an approach obscures deeper realities and long-term issues.

A great deal changed in the early twenty-first century. Religious extremism and global terrorism spread as American and European military engagement in the Muslim world escalated; anti-Americanism increased exponentially; terrorist attacks proliferated in Iraq, Afghanistan, Pakistan, Indonesia, and Europe; the Iraqi and Afghan governments and foreign militaries failed to bring security and development as the threat from Iraqi insurgents, al-Qaeda, and the Taliban grew stronger. Despite the Bush administration's call for more democracy, many of America's allies, notably Egypt and Pakistan, became more authoritarian, while others like Morocco and Jordan took detours on their paths to democratization. Failure to address the root causes of terrorism, to significantly change our perception of the world and our foreign policies, will in fact play into the hands of those enemies who believe in and seek to provoke a clash of civilizations. Much depends on what can be learned from the recent past if we want to shape a better and safer future in the new millennium. What are the major events that have shaped the turbulent Muslim politics we witness today and that affect our perceptions of Islam and the Muslim world? What can we learn from them?

ISLAM THROUGH THE PRISM OF IRAN'S ISLAMIC REVOLUTION

In the late twentieth century, Muslim politics deeply affected perceptions of Islam and relations between the Muslim world and the West, as well as the status of Muslims in Europe and America.

The initial disbelief and shock at the fall of the shah of Iran in 1979 were quickly replaced by a fear that radical Islamic fundamentalism, or Khomeini-ism, would spread like wildfire. Khomeini's call for the spread of revolutionary Islam sparked protests and uprisings in the early 1980s in the eastern oil-producing province of Saudi Arabia with its strong Shii minority, as well as in Kuwait and Bahrain.

In the 1980s, fears were focused on radical revolutionary Islam and its threat to the stability of Arab regimes, American access to oil, the security of Israel, and any future hope for peace in Israel/Palestine. In 1981, the assassination of Egypt's Anwar Sadat, who had been awarded the Nobel Peace Prize for his historic peace settlement with Israel, and who had denounced Khomeini as a madman and offered asylum to the shah of Iran, seemed proof of the extent of the "Islamic threat." Also in the 1980s, the Iran-Iraq war brought fears that Iran would topple Iraq's Saddam Hussein and further threaten the security of Gulf monarchies. Iran's role in the creation, financing, and training of Hizbollah to resist the 1982 Israeli invasion and occupation of Lebanon also worried Sunni rulers in the Gulf and Lebanon's Western allies. As we know, Hizbollah was a central player in Lebanon's (1975–90) civil war, fighting other Lebanese militias, taking hostages, and bombing embassies, often targeting American and European personnel and interests. Hizbollah's presence continues, as seen in the 2006 Hizbollah-Israeli war in Lebanon.

Today Iran has reemerged as a strategic player in post-Saddam regional politics. Its growing nuclear capability, influence in Iraq, hard-line rhetoric, and calls for the destruction of Israel, combined with Shii-Sunni conflicts not only in Iraq but from the Gulf to Pakistan, continue to underscore the importance of political Islam both locally and in Muslim-West relations. It clearly took the West many decades to begin to come to terms with the complex forces underlying political Islam. But why were Western policymakers so easily blindsided by the role of Islam in regional politics? And does this same blind spot still obstruct the understanding we need to develop effective strategies for dealing with the Muslim world?

RETREAT FROM THE SECULAR PATH/THE TRIUMPH OF ALLAH'S RULE?

Throughout much of the twentieth century the symbols and benchmarks of modernizing societies were Western in origin. We judged whether a society was "developed" by looking at its "modern" art and architecture, its Western political, legal, educational, or social institutions, and the dress and language of its people. We spoke of the "modern" (Western) skyline of a city, the new versus the old city, New Delhi versus Old Delhi. To be modern meant to adopt Western secular institutions: political, legal, and educational systems. Individuals were judged modern, as distinguished from "traditional," if they wore modern (Western) suits, dresses, and jeans and spoke a modern (Western) language. We believed that every day in every way countries were getting better and better if they implemented Western and secular ideas, languages, institutions, and values.

But by the late 1970s, the resurgence of Islam in both personal and public life seemed to turn the world on its head. Many saw this Islamic revival as evidence of an irrational, retrogressive desire to return to the seventh century. Ironically, the most striking examples of desecularization and religious reassertion occurred in the more modernized, Western-oriented countries of Egypt, Lebanon, and Iran.

Many Muslims became more religiously observant, increasingly attentive to prayer, fasting, and Islamic dress, stressing religious/family values and showing a renewed interest in Islamic mysticism, or Sufism. Publicly, Islam reemerged as an alternative to the dismal failures of secular nationalism, capitalism, and socialism. Rulers from Egypt, Sudan, Libya, and Egypt to Iran, Pakistan, Malaysia and Indonesia, as well as reform and opposition movements, appealed to Islamic symbols, rhetoric, and ideals to legitimate themselves and to mobilize popular support.

Resurgence of Religion in Muslim Politics: Why and How?

Few presidents have been great communicators. Ronald Reagan was certainly among the very best. He could connect with his audience, small or big, move, inspire, and motivate. When Reagan delivered his acceptance speech at the Republican National Convention, like a religious evangelist he called for an American revival, employing the logic of religious (and political) revivalism. Something had gone wrong in America: Khomeini had toppled the shah, and American diplomats had been held hostage for more than a year; America's economy was in serious difficulty; its power and leadership seemed in eclipse. Reagan reassured the American people that there was a formula to restore America to its rightful and righteous place. He identified our fundamental problem and provided the solution.

- The problem? America had failed because it had forgotten or departed from the principles and values of its Founding Fathers, which had made America strong at home and abroad.
- The cure? America had to renew itself, had to recapture its identity, values, and "manifest destiny." In a sense, Reagan advocated a brand of American fundamentalism! He called for a return to those fundamental American principles and values that would once again restore our success, power, and wealth and enable us to reassume America's "manifest destiny" as a global leader.

Few realized at that time that another revival was sweeping across the Muslim world in the late 1970s and 1980s. It has continued for decades, informed by politics as much as by religion, taking many shapes and forms.

Religious revivals, in America or in the Muslim world, are not just about religion. They are a response to political, economic, and social failures, to loss of a sense of identity, values, or meaning, to profound disillusionment or despair. The lure of revivalism is a return to an idealized or romanticized past, the period of the founder(s), an attempt to reappropriate those principles, beliefs, and values that represent divine guidance, a sense of purpose, meaning, and success.

By the 1970s, despite Muslim countries' gaining independence in the mid-twentieth century, the hopes and dreams of many Muslims were shattered by a series of crises across the Muslim world. Political, economic, and military failures discredited regimes, as well as Westernized secular elites and their models of political, economic, educational, and legal development. The quick and decisive routing of the strongest Arab militaries in Egypt, Syria, and Jordan and their massive loss of territory (Sinai, the West Bank and Gaza, and East Jerusalem) in the 1967 Arab-Israeli War, known as the Six Day War, were a devastating blow to Arab pride and power.

The loss of Jerusalem transformed the liberation of Jerusalem/Palestine into a transnational issue that mobilized Muslim public opinion across the Islamic world. In the aftermath of the Six Day War, the humiliating rout remembered by Arabs as "the disaster," both secular and religiously minded intellectuals struggled to answer the same question: "Why?" Why had the combined Arab forces been virtually decimated so quickly and thoroughly? What was it about Arabs that had made them so weak and vulnerable? This crisis of identity and the soul-searching that followed highlighted the failures of Arab governments.

Despite the hopes and expectations of post-independence Muslim states and their adoption of Western political, economic, and military models and institutions, authoritarianism, failed economies, growing disparities between rich and poor, and corruption, the threat of Westernization to Arab/Islamic identity and culture prevailed. Disillusionment with Western models of development in the Muslim world was intensified by America's strong political and military support for Israel in the '67 war. Many concluded that excessive dependence on the West, as a model for development or as an ally, had weakened rather than strengthened the Arab world. These crises reinforced a prevailing sense of impotence and inferiority among many Muslims, the product of centuries of European colonial dominance that left a legacy of admiration (of the West's power, science, and technology) as well as deep resentment (of its penetration and exploitation).

Islamic activist movements like Egypt's Muslim Brotherhood and South Asia's Jamaat-i-Islami (Islamic Society) remembered their founders' warnings about Western imperialism, secularism, and the institutional Church:

> The West surely seeks to humiliate us, to occupy our lands and begin destroying Islam by annulling its laws and abolishing its traditions. In doing this, the West acts under the guidance of the Church. The power of the Church is operative in orienting the internal and foreign policies of the Western bloc, led by England and America.[3]

Many urged a return to the Islamic principles and values that had made Muslim countries so powerful throughout history, insisting Muslims must reclaim their Arab-Islamic heritage, history, culture, and values. This quest for a more historic and authentic identity triggered a resurgence of religion in politics and society across the Muslim world, a force that continues to impact Muslim politics today.

In South Asia, the role of religion was also gaining strength. The 1971 Pakistan-Bangladesh civil war undermined any notion of Muslim nationalism, the glue that was supposed to hold together the ethnically and linguistically different Muslim populations of West and East Pakistan. In the war's aftermath, many Pakistanis called for a return to Pakistan's raison d'être, to be their Islamic homeland and republic. The UC Berkeley– and Oxford-educated Prime Minister Zulfiqar Ali Bhutto turned to the Arab Gulf States, less as a result of his own religious conviction than as a major source of foreign aid and jobs. To do this, Bhutto emphasized their common faith and Islamic solidarity. Yet in exchange he had to respond to the Gulf States' expectations that he would more visibly promote Islam.

Religious resurgence could be seen not only in Sunni but also in Shii Islam. Like Iran, Lebanon in the 1960s and 1970s was regarded as the most stable, modernized, and Western of Arab countries. Beirut, its capital, was a crossroads of East and West, a center of banking, commerce, and luxury hotels featuring the latest boutiques, movies, and technology. The Lebanese mosaic was celebrated as an example of the peaceful coexistence of a multireligious society of Christians, Muslims (Sunni and Shii), and Druze. However, the Lebanese civil war (1975–90) shattered the myth of this successful paradigm.

Over the years, demographic changes had quietly transformed Lebanon's Muslim minority (Shii and Sunni) into a marginalized and disaffected majority now stridently demanding a just redistribution of political and economic power held by Christians. The Shii, among the poorest and most vocal of the disenfranchised, formed militias that battled Christian Lebanese militias and the Israeli military, as well as Western interests. Two major Shii movements/militias that emerged in the 1970s and 1980s remain important today. AMAL (Lebanese Resistance Detachments) was created in 1974 as the military arm of the Shii reform organization, Movement of the Disinherited, to protect and promote Shii rights and interests. More well known and notorious is the Iranian-backed Hizbollah (Party of God) militia, created to combat the 1982 Israeli invasion and occupation of southern Lebanon. Hizbollah has been charged with responsibility for kidnappings, hostage-taking, and embassy attacks, including suicide truck bombings that killed more than 241 U.S. Marines at their barracks in Beirut, Lebanon, in 1983 (a charge Hizbollah has denied).

After the Lebanese civil war, AMAL emerged as a major force in Lebanese electoral politics. AMAL's leader, Nabih Berri, was elected speaker of the Parliament. Hizbollah remains a significant force as a militia, as seen in the 2006 Hizbollah-Israeli war, as well as a political force with elected members in the Lebanese Parliament and the cabinet. It is also a major provider of social and agricultural services to thousands of Lebanese, operating schools and hospitals as well as the al-Manar satellite television and broadcast station.[4]

THE QUIET REVOLUTION: BALLOTS, NOT BULLETS

Although the 1980s were dominated by fears of an Iranian-inspired fundamentalist wave that would destabilize governments through violence and terror, by the 1990s failing economies and widespread public unrest led to a very different result. An alternative, a quiet, nonviolent revolution led by Islamic activists, unexpectedly gained the chance to offer an Islamic solution.

The majority of governments (secular and religious) in the Muslim world have been authoritarian, a legacy of European colonial rule and postindependence regimes that have not fostered democratic governments, institutions, or values. However, during the late 1980s and early 1990s in response to "food riots," protests, and mass demonstrations, elections were held in a number of countries including Jordan, Tunisia, Sudan, Algeria, and Egypt. Nowhere has the impact of the Islamic revival been seen more clearly than in these emerging electoral and social politics. Islamic candidates won in local and national elections and assumed leadership in professional associations and trade unions. Islamic activists provided schools, clinics, hospitals, day care, legal aid, youth centers, and other social services. Private (not government-controlled) mosques and financial institutions such as Islamic banks and insurance companies also proliferated.

Islamic activists' and movements' peaceful participation in government also produced intense opposition. For example, in 1991 elections in Algeria stunned both its government and the West when Algeria's main Islamic party, the Islamic Salvation Front (FIS), won a first-round victory in the country's inaugural multiparty general elections. Although FIS leaders were arrested and imprisoned after they won municipal elections, other FIS candidates nevertheless swept parliamentary elections, and their party was poised to come to power. The specter of an Islamic-movement governance through ballots rather than bullets nevertheless triggered a radical response. The Algerian military canceled the FIS's election victory, imprisoned and outlawed its members, and installed its own, new government. This set in motion a spiral of violence and counterviolence that polarized Algerian society and produced a prolonged civil war (1992–99), costing more than a hundred thousand lives.

Democratic elections elsewhere in the Muslim world during the 1990s successfully brought Islamically oriented candidates into top levels of government. In Turkey, the bastion of secularism in the Middle East, Dr. Necmettin Erbakan became the first leader of an Islamic party to become a prime minister (1996–97); in Malaysia, Anwar Ibrahim, the founder in 1971 of ABIM (Muslim Youth Movement of Malaysia) served as the deputy prime minister from 1993 to 1998; Abdurrahman Wahid in Indonesia, head of the country's largest Islamic movement, Nahdlatul Ulama, was elected president by the People's Consultative Assembly in 1999. The trend continues into the twenty-first century.

In recent years, religiously oriented parties and candidates have continued to prove successful at the polls. In Iraq's general elections in late 2005, the Shiite alliance won 128 of 275 seats.[5] Islamic activist candidates performed strongly in Saudi Arabia's 2005 polls, winning all the seats on the municipal councils in the cities of Mecca and Medina.[6] In Egypt, the outlawed Muslim Brotherhood won an unprecedented fifth of Parliament's seats in late 2005. In the Palestinian territories' first elections in a decade, Hamas overwhelmingly defeated the secular ruling party, Fatah, in early 2006. Islamic activists strengthened their grip in Kuwait's National Assembly, winning twenty-one of fifty seats. In Turkey's secular republic, the Justice and Development Party (AKP), which had won a landslide victory in 2002 parliamentary elections, was reelected in July 2007 with a stunning victory in which the AKP took 47 percent of the vote, far more than the 34 percent the party received in the 2002 election.

The AKP's electoral victories in Turkey are especially remarkable in that it won a parliamentary majority in a Muslim country long regarded as a symbol of secularism in the Middle East. Though its founders, Recep Erdogan (prime minister) and Abdullah Gul (foreign minister and now president of Turkey), were key figures in the Islamic party Welfare and its successor, the Virtue Party, the AKP, chose to create a more inclusive pluralistic (non-Islamic) party with a strong emphasis on economic development and social conservatism. The AKP is a moderate, pro-Western party that advocates a liberal market economy and Turkey's membership in the European Union. Its history and performance demonstrate that the realities of politics can lead Islamists to learn from experience, broaden their vision, adapt to multiple constituencies, and govern effectively.

Taking office in 2002 when Turkey was still reeling from a huge financial crisis, the AKP improved Turkey's economy significantly in the next four years. Inflation dropped dramatically amidst four years of strong growth, from high double digits sometimes approaching 100 percent to 6.9 percent, the lowest since 1970. Investment and corporate growth surged. The party also implemented strong social programs for the urban and rural poor.

The AKP-led government also proved more successful than its predecessors internationally, working with Europe on Turkey's admission to the EU and other shared concerns involving the United States and Muslim countries, while upholding Turkey's independence. Domestically, fears expressed by the military and secular opposition to an "Islamically oriented" government have proven hollow. The AKP leadership have reaffirmed commitment to Turkish secularism. However, their notion of secularism, separation of state and institutional religion, contrasts strongly with hard-line secularists' antireligious approach. Fear of religion is well illustrated in the tension over women's right to wear a hijab. Secularists who dramatize a concern that loosening restrictions on wearing the hijab may result in forcing all women to wear a headscarf seem to gloss over the other side of this human rights issue. For example, Turkish women who wear the hijab are banned from serving in Parliament, from entering or working in government buildings, and from attending university. An even more glaring example occurred when the AKP came to power. The wives of the prime minister and of the majority of cabinet and Parliament members were unable to attend an annual reception given by the "secular-oriented" president of Turkey because they wore headscarves. Moreover, the prime minister's daughters could not attend university in Turkey because of their headscarves; instead, they studied in the United States.

POLICIES OF MUSLIM GOVERNMENTS

Despite the achievements of some Islamist parties and hopes of other Muslim democrats, autocrats are still far more prevalent than democrats in the Muslim world. Only one in four Muslim-majority countries has a democratically elected government. Rulers in countries with allegedly democratic elections routinely win by roughly 90 percent to 99.9 percent. Tunisia's president, Zeine Abedin Ben Ali, won 99.4 percent of the vote in the 1999 elections and 94.5 percent in 2004. In Egypt, President Hosni Mubarak won in 1999 with 94 percent and in 2005 with 88.6 percent of the vote. These facts have led to a prevailing view that Muslims reject democratic freedoms and that Islam is incompatible with democracy. However, it's important to ask if the opportunity for such freedoms is available. A majority of Muslim governments control or severely limit any opposition to their established political parties and NGOs. They have the power to license and ban or dissolve all organizations as well as to control the group's ability to hold public meetings and to access the media.

Authoritarian and repressive regimes in Iraq, Egypt, Syria, Algeria, Tunisia, and Uzbekistan have created contexts in which nonviolent opposition cannot function or is ineffective, leaving only alternative strategies that spawn a violent response. The war against global terrorism has been used by governments (Egypt, Tunisia, Saudi Arabia, Uzbekistan, Pakistan, and Israel) as an excuse to limit democratic forces, to restrict the rule of law and civil society, and to repress nonviolent reform movements. All opponents, secular and Islamic, extremist and moderate, are branded as extremist to control elections and enhance the legitimacy of their authoritarian rule. For example, when he ran for reelection in Egypt's first-ever contested presidential election in 2005, Mubarak promised to repeal Egypt's infamous emergency laws, which allow arbitrary arrests and detentions. These laws have been in place since Mubarak came to power in 1981 and are likely to remain in place since he later reneged on this campaign promise, claiming "security" concerns: living in "an inflamed region," he said, "we have to appreciate that Egypt, from time to time, is targeted."[7] The Mubarak government has continued to intimidate, arrest, and detain its critics in the NGO community, the media, political parties, and the Muslim Brotherhood.

Thus many countries remain "security states" where freedom of association and assembly and freedom of thought and expression are severely limited. In the ongoing struggle and critical choice between ballots or bullets to achieve political change, independent-minded intellectuals, secular and Islamic, continue to be silenced on the one side by fear of state security and on the other by radical Islamic groups. These conditions create an ongoing stream of new recruits willing to fight against what they regard as un-Islamic and oppressive regimes and their foreign allies. So when we think of Islamic political and social movements as a threat now and in the future, we should consider the fact that continued authoritarian regimes are as harmful to our security.

The realities of the Muslim world create a fertile field for growth of a jihad ideology that has been developing since the mid-twentieth century, starting in Egypt, where policies have contributed significantly to the kindling of the terrorist fires, first within the country and later, with impetus from Saudi and Gulf petrodollars, throughout much of the world.

The Birth and Growth of a Jihad Ideology

The events of 9/11 brought into sharp focus a militant struggle within Muslim societies that had been growing for many years. Today terms like "jihadist" and "jihadist movements" are widely used, although not necessarily always understood. Even less understood is the development of religious extremism and terrorism from a local to a global threat.

Anti-Americanism and anti-Western violence and terror that have surfaced globally have deep roots developed over several decades, spawned by ideologues like Egyptian Sayyid Qutb and Palestinian Abdullah al-Azzam and empowered by militant political and religious leaders like Ayatollah Khomeini, Muammar Qaddafi, and Saddam Hussein, as well as al-Qaeda's Osama bin Laden and Ayman al-Zawahiri. While in Western minds these names conjure up dark images of evil predators, some, especially Osama, can be highly regarded heroes in segments of the Muslim world, as reflected in popular culture by T-shirts, posters, and audio, video, and DVD recordings. What accounts for the accolades such leaders receive in the Muslim world?

Sayyid Qutb (1906–66), the godfather (what Marx was to Communism) of radical Islam, has been the major influence on the worldview of radical movements across the Muslim world. His writings have inspired jihadists, who see their struggle as a holy war, fighting occupation, oppression, and American/Western neo-colonialism. His life tells us something important about the making of religious extremists.

Few would have predicted that this well-educated man of letters, a teacher, literary critic, and government official, would become an advocate for militant Islam. Like many other young intellectuals of the time, he studied Western literature and grew up an admirer of the West. Qutb traveled to the United States in 1949 to study educational organization; what he observed proved a turning point in his life and thought. Although he had come to the United States out of admiration, he experienced a strong dose of culture shock and disillusionment. His encounters convinced him of America's (and Western civilization's) materialism, racism, social injustice, and sexual permissiveness, as well as anti-Arab bias, which he perceived in U.S. government and media support for Israel. Shortly after his return to Egypt in 1951, Sayyid Qutb joined the Muslim Brotherhood.

Qutb's militant interpretation of Islam grew out of the confrontation between the repressive Egyptian state and the Brotherhood in the 1950s and 1960s. During the 1950s, Qutb emerged in the Muslim Brotherhood as most influential, among younger, more militant members. His imprisonment (1954–64) and torture were major catalysts in transforming him from an intellectual and prominent mainstream religious writer to a militant radical condemning both the Egyptian and American governments and defending the legitimacy of militant jihad.

Qutb's revolutionary vision is captured in his most influential tract, *Milestones*, a small book he wrote in prison that was used as evidence against him and that led to his being sentenced to death in 1966. Qutb's writings and ideas created the religious worldview and stimulated the discourse for generations of activists, moderate and extremist, including the radical group al-Jihad (Islamic Jihad), which assassinated Egypt's President Anwar Sadat, as well as Osama bin Laden and al-Qaeda. Qutb's teachings recast the world into black-and-white polarities. There were no shades of gray. More than a pious alternative to be achieved in the distant future, creating an Islamic government was a divinely mandated imperative that Muslims must strive to implement immediately:

> There is only one place on earth which can be called the home of Islam (Dar-ul-Islam), and it is that place where the Islamic state is established and the Shariah is the authority and God's limits are observed and where all the Muslims administer the affairs of the state with mutual consultation. The rest of the world is the home of hostility (Dar-ul-Harb).[8]

Given the authoritarian and repressive nature of the Egyptian government and many other governments in the Muslim world, Qutb concluded that change from within the system was futile and that Islam was on the brink of disaster. He saw jihad as armed struggle defending Islam against the injustice and oppression of anti-Islamic governments and the neo-colonial West and East (Soviet Union), necessary to implement a just Islamic order. It was incumbent upon all Muslims. Muslims who refused to participate should be counted among the enemies of God, apostates to be excommunicated (*takfir*), to be fought and killed like the other enemies of God. Many radical extremist groups, for decades after Qutb's death, have kept his vision alive in their ideologies and tactics. Abdullah al-Azzam and Osama bin Laden would transform and implement Qutb's ideas into a global jihadist ideology and movement.

Abdullah al-Azzam (1941–89) has been described as the emir (prince or leader) of global jihad. A mesmerizing speaker, he preached a message of militant confrontation: "Jihad and the rifle alone: no negotiations, no conferences and no dialogues."[9] As with Qutb, political realities, and his personal experiences of the occupation of Palestine and of Afghanistan, conditioned his jihadist worldview. He met his student and protégé Osama bin Laden in Saudi Arabia and later became his mentor in Afghanistan.

Born and educated in Palestine, after the 1967 Arab-Israeli Six Day War, al-Azzam emigrated with many other Palestinians to Jordan, where he continued to fight in the jihad against Israel. Disaffected with Yasser Arafat's

Palestinian Liberation Organization (PLO) in the early 1970s, he went to study in Cairo, where he met Sheikh Omar Abdel Rahman, the spiritual guide for Egypt's al-Jihad, and Dr. Ayman al-Zawahiri, who would later become Osama bin Laden's number two in al-Qaeda.

After earning a doctorate in Islamic jurisprudence at Egypt's al-Azhar University in 1973, al-Azzam taught at King Abdul Aziz University in Saudi Arabia, where he met the student Osama bin Laden. In 1984 al-Azzam and bin Laden founded Maktab al-Khidamat to recruit and assist Arab jihadists, so-called Afghan Arabs. For al-Azzam, Afghanistan was but the first step in a global jihad: "This duty will not end with victory in Afghanistan; jihad will remain an individual obligation until all other lands that were Muslim are returned to us so that Islam will reign again: before us lie Palestine, Bokhara, Lebanon, Chad, Eritrea, Somalia, the Philippines, Burma, Southern Yemen, Tashkent and Andalusia [southern Spain]."[10]

In contrast to Islamic law and tradition, which viewed jihad as a community obligation, al-Azzam issued a fatwa (as would Osama) that the jihad in Afghanistan and globally was an obligatory duty for all able-bodied Muslims. The fatwa, *Defense of Muslim Lands*, would later be published with a preface from Sheikh Abdul Aziz bin Baz, the Grand Mufti of Saudi Arabia, who had also issued a similar fatwa.

Central to al-Azzam's fund-raising and preaching was a cult of jihad and martyrdom, a romanticized and sanctified path of sacrificing one's life for God and receiving the eternal rewards of paradise: "I traveled to acquaint people with jihad. . . . We were trying to satisfy the thirst for martyrdom. We are still in love with this."[11] His ideas were developed and disseminated in books, audiotapes, videos, and a magazine, *Jihad*, distributed internationally. Abdullah al-Azzam's life was cut short when a bomb blew up his car. However, his global jihadist ideology would be carried on and implemented by Osama bin Laden and al-Qaeda.

Who could have predicted that the son of the Saudi establishment would become the world's most wanted terrorist? Born in Riyadh, Saudi Arabia, in 1957 to a prominent family with close ties to the king and one of the largest construction companies in the Middle East, Osama bin Laden studied management and economics at King Abdul Aziz University, receiving a degree in public administration in 1981. The young bin Laden's worldview was deeply influenced by the religious environment of the Saudi Islamic state with its rigid, puritanical Wahhabi brand of Islam, the militant ideas of Qutb and al-Azzam, and political conditions and conflicts in the Middle East. These included an increase in the power and visibility of internal Islamic opposition movements like the Muslim Brotherhood and a series of radical groups in Egypt, as well as Iran's Islamic revolution that rallied Islamic activists across the Muslim world. Saudi Arabia itself was rocked by the seizure of the Grand Mosque in Mecca in 1979 by well-educated, pious activists who denounced the wealth and corruption of the "infidel" House of Saud as well as the corrosive impact of the West on religious and social values. They wanted to purify and return to true Islam, recreating a true Islamic state.

A major turning point in bin Laden's adult life occurred in 1979 when the Soviets occupied Afghanistan. From 1979 to 1982, he used his financial resources to vigorously support the jihad resistance against the Soviets, providing construction materials, building roads and airfields, and then moving to Afghanistan to set up a guesthouse and camps for Arab mujahidin forces. Bin Laden later created al-Qaeda, "the base," to organize and track the channeling of fighters and funds for the Afghan resistance.

Bin Laden returned to Saudi Arabia as a hero after the Soviets withdrew from Afghanistan in 1989, but when he offered to use the Afghan Arab mujahidin to defend Saudi Arabia from invasion by Kuwait in 1990, he received only deafening silence from King Fahd, along with devastating news. America would lead a coalition in the Gulf War of 1991 to oust Saddam Hussein from his occupation of Kuwait. Bin Laden admitted later that seeing the American-led coalition "occupy" Islam's holy land and anticipating America's greater presence and influence in postwar Saudi Arabia and the Gulf transformed his life completely. It put him on an inevitable long-term collision course with the Saudi government and the West.

In 1994 the Kingdom of Saudi Arabia revoked bin Laden's citizenship and moved to freeze his assets because of his support for militant fundamentalist movements.[12] Pushed to the fringe, he left Saudi Arabia for Sudan and then joined other dissident activists and religious scholars in Afghanistan in 1996. Bin Laden found the Taliban's Afghanistan a comfortable haven and useful base of operations. The Taliban leader, Mullah Omar, had been quick to offer sanctuary and express his admiration for bin Laden's sacrifices and dedication to jihad. Bin Laden skillfully cultivated his relationship with Omar and the Taliban, providing financial support, building roads and facilities, and sending his Afghan Arabs to fight alongside the Taliban in critical battles.

Bin Laden's followers grew steadily. He attracted Arab and other Muslim dissidents, many who had had to flee their native countries. They included prominent Egyptian radicals: Dr. Ayman al-Zawahiri, a physician and a leader of the banned Islamic Jihad in Egypt, Rifai Taha Musa, leader of Egypt's banned Gamaa Islamiyya, and two sons of Sheikh Omar Abdel

Rahman, the blind Egyptian preacher indicted for involvement in the assassination of Anwar Sadat, suspected of involvement in the World Trade Center bombing of 1993, and later found guilty of conspiring to blow up major sites in New York City. Ayman al-Zawahiri, with decades-long experience as a jihadist, became bin Laden's mentor and spokesperson, seen in videos denouncing the West and promising further attacks against the West.

In 1996, bin Laden and al-Zawahiri issued a clear manifesto, a Declaration of Jihad to drive the United States out of Arabia, overthrow the Saudi government, liberate Islam's holy sites of Mecca and Medina, and support revolutionary groups around the world. In 2000, he formed the World Islamic Front for the Jihad Against Jews and Crusaders, an umbrella group of radical movements across the Muslim world, and issued a fatwa emphasizing the duty of all Muslims to kill U.S. citizens and their allies. The significance and threat of al-Qaeda would go beyond the organization itself. Bin Laden and al-Qaeda have become the primary symbol, example, and model for many Muslim global terrorists. But is religion their primary driver?

Religion and Terrorism

The primary causes of global terrorism, political and economic grievances, are often obscured by the religious language and symbolism used by extremists. Religion has become an effective way to legitimate the militants and mobilize popular support. As can be seen in Northern Ireland, Sri Lanka, India, Israel, Palestine, post-Saddam Iraq, Kashmir, Chechnya, or in the global strategy of Osama bin Laden and al-Qaeda, the grievance and goal are often primarily nationalist: to end the occupation of lands or to force "foreign" military forces from what these movements regard as their homeland.[13] However, using religious symbolism, referring to moral justifications and obligations, and adding the certitude that comes from moral authority and heavenly rewards can strengthen recruitment and enhance a willingness to fight and die in a sacred struggle.

Secular movements often appeal to the power of religious symbolism. Yasser Arafat, leader of a secular nationalist movement (PLO and then PNA, Palestinian National Authority), used the terms *jihad* and *shahid* (martyr) to dramatize and enhance his cause when he was under siege in Ramallah. The Palestinian militia (not just Hamas) calls itself the al-Aqsa Martyrs Brigade, drawing on the religious symbolism of the al-Aqsa Mosque in Jerusalem, jihad, and martyrdom. Moreover, while religious and nonreligious organizations and movements (whether al-Qaeda or the Marxist Tamil Tigers) share a common strategy, those that are Muslim often identify their goal as Islamic, to create an Islamic government, either a caliphate or simply a more Islamically oriented state and society.

Another factor that obscures understanding of terrorism is the seemingly logical profile of terrorists as unemployed, uneducated psychological or social misfits. In contrast, like people joining many social movements throughout the world, members of terrorist organizations are not solely the "have nots," the poor and oppressed; very often they are bright, educated, motivated individuals responding to what they see as grave political or social injustices. With some exceptions, the new breed of militants and terrorists responsible for violence, from the 9/11 attacks to the London bombings, are educated working-class and middle-class people. Most were not graduates of religious schools like madrasas or seminaries but of private or public schools and universities. Bin Laden was trained in management, economics, and engineering. Al-Zawahiri, a surgeon, and other al-Qaeda leaders, as well as those responsible for the World Trade Center and Pentagon attacks, like Muhammad Atta, were well-educated, middle-class professionals. British-born Omar Sheikh, who was convicted and sentenced to death for the kidnapping and murder of *Wall Street Journal* reporter Daniel Pearl, was educated at elite private schools including the London School of Economics. Five physicians, including Dr. Bilal Abdulla, a U.K.-born and -educated doctor working at the Royal Alexandra Hospital, were arrested in connection with the abortive car bomb attack at Glasgow International Airport on June 30, 2007. This portrait should not have been a surprise. It matches that of groups like Egypt's al-Jihad, Hamas, and others. As studies of the assassins of Egypt's President Anwar Sadat in 1981 concluded:

> The typical social profile of members of militant Islamic groups could be summarized as being young (early twenties), of rural or small town background, from middle and lower middle class, with high achievement motivation, upwardly mobile, with science or engineering education, and from a normally cohesive family. . . . Most of those we investigated would be considered model Egyptian youth.[14]

Religion plays a multidimensional role for those engaging in acts of global terrorism. Some terrorists truly believe and are religiously observant, if distorted in their vision and tactics. Others are less observant, cultural Muslims, who see being Muslim as part of their nationalist or social/cultural identity but may retreat to their religious tradition when under siege or faced with death. Still others appeal to religion primarily as a tactic to legitimate their struggle and mobilize popular support. We find examples of the diverse use of and appeal to religion in conflicts among people of many faiths: Catholics and Protestants in Northern Ireland; Bosniak Muslims, Serbian Orthodox, and Croat Catholics in the Balkans; Tamil and Sinhalese in Sri Lanka; Christians and Muslims during the Lebanese civil war; Sunni and Shii in post-Saddam Iraq as well as among the 9/11 terrorists.

A critical issue is the relationship of religion to violence and warfare. While we commonly reject violent groups and movements, in fact most religions and nations have resorted to violence in their "just" struggles, wars, and revolutions: the holy wars of the Bible, the Crusades, the French and American revolutions, the Afghan jihad, the war on global terrorism. The critical distinction is between the legitimate and illegitimate use of religion to justify the use of violence. This criterion and others are used to determine "just" wars and legitimate resistance or liberation movements versus terrorist movements. The problem is not only adequate criteria but who makes the judgment. "Just wars" are often like beauty in the eye of the beholder. The common position of all sides in political conflicts is that they are fighting a defensive war against aggression and injustice. Similarly, religious leaders have often supported contesting groups in the major wars of the twentieth century: conflicts in Bosnia, Serbia, Croatia, Kosovo, Palestine/Israel, and Northern Ireland, and in the U.S.-led invasion and war in Iraq. While the majority of major religious leaders in the United States, as well as the pope and other international religious leaders, condemned the invasion of Iraq, maintaining that it did not meet "just war" criteria, major Christian Right leaders supported President Bush.

A common charge is that the fight against Muslim extremism and terrorism is affected by Islam's lack of a central religious authority. Muftis (legal experts) can render different legal opinions (fatwas) involving both personal and public life, in business contracts or obligations in marriage and divorce, as well as in fighting and warfare. Moderate religious leaders can counter the fatwas of those who support extremists, but fatwas on both sides may still be considered valid by their followers. Fatwas by radical ulama like Sheikh Omar Abdel Rahman to legitimate terrorism in Egypt and in New York and fatwas from Osama bin Laden and al-Qaeda justifying their global terrorism represent major problems in recent decades. Thus a source of healthy diversity and flexibility in Islam can have a dangerous downside. The "war of fatwas" is reflected in diverse and conflicting rulings about suicide bombing; in sharp differences between mainstream senior religious leaders in Iraq like Ayatollah Ali al-Sistani and militants like Moqtada al-Sadr or the now deceased terrorist leader of al-Qaeda in Iraq, Abu Musab al-Zarqawi; and in the rulings of recent Grand Muftis of Saudi Arabia, the home of Wahhabi Islam, condemning violence and terrorism versus the views and actions of al-Qaeda in that country.

The dilemma of fatwas that legitimate violence and terrorism, coupled with the lack of a central authority, has become an important Muslim issue in the struggle for the soul of Islam, a struggle with obvious implications for global affairs. A number of major efforts have been launched to deal with this issue. High-ranking Muslim religious authorities and scholars are refuting and marginalizing religious extremists by more clearly defining who is qualified to issue a fatwa and what the criteria are for a legitimate fatwa. Proposals have been made for greater centralization through the use of regional councils of muftis. These are important steps in a necessary process of reform.

At the same time, the notion that a lack of central authority is a problem peculiar to Islam and thus makes it more vulnerable to abuse is exaggerated. While it is common to contrast Islam to the papacy in Catholicism, the pope does not speak for Protestants or for Orthodox Christians. There is no central authority in Christianity, nor in Judaism, Hinduism, or Buddhism. Thus, for example, no single authority speaks for Reform, Conservative, Reconstructionist, and Orthodox Judaism. In many cases, local rabbis and their synagogue's board make decisions for their communities.

In addition to fatwas, other forces undercut Muslim terrorists. The violent acts of militants can boomerang and result in a loss of support for terrorists, alienating segments of a society that might otherwise be sympathetic. A major turning point in the Egyptian government's war against organizations like al-Jihad and the Gamaa Islamiyya occurred when attacks in Luxor and elsewhere indiscriminately slaughtered innocent foreigners and civilian Egyptians. Similarly, the Saudis became really aggressive in combating al-Qaeda not in the immediate aftermath of 9/11 (despite the fact that the vast majority of those responsible for attacks against the World Trade Center and the Pentagon were Saudis) but after major attacks in Saudi Arabia targeted and slaughtered not just foreigners but Saudis themselves, including women and children.

THE ROLE OF WAHHABI/SALAFI ISLAM

Pre 9/11, "Islamic fundamentalism" was the common term used to identify radical Islam. Post 9/11, it was replaced by the more specific terms "Wahhabi Islam" and "Salafi Islam." Wahhabi Islam takes its name from Muhammad ibn Abd al-Wahhab, an eighteenth-century religious leader and leader of a sociomoral movement for the reform of society, who formed an alliance with a tribal chieftain, Muhammad ibn Saud, that laid the basis for what would later become Saudi Arabia. The Wahhabi religious vision or brand of Islam is a strict, puritanical faith that emphasizes literal interpretation of the Quran and the absolute oneness of God (monotheism), and it has been a staple of the Saudi government, a source of its religious and political legitimation. Wahhabis denounced other tribes and Muslim communities as polytheists or idolaters. Anything the Wahhabis perceived as un-Islamic behavior constituted unbelief (*kufr*) in their eyes, which must be countered and suppressed.

It was Muhammad ibn Saud's son Abdulaziz who framed the development of Saudi Arabia, using stories and symbols drawn from the life and struggles of the Prophet. He recruited Bedouin tribesmen to join the brotherhood of believers and, like Muhammad's community, engaged in a process of hijra and jihad. Like Muhammad and the early community, they emigrated to new settlements where they could live a true Islamic life and be trained religiously and militarily. They combined missionary zeal, military might, and a desire for booty to once again spread Islamic rule in Arabia, waging jihads approved by their religious leaders. Abdulaziz used the banner of the puritanical Wahhabi to legitimate fighting other Muslim tribal leaders and the seizure of Mecca and Medina. Wahhabi history and paradigms were an essential part of Osama bin Laden's religious faith and sense of history, a heritage he would turn to in later life for inspiration and guidance.

Beyond "Wahhabi," "Salafi Islam" has become the popular term for a movement that has spread beyond Saudi Arabia and the Gulf. The term "Salafi" reflects the claim to return to the pristine Islam of the first generation of Muslims (*salaf*, or pious ancestors). However, both "Wahhabi" and "Salafi" are complex and multilayered terms that can be misleading. They are often used as umbrella terms to identify diverse theologies, ideologues and movements, medieval and modern, nonviolent and violent.

Wahhabis and Salafis idealize the period of Muhammad and his Companions as an uncorrupted time for the religious community. They believe that Islam's decline after the early generations is the result of un-Islamic religious innovations (*bidah*) and that an Islamic revival requires emulating the early generations and purging foreign influences from the religion. Salafis, like Wahhabis, emphasize monotheism (*tawhid*) and insist on the inerrancy of Shariah, or Islamic law. They condemn many common Muslim practices as polytheism (*shirk*) and are opposed to Sufi and Shia doctrines and to most Islamic movements, which they regard as innovations of "true Islam" and therefore "heretical."

Although associated with the Gulf States, Salafism includes many groups and shades of belief. It is found in most Muslim-majority countries and in European and American communities, where it serves as an attractive alternative for disaffected second-generation Muslim youth who want to define their identity and differentiate themselves from the Islam practiced by their parents and grandparents. They see themselves as embracing an authentic, original, "pure" form of Islam that transcends a specific culture and underscores Islam's universality.

Is the Wahhabi/Salafi message necessarily violent and terrorist? True, Wahhabi refers to an ultraconservative, puritanical, absolutist theology based on an uncompromising, polarized view of the world. It pits good against evil, believer against nonbeliever, and Sunni against Shia. Wahhabi zeal resulted in a puritan iconoclasm that historically led not only to the destruction of the tombs of the Prophet and his Companions in what is modern-day Saudi Arabia but also to the destruction of the tomb of Hussein and other major Shia holy shrines and places of pilgrimage in Iran. This inflamed Wahhabi-Shia relations and led to conflicts between Sunni Saudi Arabia and Shia Iran as well as frequent clashes between the Sunni majority and the Shia minority within Saudi Arabia since the late 1970s and between the Taliban and the Shia minority in Afghanistan.

From the late 1960's Wahabbi/Salafi Islam has had a global reach and impact. Saudis, both government-sponsored organizations and wealthy individuals, have supported the export of both the mainstream and extremist forms of Wahhabi Islam to other communities in the Muslim world and the West. Like Libya and Iran, Saudi Arabia has funded international conferences and built mosques, Islamic centers, schools, and libraries. It has paid preacher-missionary salaries and distributed religious texts, all to spread its ultraconservative message.

Gulf States funding to Islamic groups worldwide accelerated dramatically in the 1980s after the Iranian revolution to counter the challenge from Shii Iran's alternative revolutionary Islamic system. Saudi Arabia had developed close ties with major Islamic movements like the Muslim Brotherhood and the Jamaat-i-Islami. In the late 1960s and 1970s Saudi Arabia, Qatar, and other Gulf States gave asylum to Muslim Brothers such as Muhammad Qutb, the brother of Sayyid Qutb, who were well-educated professional Islamic activists with other needed technical skills. Petrodollars enabled movements to internationalize, to create, translate, and distribute worldwide the Islamic ideology of Muslim Brotherhood founder Hassan al-Banna, Sayyid Qutb, and Mawlana Mawdudi, founder of South Asia's Jamaat-i-Islami.

Saudi Arabia's funding efforts were motivated by its desire to project itself as the homeland of Islam, the protector of Mecca and Medina, Islam's holiest sites, and the leader and spokesman for the Muslim world in the international arena. However, at the same time, some wealthy businessmen and organizations in Saudi and the Gulf have provided financial support to radical Wahhabi or Salafi groups representing a jihadist culture that promotes a militant, violent brand of Islam.

Wahhabi/Salafi religious exclusivism is clearly antipluralist and often religiously intolerant of other believers, both other Muslims—in particular Shia, whom they despise—as well as non-Muslims. Wahhabis seek to promote and impose their strict beliefs and interpretations, which are not commonly shared by other Sunnis or by Shii Muslims throughout the Muslim world. In itself, exclusivist Wahhabi theology is not necessarily violent, but its worldview, like that of radical Christian Right preachers, can lend itself to extremism and violence when religious fundamentalists believe they have a mandate from God to impose his will. While those who simply adopt an exclusive theology might tell others, "You're going to hell," religious terrorists say, "I not only know you're going to hell, but I believe that a good Muslim has an obligation to God to send you there now." Global terrorists like Osama bin Laden and Ayman al-Zawahiri, are primary examples of this outlook. Post-9/11 attacks by al-Qaeda within Saudi Arabia and the Saudi jihadists in Iraq have exemplified the militant Wahhabi/Salafi threat.

Wahhabi/Salafi interpretations remain strong but not predominant in many Muslim communities. Their exclusivist, isolationist and often intolerant theologies are no more dangerous than fundamentalisms in other faiths, but their followers will surely be ill equipped to respond to the need for religious pluralism in an increasingly globalized world, a world where millions of Muslims live in non-Muslim-majority countries. However, jihadist movements do constitute an ongoing and direct threat to the security of Muslim countries and the West and will continue to validate those who see Islam as the problem and global jihad as the preeminent threat.

Globalization of Jihad

From the 1970s to the early 1990s, Muslim extremist groups primarily focused within their own countries. With the exception of bombings at the World Trade Center in 1993 and in Paris in 1995, most attacks against Westerners or embassies had occurred within Muslim countries, from

Morocco, Egypt, Saudi Arabia, and Turkey to Iraq, Yemen, Pakistan, and Indonesia. Meanwhile, America and Europe remained secondary targets, "the far enemy," but because of their military and economic support for oppressive regimes, hatred and fear of them continued to build.

In the twenty-first century, most experts expect that attacks globally will continue to grow, making strategies that weaken jihadist groups and their pool of recruits even more crucial. Why the transformation from a local to a global jihad? And what does this transformation mean for future generations?

Although jihad has been an important source of inspiration for Muslims throughout the centuries, as we have seen, the last half of the twentieth century witnessed a globalization of a "new" jihad that has been exploited internationally to powerfully mobilize individuals as well as political and social movements, mainstream and extremist. This term has been central in resistance and liberation struggles, in holy and unholy wars, and there is no indication that its power will diminish in the future. What are the origins of today's global jihad? How was the new jihad born?

THE AFGHAN JIHAD

The 1979–89 Afghan-Soviet war was waged during the Cold War, at the very time that Western and many Muslim nations feared not only Communism but also Khomeini's export of the Iranian revolution. The Afghan war was special because of the countries that supported it, the mass communications that covered it, and the way in which the mass media made it an immediate reality. While many in America, Europe, Pakistan, Saudi Arabia, and the Gulf States feared Iran's evil jihad, both Western and Muslim governments embraced and were anxious to support Afghanistan's "good" jihad with money, weapons, and advisers. And this support was clearly seen through instantaneous global coverage, which enabled Arabs and Muslims to identify with this righteous struggle. Instant coverage helped to raise Muslim consciousness, renewing the sense of belonging to a global transnational community, the *ummah*, and motivating action: many individuals sent financial contributions; some went to Afghanistan to join the jihad.

Globalization of the Afghan war and the inspiring victory of the mujahidin against the powerful Soviets strongly encouraged Muslims to use their religious symbols for the many other struggles they were engaged in globally. Whether resistance or terrorist movements, religious or secular, holy or unholy wars in Bosnia or Kosovo, Chechnya or Kashmir, Iraq or Palestine, all were called jihads, and those who died were identified as martyrs. Unwittingly, the Afghan war had also provided a reality-based training ground for future jihadists, those who came to be called Afghan Arabs, young men whose experiences and victory in battle encouraged them to seek jihads at home or in other Muslim lands. The policies of many Muslim governments have proved to be catalysts for radicalism and terrorism directed both within their countries and toward their Western supporters.

Sunni-Shia Sectarianism

Just as we too often paint the war against a monolithic "global terrorism" and its "terrorist jihadists" with a single brushstroke, we also simplistically ignore the diversity of Muslims and Muslim countries. Not understanding the origins and saliency of Sunni and Shia sectarianism in the Muslim world led us to what we now understand as disastrous results in the invasion and occupation of Iraq and for the future will threaten our ability to effectively handle Sunni-Shia politics in the rest of the Muslim world, especially in the Gulf and in Pakistan.

Sunni-Shia conflicts in modern Muslim politics need to be understood within a political context. Frequently Sunni governments have used what they call a "Shia threat" as an excuse to maintain Sunni dominance. For example, in 1998 the government of General Sani Abacha in Nigeria accused Muslim Brotherhood leader Sheikh Ibrahim al-Zak Zaki of being a Shia before his trial for antigovernment activism. In Malaysia, government clampdowns on and arrests of Islamic activists have often utilized the pretext of protecting Sunni Islam from alleged Shia nefarious activities. Sunni ulama in India and Pakistan condemned Khomeini's trenchant criticisms of the House of Saud as a source of *fitna* (a source of disunity, schism, anarchy), thus evoking memories of Shia rebellions against Sunni Umayyad and Abbasid caliphates in early Islamic history.

Historically, Sunni-Shiite tension has been exacerbated by the often violent repression of Shia in Bahrain, Iraq, Kuwait, Pakistan, and Saudi Arabia, where Shia demonstrations and protests were perceived and portrayed as threats to Sunni rulers. The regimes of Zia al-Haq in Pakistan and Saddam Hussein in Iraq sanctioned the use of sectarian violence to eliminate potential Shia dissent. In Iraq, thousands of Shiites died in assassinations, mass killings, and executions.[15]

Despite the U.S. occupation of and involvement in post-Saddam Iraq, American policymakers continued to be hampered by a dangerous ignorance about Sunni and Shii Islam. The very administration and military that planned the invasion of Iraq was totally blindsided by the important role that Shii Islam and its clergy and militias would play after the "shock and awe." The early years of the American occupation demonstrated the extent to which the Bush administration and Ambassador Paul Bremer, head of the Coalition Provisional Authority (2003–4), did not understand the historical and political context. They could not even identify potential friends or foes among the major Shia leaders, and therefore could not hope to deal effectively with militants like Moqtada al-Sadr or work with potential allies like Ayatollah Sistani. Making sense of the continuing sectarian violence in Iraq, the intricacies of Sunni-Shia politics, and potential conflicts in the Gulf and in Pakistan is critical.

Sectarian violence in Iraq was not simply the product of increasing Shia power in Iraq but the product of both old and recent conflicts and grievances in Shia-Sunni relations described in chapter 1. Under the Sunni dictator Saddam Hussein, the majority of the population, who are Shia, had been excluded from positions of power and purged from the military and government agencies. In 1991 alone, some thirty thousand Iraqi Shia were the victims of executions, assassinations, and mass killings.[16] The fall of Saddam reversed the political fortunes of the Sunni minority (32 percent of Arabs and Kurds) and the Shia majority (65 percent) and rekindled a historic sectarian conflict. The lack of political stability in Iraq after the U.S. invasion in 2003 and the emergence of the Shia as the dominant political force provided fertile ground for massive sectarian conflict and violence, which took hold in Iraqi politics in 2005. Initiated primarily by Sunni insurgents, attacks and counterattacks were justified by both Sunni and Shii using their sectarian identity and religious ideology.

Al-Qaeda Iraq, one of the most prominent Sunni insurgent groups, was founded by the Jordanian-born Sunni Abu Musab al-Zarqawi (d. 2006), who despised Shia and denounced them as apostates. Zarqawi was responsible for some of the bloodiest bombings of Shia mosques and for the killing of Shia religious leaders and civilians as well as Iraq's security forces and U.S. military personnel.[17] Sunni targeting of Shia sacred shrines was intended to weaken a powerful source of Shia strength and resolve, their belief in the return of the Mahdi. As Juan Cole points out:

> The Sunni Arab guerrillas know that this millenarian hope and fervor sustains many Shiites and that they are touchy about it. That is why they have twice bombed the shrine at Samarra, dedicated to the father and grandfather of the Imam Mahdi, and now have hit in such

> a powerful and gruesome way the mosque-shrine of the Imam Mahdi's second Deputy.[18]

Many Shia blamed not only Iraqi Sunnis but also the United States for the desecrations of some of Shii Islam's most holy places. In fact, many Iraqi Shia viewed both the Sunni militia and the Americans as the Anti-Christ, the figure preventing the return of the Mahdi and Jesus Christ. Cole says:

> Ironically, some of the US troops fighting the Shiite millenarians may be evangelicals who also believe that the Return of Christ is near; Iraq is a wonderland for apocalypticism.[19]

The Sunni insurgency's use of sectarian violence and terrorist attacks to capitalize on Sunni fears of the Shia majority was matched by the Shia armed militias' death squads, whose reprisals and ethnic cleansing of Sunni families and neighborhoods have been just as ruthless. The strongest Iraqi Shia militia, the Medhi Army, was led by the young, radical cleric Moqtada al-Sadr, whose father, a revered Shia cleric, was assassinated by Saddam's security forces in 1999. Using Iraqi nationalism and Shia radicalism he mobilized Iraq's poor Shia community to stage intense uprisings against U.S.-led forces. Believed to have the support of up to 15 percent of Iraq's Shia community, or approximately 2.5 million people, al-Sadr also became involved in the political process, controlling thirty seats in the 128-seat Shia bloc that dominated the 275-member Parliament after the December 2005 elections.[20]

The Mehdi Army became one of the major armed forces on the ground in Baghdad, protecting and controlling predominantly Shia areas. According to some U.S. Army commanders, Sadr's militias heavily infiltrated the Iraqi police and army units.[21] Mosque bombings, kidnappings, suicide attacks, and car bombings occurred daily. Iraq, where no evidence of al-Qaeda had existed, threatened to become a training ground for al-Qaeda's future jihads worldwide.

American Foreign Policy: A War Against Global Terrorism or Against Islam?

In the aftermath of the September 11 attacks, President Bush and many other policymakers were careful to emphasize that America was waging a war against global terrorism, not against Islam. However, America's pursuit internationally and domestically of its broad-based war against what are broadly called "terrorists," the rhetoric and policies of the administration that accompanied its actions, mass arrests and detention of Muslims, and the erosion of civil liberties of American Muslims have convinced many Muslims that the war is indeed a war against Islam and Muslims.

The trajectory of American foreign policy and military action—the broadening of the American-led military campaign's scope beyond the invasion and occupation of Afghanistan to second frontiers, the identification of an "axis of evil" (comprised of a majority of countries that were Muslim), the invasion and occupation of Iraq, and the Bush administration's failed leadership in the Palestinian-Israeli conflict and the Hizbollah-Lebanon and Gaza wars—has fed anti-American sentiment among the mainstream as well as the hatred of America among militant extremists. America has come to be seen as a neo-colonial, imperial country, whose overwhelming military and political power has been used unilaterally, disproportionately, and indiscriminately.

Osama bin Laden, like a Hitler or a Stalin, did not mobilize people simply by calling upon them to be terrorists; rather, like the secular Saddam Hussein and the Ayatollah Khomeini before him, bin Laden cleverly identified political grievances against Muslim regimes and America that were shared across a broad spectrum of Muslims, most of whom are not extremists. He then used religious texts and doctrines to justify his jihad of violence and terrorism.

Anti-Americanism has been driven not only by the arguments of terrorists but also by a frustration with American foreign policy among many in Arab and Muslim societies: government officials, diplomats, the military, businessmen, professionals, intellectuals, and journalists. Among Muslim democrats—those who believe democracy is important to their progress and future—very small percentages (only 5 percent to 10 percent) say they believe the United States is trustworthy, friendly, or treats other countries respectfully.[22]

The grievances of mainstream and potential extremists vary from one Muslim country to another, but a prominent concern involves America's longtime support for authoritarian Muslim regimes over the years from Hosni Mubarak's Egypt and Zeine Abedin Ben Ali's Tunisia to Saddam Hussein's Iraq (1980–88) and Parvez Musharif's Pakistan. Critics point out America's double standard in promoting its fundamental principles and values (democracy, political participation, human rights, and basic freedoms of speech, assembly, and the press) selectively or not at all when it comes to the Muslim world. Majorities in virtually every majority Muslim nation surveyed in a Gallup World Poll said they disagreed that the United States is serious about establishing democratic systems in the region. The exceptions were Lebanon (54 percent agreed), Sierra Leone (68 percent), and Afghanistan (53 percent).[23]

Muslims had to look no further than the Bush administration to find corroboration for their concerns. When weapons of mass destruction were not found in Iraq, the administration boldly declared that the U.S.-led invasion and toppling of Hussein were intended to bring democracy to Iraq as part of a broader policy of promoting democracy in the Middle East. In a major policy address, Ambassador Richard Haass, a senior State Department official in the George W. Bush administration, acknowledged that both Democratic and Republican administrations had practiced what he termed "democratic exceptionalism" in the Muslim world: subordinating democracy to other national interests such as accessing oil, containing the Soviet Union, and grappling with the Arab-Israeli conflict.[24] Nevertheless, majorities of Muslims and others in the world saw the invasion of Iraq as a war of occupation. Claims of a commitment to democratization are dismissed as at best a "guided democracy" under American trusteeship. Outside of Iraq, majorities in most of the countries surveyed agreed that the American Iraq initiative has done more harm than good.[25]

The war in Iraq, waged without the support of a broad-based coalition, did not remove a major regional or global threat that possessed WMDs, nuclear weapons, or a major supporter of Osama bin Laden and al-Qaeda. The occupation reduced substantially the quality of life (employment, electricity, water), safety, and security of many Iraqis, pushed Iraq to the brink of civil war, inflamed sectarianism, and ironically transformed Iraq into a training ground for terrorists. It created political and economic conditions that fed radicalization and terrorism, threatened the stability of Turkey, Jordan, Syria, Saudi Arabia, Kuwait, and other Gulf States, and enhanced Iran's stature as a major political player in the Middle East.

Abuses in Iraq, Abu Ghraib, and Haditha, as well as Guantanamo Bay and the rendition of prisoners (that is, transfer of suspected terrorists to "CIA prisons" in countries employing harsh interrogation techniques and torture), undermined the U.S. record on human rights and outraged not only Muslims but many others across the world. This war, condemned by the heads of many mainstream religious faiths, including President Bush's own Methodist denomination, as unjust but supported by the political power of neo-conservatives and the hard-line Christian Right, led to U.S. attempts to circumvent international law: embrace the doctrine of preemptive strikes, sidestep the Geneva Accords, and try to exempt itself from accountability before international tribunals.

The deterioration of Palestinian-Israeli relations and perception of a U.S. bias, diplomatically, politically, and economically, in support of Israel's invasion and wars in Lebanon and Gaza further undercut America's credibility in the Muslim world and internationally. President Bush consistently failed to match his denunciation of Hizbollah's and Palestinian acts of terrorism with an equally tough stand against Israel's use of violence and terror in Lebanon, Gaza, and the West Bank.

The Bush administration unconditionally supported Israel's massive, disproportionate military response, a thirty-four-day war in Lebanon in 2006, to (ostensibly) Hizbollah's July 12 seizure of two soldiers and killing of three others. The day after UN Secretary-General Kofi Annan criticized Israeli bombardment of Lebanon as "excessive use of force," the *New York Times* headline read, "U.S. Speeds Up Bomb Delivery for the Israelis." In response to Hizbollah rocket attacks targeting northern Israeli cities, Israel dropped more than a million cluster bombs, whose primary victims were innocent Lebanese civilians, not terrorists. The air strikes on Lebanon's airport, runways, gas stations, lighthouses, bridges, buses, residences, and power plants left an estimated twelve hundred Lebanese killed, most of them civilians, and a million people homeless.[26] Israel lost 117 soldiers and 41 civilians in the war. Amnesty International accused Israel of attacking and destroying infrastructure indispensable to the survival of the civilian population, entire civilian neighborhoods, villages, and bridges with no strategic value.[27]

THE ISRAELI INVASION AND WAR IN GAZA

America's firm and at times uncritical commitment to Israel's existence, safety, and security were put to the test yet again when Israel on December 27, 2008, launched a twenty-two-day war in Gaza.

While the track record of most American presidents, as witnessed by the U.S. voting record in the UN, has demonstrated the nation's consistent tilt toward Israel, George W. Bush had taken America's relationship with Israel to the next level. The administration's uncritical alignment with Israel supported Israel's reliance on military might rather than diplomacy, ignored its sidestepping of international law, and risked America's complicity in war crimes. The timing of Israel's war in Gaza was calculated, executed on George Bush's "watch," rather than during an unknown Obama administration that might prove less sympathetic. Israel counted on a Bush administration that had supported, but failed to intervene during, the Israeli war in Lebanon.

Reports had circulated in the Israeli press that the Israeli military was planning for and looking for a pretext or provocation to strike. The pretext chosen for the bombings and ground invasion of Gaza was Hamas's violation of a six-month cease-fire by shelling Israel. However, Hamas started shelling only after talks to renew the cease-fire had failed. Despite the fact that the shellings had not killed a single Israeli, Israel maintained that the terror of daily Hamas rocket fire had driven it to war in a "fight to the bitter end."

Israel ignored the fact that during the cease-fire, it had put up blockades to stop essential goods from getting into Gaza. This created a humanitarian catastrophe for Gaza's 1.5 million Palestinian residents by restricting the provision of food, fuel, medicine, electricity, and other necessities of life. The United States and Europe were complicit in the blockade of a democratically elected Hamas government, a siege whose primary victims were Gaza civilians. Hamas militants vented their anger by firing rockets.

Following its pattern in the Israeli-Hizbollah war, the Israeli military engaged in an all-out attack that ignored moral and international standards of warfare. As in Lebanon, so too in Gaza the Bush administration supported an Israeli invasion and war whose major victims were civilians, mainly women and children, condoned destruction of the infrastructure and institutions of society (homes, neighborhoods, universities and schools, mosques, police stations, hospitals), and inflamed the hatred and radicalization of a future generation of Palestinians.

The dead numbered more than thirteen hundred Palestinians, and at least five thousand were injured. Many of the victims were civilians, including at least four hundred children. The proportion of Palestinians killed to Israelis was 100 to 1. The United States provided Israel with the F-16s, Apache helicopters, and bombs used to massacre Gaza civilians and even abstained from a UN vote for a cease-fire that it helped draft. It followed the Israeli government in blaming Hamas solely for civilian deaths in Gaza just as it blamed Hizbollah for the high civilian casualty count in Lebanon.

Despite calls from the international community (including the UN, the EU, international human rights organizations, and many religious leaders, among them Pope Benedict XVI) for an immediate cease-fire, Israel, with the blessing of the Bush administration, continued, even escalated, its air and ground war, flouting international law and the criticism of Amnesty International for its "war crimes." Its conduct led critics to declare that Israel had become a "rogue state." As Professor Avi Shlaim, an Israeli and a distinguished professor of international relations at Oxford, concluded:

> A review of Israel's record over the past four decades makes it difficult to resist the conclusion that it has become a rogue state with "an

utterly unscrupulous set of leaders." A rogue state habitually violates international law, possesses weapons of mass destruction and practises terrorism—the use of violence against civilians for political purposes. Israel fulfils all of these three criteria; the cap fits and it must wear it. Israel's real aim is not peaceful coexistence with its Palestinian neighbours but military domination.[28]

Cardinal Renato Martino, head of the Pontifical Council for Justice and Peace, has also severely criticized Israel's conduct of the war: "We are seeing a continual massacre in the Holy Land where the overwhelming majority has nothing to do with the conflict, but it is paying for the hatred of a few with their lives.... Let's look at the conditions in Gaza: It's looking more and more like a big concentration camp."[29]

Demonstrations throughout the Arab world, popular political discourse, and the Internet discredited the ambivalence and failure of Arab leaders and the Arab League to respond effectively and reinforced for many the belief that, as in Palestine, Islam is the only viable political alternative in the Arab world. The failures of Arab and Western governments and resultant inflamed anti-American/Western popular sentiment provided fodder for militants and threatened the security of mainstream Muslim societies and the West.

The Ongoing Challenge

Since the 1970s, Islam has emerged as a powerful force in Muslim politics, mainstream and extremist. Governments and Islamic movements, mainstream reform and opposition and terrorist, have appealed to religion as a source of identity, legitimacy, and mobilization. Religious extremist and terrorist movements today are both local and global. Today, Muslims face a twofold challenge of religious and political reform, both of which are integral to the development of Muslim communities and the marginalization and containment of religious extremism and terrorism.

Religious leaders and intellectuals play a critical role in this struggle for the soul of Islam. They bring to bear a religious authority and interpretations of Islam that better enable Muslims to face the many challenges of the relationship of faith and life in today's rapidly changing environment and discredit theologies of hate. The ongoing challenge is to formulate and implement doctrinal and educational reforms (in schools, madrasas, and universities) that more effectively respond to the challenges of globalization in the twenty-first century with its need for all religious faiths to emphasize inclusive rather than exclusive theologies, theologies that foster mutual understanding, respect, and religious pluralism.

As we shall now see in the next chapter, a globally and intellectually diverse group of reformers do exist, working and speaking out on issues of religious and political reform. Who are some of these major reformers? What do they identify and address as key issues in Islam and in relations between Muslims and (and in) the West in the twenty-first century?

Chapter Three

Where Are the Muslim Reformers?

"We need a new theology, a period similar to the Protestant Reformation; the lesson of Luther's movement should not be lost."

Mohammad Iqbal, *The Reconstruction of Religious Thought in Islam*

Is Islam Capable of Reform?

In Japan more than a decade ago, Indonesia's Abdurrahman Wahid (then leader of a thirty-million-strong Islamic movement and later to become democratic Indonesia's first president) and I faced a ballroom of Japanese businessmen and diplomats. Islam's supposed incompatibility with modern science and technology and its inability to reform dominated their comments and questions. Echoing many who in the mid-twentieth century doubted whether Muslims could choose between "Mecca and mechanization," the Japanese expressed strong doubts that Muslims would embrace modernization, given their religion and culture. In an attempt to break through their stereotypes, I told them how as a young boy I was disappointed when I received a gift made in Japan. The "wisdom" of the time was that a product "made in Japan" was cheap and inferior to anything made in America; it was inconceivable that the Japanese would ever challenge American technological superiority. Yet here I was today, I announced, the proud owner of a Lexus! The light suddenly went on for many of our listeners.

At one level, the questions "Is Islam capable of reform?" and "Are there Islamic reformers?" are, like many asked about Islam today, strange, even absurd. They seem to start with an assumption of "Islamic exceptionalism," the conviction that Islam is unlike any other religion. As any student of the history of religions can tell you, all of the major world religions have changed and continue to change. Given human nature and dynamic historical and social contexts, change is inevitable. The issue, even among conservatives or fundamentalists, has not been whether there will be change but rather how much and what kind.

Post 9/11, the call to reform Islam, to strengthen its relevance in a rapidly changing twenty-first-century world, has intensified. If some say that Islam is a perfect religion that doesn't need to change or adapt, others stress that Islam is inherently dynamic and that reinterpretation and reform are critical in the struggle to respond to the demands of our times, to marginalize extremists, and to promote gender equality, religious pluralism, and human rights. This debate has been intensified by a number of forces, from modern technology and mass communications to the growth of religious extremism and terrorism in the name of Islam. But, if this is the case, who and where are the Islamic reformers, the Muslim Martin Luthers of today?

For several decades, an influential group of vibrant Muslim intellectuals and religious leaders, from Africa to Asia, from Europe to America, have addressed the role of Islam in contemporary society: How do religion and Islamic law contribute to the modern nation-state? Where do Islamic values apply to key issues of today, like democracy, secularism, gender equality, human rights, free market economies, modern banking? What is the role of the clergy (ulama); are they the preeminent authoritative voices who speak for Islam?

Reformists are clergy, as well as intellectuals and activists; rulers and citizens, both traditionalist and modernist. They can be found at Islamic institutes and universities, at academic and religious conferences, and in parliamentary debates. Reformist ideas proliferate in hundreds of books and articles, audios, videos and DVDs, in newspaper editorials, in muftis' fatwas, and on the Internet. As in Christianity, change in Islam is not limited to debates in theology and law but also involves struggles in politics and society, and at times violence and terror.

Most of us have forgotten that Christianity struggled mightily over many centuries to bring about change. The Protestant Reformation started as an attempt to reform Roman Catholicism on issues as diverse as the papacy, the priesthood, the Eucharist, devotion to the Virgin Mary and the saints, the existence of purgatory, and the sale of indulgences. It is common to think of these controversies in terms of theological discussion and debate, which resulted in "the Enlightenment" and "the Protestant Reformation." What we may not remember is that this religious reform was part of a centuries-long process that included the bloody "Thirty Years Wars" between Protestants and Catholics, engulfing popes and monarchs, clergy and laity, in a struggle that was as much about religious and political authority and power as it was about doctrine and ritual. This was a time of religious rebellion and persecution, of violence and terror in the name of God. Both sides suppressed, imprisoned, tortured, and executed their opponents; destroyed churches, cathedrals, schools, and libraries.

Conflict has persisted in post-Reformation Christianity. Christians battle over issues that include modern biblical criticism versus the inerrancy of the Bible, creationism versus evolution, the search for the historical Jesus versus the Jesus of faith, the trinity, religious pluralism and dialogue, relativism, women and gays in the ministry, birth control, abortion, stem cell research, and finally, defining new roles for the laity in the churches. Today, after all the debates and battles, Christians still hold positions that range from fundamentalist and evangelical to Roman Catholic (conservative and liberal), mainline Protestant, Eastern Orthodox, and Unitarian.

Just like Christians, Muslims represent many diverse orientations, from literalist/fundamentalist, conservative, and traditionalist to secular and reformist. In contrast to Christian reforms that grew out of and were influenced primarily by conditions in the West over several centuries, Islam and Muslims have decades, not centuries, to make significant progress in a globalizing world characterized by Western political, military, and economic hegemony. Many Muslims today pursue reform not from a position of power and strength but from one of relative weakness, struggling for change in the face of authoritarianism and repression, limited freedom of speech and the press, and in some cases war and terror.

The Legacy of Islamic Modernism

Reform has been an integral part of Islam's history. The Prophet-Reformer Muhammad and his early community struggled to improve their world by establishing an Islamic order. In every age, the glaring disparities (real or perceived) between God's will and the state of the world have inspired religious reformers (*mujaddids*) and movements that called Muslims to reform their society and follow Islam more faithfully. This was supported by the belief, from a hadith, that in every century "God will send to His community one who will renew its religion." In times of division and decline, religious scholars and movements (most mainstream but some extremist) have risen up to call the community back to its fundamental message and mission.

From its earliest days, Islam possessed a rich tradition of reform. The concepts of renewal *(tajdid)* and reform *(islah)* are fundamental components of Islam's worldview, rooted in the Quran and the Sunna of the Prophet.[1] Both concepts involve a call for a return to the fundamentals of Islam (the Quran and Sunna). *Islah* is a Quranic term (7:170; 11:117; 28:19) used to describe the reform preached and undertaken by the prophets when they warned their sinful communities and called on them to return to God's path by realigning their lives, as individuals and as a community, within the norms of the Shariah. This Quranic mandate, epitomized in the lives and preaching of the prophets, especially of Muhammad, coupled with God's command to enjoin good and prohibit evil (3:104, 110), provides the time-honored rationale for Islamic reformism, however diverse its manifestations in history.

Renewal *(tajdid)* is based on a tradition of the Prophet: "God will send to this *umma* [the Muslim community] at the head of each century those who will renew its faith for it." The renewer *(mujaddid)* of Islam is believed to be sent at the beginning of each century to restore true Islamic practice and thus regenerate a community that tends, over time, to wander from the straight path. The two major aspects of this process are, first, a return to the ideal pattern revealed in the Quran and Sunnah, and, second, the right to practice *ijtihad,* to interpret the sources of Islam. Implicit in renewal are (1) the belief that the righteous community established and guided by the Prophet at Medina already possesses the norm, (2) the removal of foreign (un-Islamic) historical accretions or unwarranted innovations *(bidah)* that have infiltrated and corrupted community life, and (3) a critique of established institutions, in particular the religious establishment's interpretation of Islam. Down through the centuries, Muslim theologians like Muhammad al-Ghazali (d. 1111) and leaders of eighteenth-century revivalist movements (the Mahdi in the Sudan, Muhammad ibn Abd al-Wahhab in Arabia, and Shah Wali Allah in India) claimed the right to reinterpret Islam in order to purify and revitalize their societies. However, in contrast to the Islamic modernist movement of the nineteenth and twentieth centuries, the purpose of reinterpretation *(ijtihad)* was not to accommodate new ideas but to get back to or reappropriate the unique and essentially complete vision of Islam as preserved in its revealed sources.

Today, reformers rely heavily on ideas and strategies developed by Muslim leaders who faced the crisis of European colonialism and hegemony in the late nineteenth century. In the midst of political and economic decline, Muslim reformers from North Africa to Southeast Asia called for *ijtihad* of

Islam as they struggled to meet the demands of modern life. Like secular Muslims, Islamic reformers were influenced by the challenge and threat of the "success of the West." The West was strong; Muslims were weak and subject to Western domination. They called for an Islamic renaissance to respond appropriately to modern Western ideas and institutions. This renaissance, they believed, would be the first step on the road to revitalizing Islam, restoring Muslim power, and gaining national independence.

Islamic modernists argued that the decline of the Muslim community was not due to any flaw in Islam itself but rather to departure from the dynamic faith and practice of the Prophet Muhammad and the early Muslim community. Men whose names and ideas remain alive today, Jamal al-Din al-Afghani (1838–97), Muhammad Abduh (1849–1905) in Egypt, and in the Indian subcontinent Sayyid Ahmad Khan (1817–98) and Muhammad Iqbal (1876–1938), called for purification, reconstruction, and renewal of Islam to replace the prevalent static, medieval religious worldview. There were calls for theological, educational, and scientific development, an Islamic reformation. At the end of the nineteenth century, Sayyid Ahmad Khan argued the need for a new theology: "Today, as in former days, we need a modern theology by which we either render futile the tenets of modern sciences or [show them to be] doubtful, or bring them into harmony with the doctrines of Islam." Ahmad Khan devoted his life not only to religious but also educational reform, establishing Aligarh University, whose modern curriculum was modeled on Cambridge University's. Decades later in South India, Muhammad Iqbal, a philosopher-poet who had earned a law degree in London and a doctorate in Germany, called explicitly for an Islamic reformation: "We need a new theology, a period similar to the Protestant Reformation; the lesson of Luther's movement should not be lost."

Islamic modernists focused on the compatibility of Islam with reason, science, and technology. They cited impressive historical Muslim contributions to mathematics, algebra, geometry, medicine, and the sciences to show that Islam was a religion of reason and progress. They called for a bold reinterpretation (*ijtihad*) of Islamic law and theology, one that would distinguish between the fundamental and unchangeable religious observances of Islamic law (prayer, fasting, and pilgrimage) and social legislation (marriage, divorce, contracts, and even political systems) that could be reformulated and changed to meet the demands of changing societies and modern life. This led to the development of a key method for Islamic reform, which is frequently cited today: making the important distinction between unchanging, divinely revealed principles and values (Shariah) and historically conditioned human interpretations (*fiqh*), or man-made Islamic laws. These man-made laws must be able to respond to changing circumstances and new problems arising in modernity.

Interestingly, most reformers were not traditionally trained religious scholars but rather modern educated "laymen," professionals who repudiated the authority of conservative ulama as the sole "keepers of Islam," as well as the tradition that the ulama's legal doctrines and interpretations of the past were binding. They reinterpreted Quranic verses to promote greater gender equality, to restrict polygamy and a husband's unilateral right to divorce, and to promote education for women. However, their impact was limited by the influence of authoritarian regimes and an entrenched conservative religious establishment. Moreover, most reformers failed to understand the need for strong reform organizations. Their ideas did not quickly materialize into popular mass movements. Yet the power of their reinterpretations of Islam formed a strong foundation that many are building upon today. The legacies of Abduh, Khan, and Iqbal are alive among reformers working to legitimate and Islamize modern ideas of democracy and parliamentary government, human rights, and gender equality and reforms to establish educational institutions that combine "modern" curricula and Islamic studies. Islamic modernist ideas and values have entered into the stream of Muslim discourse and, as we will see, have become part of mainstream Muslim thought.

Rethinking Islam

The tradition of Islamic reform established in the early community continues today, often obscured by hard-line clerics and terrorists who receive a disproportionate amount of coverage. Muslim voices of reform, scholars (ulama and lay intellectuals), the "Martin Luthers," and televangelists, the "Billy Grahams," represent a diverse collection of Muslims: men and women, laity and clergy, professionals, scholars, and popular preachers. Their audiences extend from North Africa to the Gulf States, South to Central and Southeast Asia, and Europe to America.

This chapter will look at a sampling of Muslims across the globe who spearhead a dynamic rethinking of Islam and its role in the world. My use of terms like "Islamic reformation," "Martin Luthers and Billy Grahams," or "televangelists" is functional, referring to a major period and process of reform. But this does not imply or equate Islamic reform with specific emulation of the Protestant Reformation. Reformers are significant not only because of their ideas and orientations but also because they are debunking entrenched perceptions: Islam is medieval, static, and incapable of change; Islam is a violent religion; Islam degrades women; Islam and democracy are incompatible; Muslims do not speak out against religious extremism and terrorism; Muslims reject religious pluralism and interfaith dialogue; Muslims cannot be loyal citizens.

The number and diversity of today's reformers bely the oft-raised question (with its implied skepticism) "Are there really any Muslim reformers?" I could wish there were fewer, because I would not have faced the difficulty of selecting a representative sample. My primary criteria for selection were that each enjoys a significant following or audience and that together they provide a spectrum of religious and lay as well as traditionalist, or perhaps more accurately neo-traditionalist, and modernist voices for change in the twenty-first century. I am as concerned about their methodology as about what they say because in gaining support for Islamic reforms, how one arrives at conclusions can be as important as the conclusion itself.

Tariq Ramadan and Amr Khaled were both named to *Time* magazine's annual list of the one hundred most influential people in the world. Preeminent muftis like Sheikh Ali Gomaa, the Grand Mufti of Egypt, Mustafa Ceric, the Grand Mufti of Bosnia-Herzegovina, and Qatar's Yusuf Qaradawi are well-known senior religious officials with differing styles and perspectives. Nurcholish Madjid from Indonesia, Timothy Winter (Abdal Hakim Murad) in Britain, Farhat Hashmi in Pakistan and Canada, Amina Wadud in the United States, and Heba Raouf in Egypt are Islamically and Western-educated scholars from very diverse cultural contexts. Hashmi, Wadud, and Raouf are female reformers who often have diametrically opposed positions on women in Islam. Abdullah Gymnastiar in Indonesia, like Amr Khaled from Egypt, represents a new breed of popular televangelists addressing key questions about "How shall we live?" for Muslims around the world.

TRADITION AND MODERNITY OR LINKING PAST AND PRESENT

A major challenge for all Muslim reformers is the importance of linking, of showing continuity, between proposed changes and long-held Islamic beliefs and traditions. Other faiths (Catholic, Protestant, and Jewish) have gone through and still struggle with a similar process, as they deal with reforming traditional norms for marriage, divorce, abortion, and homosexuality or new issues like stem cell research and cloning. The legitimacy of Islamic reformist thought, its acceptance or rejection, hinges on its perceived Islamic character and authenticity. Therefore, the "how" is as important as the "what"; the process of change (methodology) is often as important as the actual reforms themselves.

Not surprisingly, reformers often emphasize that they are not advocating anything radically "new," that Islamic tradition has always recognized the need to reinterpret its sources in light of current cultural and social realities. Like Islamic modernists of the late nineteenth and early twentieth centuries, most reformers today draw a sharp distinction between obligations to God or worship (such as prayer, zakat, the fast of Ramadan) and laws that govern social and human affairs (marriage, divorce, inheritance, contracts, bank interest, mortgages) that can be changed in response to new circumstances.[2] As Tariq Ramadan puts it:

> Faithfulness to principles cannot involve faithfulness to historical models because times change, societies and political and economic systems become more complex, and in every age, it is in fact necessary to think of a model appropriate to each social and cultural reality.[3]

But what about the sacred sources, the Quran and Prophetic traditions? Do they block change, reducing religion to a sacralized static worldview?

Many reformers point out that the belief that scripture is the literal word of God does not require a literalist interpretation of texts, nor does it prevent the re-reading and reinterpretation of religious texts. "Change," according to Ramadan, requires "re-reading the scriptural sources themselves with a new eye. . . . This renewal is not a modification of the sources but a transformation of the mind and eyes that read them, which are indeed naturally influenced by the new social, political and scientific environment in which they live. A new context changes the horizons of the text, renews it, and sometimes gives it an original purport, providing responses never before imagined."[4]

Ramadan's position provides space for affirmation both of Islamic tradition and of the need and the ability to re-read sacred texts in response to changing or new historical, political, and social contexts. He seeks to demonstrate the continuity between his reformism and Islamic tradition.

The fact that Islamic tradition, law, and theology are based on the Quran and Prophetic traditions has led some reformers to embrace a methodology that sacralizes tradition or classical/medieval Islam. Many authorities, past and present, regard the major Islamic schools of law and classical Islamic law as authoritative sources that cannot be substantially questioned or altered. Indonesia's Nurcholish Madjid goes to the heart of the matter, pointedly urging Muslims to "desacralize" tradition, to distinguish between the universal and the particular, between unchanging prescriptions of God and Muslim cultures and traditions that are subject to change. Madjid, like Ramadan, is cognizant of the difficulty many Muslims face when the boundaries between the transcendent (unchanging) and the particular (subject to change) are blurred.[5] The result is a sacralized and static religious worldview.

The power of tradition or the classical formulation of Islam affects many critical issues. In Sunni Islam, the consensus (*ijma*) of past religious scholars is considered authoritative. Therefore the requirement that women wear the hijab or are forbidden to lead mixed gender prayers is seen as authoritative, even if the Quran does not speak to these issues and even if the Prophetic traditions can be cited to show that such restrictions are not required. (This is similar to the denial of women's right to be ordained a priest in the Catholic Church based on tradition even though no supportive specific New Testament text exists.) For Muslim traditionalists, failure to establish a link or continuity between the authoritative consensus of the past and modern reform is unacceptable. At Cairo's al-Azhar University (a major center of Islamic learning and religious authority) a popular saying encapsulates this outlook: "Consensus is the stable pillar on which the religion rests."

Modern reformers like Nurcholish Madjid or Mustafa Ceric respect tradition but advocate a creative synthesis of traditional and modern scholarship. While emphasizing the merit of classical Islam and its legacy, they maintain that tradition is not an absolute reference point or religious authority but rather a tool for solving modern problems.[6] Thus, when necessary, they go directly to the Quran. They feel free to reject past interpretations that they see as conditioned by historical and social contexts, no longer relevant or useful and, most important, not based on a Quranic prescription. They re-read sacred texts in today's context and produce new or fresh interpretations of the Quran.

Nurcholish's treatment of apostasy in Islam provides a timely, and controversial, example of the process of desacralization and reform. He maintains that the Islamic law on apostasy, which prescribes the death penalty, has no basis in the Quran. Rather, it was a man-made effort in early Islam to prevent and punish the equivalent of desertion or treason. Times have changed, he argues, and so must the law. Citing Quran 3:85 and 18:29, Nurcholish argues that punishment for leaving the faith is not a matter for the state but God's decision on the Day of Judgment.

Reformers like Ramadan and Nurcholish might be dismissed by conservative ulama and other Muslims as laymen whose modernist agenda is influenced by their education and exposure to the West, but there are also prominent ulama who reflect reformist ideas. In a response published by the "On Faith" online forum of the *Washington Post* and *Newsweek* magazine, Sheikh Ali Gomaa, the Grand Mufti of Egypt, declared that God has given freedom to all of humanity; this includes the right to choose their own religion without it being imposed upon them from the outside.[7] Ali Gomaa cites the Quran to argue that Muslims are free to choose another religion: "The essential question before us is can a person who is Muslim choose a religion other than Islam? The answer is yes, they can because the Quran says, 'Unto you your religion, and unto me my religion,' [Quran, 109:6], and, 'Whosoever will, let him believe, and whosoever will, let him disbelieve,' [Quran, 18:29], and, 'There is no compulsion in religion. The right direction is distinct from error,' [Quran, 2: 256]."[8] But freedom, Ali Gomaa stresses, also means responsibility. Choice means freedom, including the freedom to abandon one's religion, although it is a sin punishable by God on the Day of Judgment.

Not only modern reformers but also some avowed traditionalists distinguish between religious observances and social obligations. Sheikh Yusuf Qaradawi is one of the Muslim world's most senior and esteemed religious authorities. Trained at al-Azhar, Qaradawi is a scholar and mufti for whom the classical Islamic tradition is central and authoritative. Yet he too accepts a methodology that distinguishes between a Muslim's duties to God or worship, the required rituals of Islam where no room for reform exists, and other areas of Islamic law. Thus, for example, religious obligations like zakat (almsgiving) cannot be replaced with modern governmental taxes; the fast of Ramadan cannot be observed during a different month. Likewise, Friday congregational prayer cannot happen on another day. However, "in relation to acts other than the purely devotional ones," Qaradawi writes, "we may examine them in light of their underlying meanings and purposes. Once we grasp such meanings, we can base verdicts thereon and either accept or reject them."[9] A legal doctrine or authoritative interpretation might have been appropriate in the past but not respond adequately to new social realities and circumstances.

Tariq Ramadan, conscious that any criticism of the classical tradition risks undermining his credibility and reformist agenda among large sectors of Muslims, avoids taking on the question directly and tries to walk down the middle. Ramadan finds "space" for reform, by maintaining that the Quran permits everything except what is explicitly forbidden by a revealed text or the consensus of religious experts. Thus, for Ramadan, "the scope for the exercise of reason and creativity is huge."[10]

Qaradawi similarly claims that everything is acceptable (*halal*) unless proven forbidden (*haram*) by an explicit Quranic or Prophetic text.[11] This not only positions him as a neo-traditionalist religious scholar but also places him in direct conflict with many Salafi Muslims, puritanical, ultraconservative, or fundamentalist, who maintain that "everything is forbidden unless proven acceptable."

Qaradawi's traditionalist but also reformist vision is popularized in his *The Lawful and Prohibited in Islam,* a basic and authoritative guide followed by many Muslims in the Arab world and in the West. He speaks to the everyday problems and issues Muslims encounter in life—from marriage, divorce, and raising children to business transactions and Islamic dietary requirements. In contrast to the fatwas of more conservative ulama, Qaradawi's are informed by his belief, based, he says, on the Quran and Prophetic traditions, that the purpose of Islamic jurisprudence is to make things easy for people, not difficult. In penal law, Qaradawi maintains that the least rather than the maximum punishment should be applied; for example, repentance is sufficient to rescind the *hadd* punishment (amputation for theft, stoning for adultery, etc.), and the punishment for drinking wine ought to be discretionary.[12] Similarly, Qaradawi insists that the job of Islamic legal experts is to facilitate change rather than to cling to the past, opposing reforms in areas as diverse as financial transactions, women and the family, the arts, and entertainment.

Sheikh Ali Gomaa, Grand Mufti of Egypt, also emphasizes the importance and centrality of the Islamic legal tradition. But he carefully mines the tradition to find fresh legal responses to new situations and issues. In contrast to those who view the sacred sources of Islam and the principles of Islamic jurisprudence as fixed and unchanging, he believes that specific laws are conditioned by their historical context and subject to change. He is careful not to challenge the interpretations of major scholars of the past, but instead argues that current times and conditions render some interpretations unsuitable and require new solutions:

> We hold the sources of knowledge sacred because we believe they are from God. So we cannot say that the legal questions produced by scholars are incorrect, but rather they were correct due to their relation to their time and place. . . . We hold a different opinion [today] due to the difference in time, place, persons, or conditions. From here stemmed the theory of *the obligation of one's time*, which means that every age carries with it a duty with which the scholars must be occupied. This duty changes with the change of time and conditions of the people. . . . While we believe legal questions may be constrained by their time or place, for example, we also believe they were correct for that time or that place, even if they are no longer suitable for our current times. From here came the rule that we respect the tradition but we do not hold it sacred, meaning by "tradition" the intellectual output of scholars and their scholastic efforts throughout the ages.[13]

"TRUE ISLAM" AND "EXTREMIST ISLAM": DRAWING THE LINE

Consumed by our own fears of terrorism and extremism in the West, we sometimes forget that such violence represents an even more destructive force against Muslims. Not only are Muslims the majority of victims in terrorist attacks, but fear of continued violence across the world has linked their religion with all that is threatening and evil and painted all Muslims as people who do not fight these evils or speak out against them.

September 11 and its aftermath have been a wake-up call for many Muslims. While some have been and may still be in a state of denial, many others recognize the global threat of religious extremism and understand the need to join the worldwide struggle to delegitimate and marginalize extremists. Reform is the key to Muslims' future, a future in which the distinction between "true" and "extremist" Islam will be critical.

Many Muslim leaders denounce the attacks of 9/11 and other acts of terrorism and draw a sharp line between "true" Islam and "extremist" Islam. However, they differ considerably in their definitions of legitimate and illegitimate violence and what constitutes terrorism. Suicide bombing in Palestine is a particularly contentious issue.

Timothy Winter, a Cambridge University professor and prominent Muslim religious leader, represents many Muslims in his clear and straightforward rejection of extremists like al-Qaeda as religiously illegitimate and inauthentic. A traditionalist, Winter decries extremists' failure to adhere to the classical canons of Islamic law and theology and denounces their fatwas as "neither formally nor in their habit of mind deducible from medieval exegesis."[14] Moreover, unlike some Muslims, he unequivocally rejects suicide bombing as an act of suicide as well as the killing of noncombatants as always forbidden, noting that some sources regard it as worse than murder. Winters dismisses bin Laden and his right-hand man, Ayman al-Zawahiri, as unqualified, un-Islamic vigilantes who violate basic Islamic teachings:

> Their proclamations ignore 14 centuries of Muslim scholarship.... [They use] lists of anti-American grievances and of Koranic quotations referring to early Muslim wars against Arab idolators.... All this amounts to an odd and extreme violation of the normal methods of Islamic scholarship.... An insurrectionist who kills non-combatants is guilty of *baghy*, "armed transgression," a capital offence in Islamic law. A jihad can be proclaimed only by a properly constituted state; anything else is pure vigilantism.[15]

Like Winter, Yusuf Qaradawi denounces religious extremism, from the literalism and narrow-mindedness of some fundamentalists to the ideologies and acts of terrorists. Qaradawi roundly criticizes Salafi Muslims and those Islamists who subscribe to a negative Islam: "To them, the whole of society is an embodiment of *jahiliyya* (ignorance of Islam); everything in life is a sin; people are either unbelievers or hypocrites and the world is full of monsters and the universe is full of evil."[16]

Although Qaradawi, himself a former Egyptian Muslim Brother, is sympathetic to the Muslim Brotherhood and the Islamic movement in general, he blames the Salafi outlook on Sayyid Qutb and Sheikh Saeed Hawwa, two of the Muslim Brotherhood's most prominent ideologues. Acknowledging the influence that government oppression and imprisonment in the 1950s and 1960s had on their worldview, Qaradawi nevertheless criticizes their militant ideology, which "advocated the rejection of everything, pessimism and suspicion, accusation of others regardless of their beliefs and tendencies, including Muslims."[17] Qaradawi stresses that the Islamic movement (activist organizations like the Muslim Brotherhood) must see the various shades of gray rather than a black-and-white world and embrace a "balanced" and moderate vision of Islam. Islam, says Qaradawi, is "the middle way" (*al-wasat*) between extremism and secularism that rests on religious interpretations emphasizing "moderation."[18]

One of the first leading Muslim scholars to condemn the 9/11 terrorist attacks, on September 12, 2001, Qaradawi encouraged Muslims to donate blood to the victims. Muslims are not allowed to kill anyone except those fighting Muslims directly, Qaradawi asserted, clarifying that it is immoral to kill innocent civilians for their government's actions:

> Islam, the religion of tolerance, holds the human soul in high esteem, and considers the attack against innocent human beings a grave sin, this is backed by the Qur'anic verse which reads: "Who so ever kills a human being for other than manslaughter or corruption in the earth, it shall be as if he has killed all mankind, and who so ever saves the life of one, it shall be as if he had saved the life of all mankind" (Al-Ma'dah:32). . . . I categorically go against a committed Muslim's embarking on such attacks.[19]

So far so good; but Qaradawi goes further, and for his critics crosses the line. He adds that Arab Muslims can sympathize with the 9/11 victims because of their own experience of Israeli oppression: "We share the suffering experienced by innocent Palestinians at the hands of the tyrannical Jewish entity who raze the Palestinian homes to the ground, set fire to their tilth, kill them cold-bloodedly, and leave innocent orphans wailing behind."[20] This perspective, as we shall see, influences his position on suicide bombing in Israel-Palestine, casting him as a hero for some and a villain for many others.

While reformers like Winter and Qaradawi may be critical of Muslim terrorists, they do not regard Western countries as innocent bystanders. Though unsparing in his criticism of al-Qaeda and other terrorists, Winter nevertheless sees Western ideology and tactics as reflecting a military ethic that justifies airpower to terrorize civilians: "The 777 has become the poor man's nuclear weapon, his own Manhattan Project. Again, he has turned traitor to the East by embracing the utilitarian military ethic of his supposed adversary. He, even more than the regimes [Arab governments], shows the cost of Westernisation."[21]

Because of his belief that mainstream Islam is traditionalist Islam, Winter labels all Islamist movements, nonviolent and violent, as an aberration and a reflection of Western foreign policies in the Middle East:

> Twenty or thirty years ago, nobody had really heard of the kind of fundamentalist movement [or] . . . this kind of targeting of civilians. . . . It hasn't gained much inroad into the leadership of the religion, but in the masses on the streets, as it were, particularly in very tense, unnatural places like Gaza, the slums of Baghdad and other places, it does have a certain standing unfortunately. And this is the great challenge of the leadership of the religion—how to reassert orthodoxy in the face of a growing groundswell of fundamentalist revolt.[22]

While faulting Western policies for fueling anger and resentment in the Muslim world, Winter is equally critical of Saudi Arabia's Wahhabi ideology, which gives Muslim extremists a theological pretext for their extremism and violence: "It is unfair and simplistic, however, to claim that it is Western policy that lit the fuse for last month's events [9/11]. Without a theological position justifying the rejection of the mainstream position [which condemns suicide attacks and terrorism], the frustration with orthodoxy would have led to a frustration with religion—and then to a search for secular responses. That alternative theology does, however, exist."[23]

In recent decades, Saudi Arabia and wealthy Saudi businessmen have provided funding for mosques to be built around the world, to pay the salaries of Wahhabi-influenced imams, and to distribute thousands of copies of the Quran and other religious literature. Winter believes that, although historically Wahhabi Islam's "alternate theology" has been rejected by the majority of the Muslim world, today its acceptance "allows young men whose anger has been aroused by American policy in the Middle East to ignore the scholarly consensus about the meaning of the Koran, and read their own frustrations into the text."[24] To respond to fundamentalist threats, Winter calls for a counter-reformation, "driven by our best and most cosmopolitan heritage of spirit and law." This solution, he stresses, is "the primary responsibility of the Islamic world, not the West to provide."[25]

For Winter, global terrorism is the product of both Muslim and Western extremists. The two major protagonists are American neo-conservative war hawks and the Muslim terrorists, who share glaring similarities. Both have appropriated the past only to glorify the present, but neither is "validly linked to the remnants of established religion, or shows any sign of awareness of how to connect with history."[26]

Muslim extremism, Winter contends, is a by-product of modernity and globalization. The validation of "soft targets" in time of war, he maintains, is rooted in modern Western history and Enlightenment philosophy, rather than Islam, as seen in Britain's "terror bombing" of Hamburg in the 1940s and the carpet-bombing of Dresden in 1945.[27]

Yusuf Qaradawi takes a very different approach, attributing religious extremism to arrogance and intellectual shallowness, a lack of knowledge and religious insight. This leads Muslim extremists to their preoccupation with marginal issues (growing a beard, wearing clothes that reach below the ankle) and their focus on the negative: "They are hasty to prohibit things without reservation, if we take them to be well-meaing, or possibly out of other motives known to God. If there are two opinions on Islamic jurisprudence on a certain thing, one declaring it indifferent (*mubah*) and the other undesirable (*makruh*), the extremists abide by the latter."[28] These preoccupations, says Qaradawi, distract from major issues such as secularism, Zionism, and "Crusader-like" Christianity.[29]

SUICIDE BOMBING: THE WAR OF THE FATWAS

Few issues in recent years have been more contentious among Islamic religious authorities than suicide bombing. The question of whether suicide bombing is legitimate or illegitimate crystallized in the Israeli-Palestinian conflict during the second intifada. Increased Israeli military violence and targeted assassinations and the lack of comparable weapons to fight and defend (in their eyes) themselves reinforced the belief among many Palestinians that suicide bombers were committing not an act of suicide but one of self-sacrifice, their only option for resisting and retaliating against an enemy with overwhelming military power and foreign support. As student posters at universities in the West Bank and Gaza declared: "Israel has nuclear bombs, we have human bombs."

Suicide attacks that target innocent civilians or noncombatants spark sharp debate among prominent religious authorities in the Muslim world. Sheikh Ahmad Yassin, the late religious leader and founder of Hamas in Palestine, and Akram Sabri, the Grand Mufti of Jerusalem, along with many other Arab and Palestinian religious leaders, have argued that suicide bombing is necessary and justified to counter Israel's illegal occupation and overwhelming military power. Likewise, although Yusuf Qaradawi had condemned acts of terrorism and suicide bombings, in 1995, he was also one of the first religious scholars to issue a fatwa justifying such attacks in Israel, based on the premise that Israelis were not civilians but combatants in a war of occupation waged against the Palestinians.

In sharp contrast, Abdulaziz al-Shaikh, Grand Mufti of Saudi Arabia, condemned all suicide bombing without exception as un-Islamic and forbidden by Islam. Shortly after 9/11, on September 15, 2001, he stated:

> Enmity and hatred do not justify aggression or injustice. . . . Firstly: the recent developments in the United States including hijacking planes, terrorizing innocent people and shedding blood, constitute a form of injustice that cannot be tolerated by Islam, which views them as gross crimes and sinful acts. Secondly: any Muslim who is aware of the teachings of his religion and adheres to the directives of the Holy Qur'an and the sunnah (the teachings of the Prophet Muhammad) will never involve himself in such acts, because they will invoke the anger of God Almighty and lead to harm and corruption on earth. Thirdly: it is the duty of the Muslim ulema (religious scholars) to make facts clear in this respect, and to clarify that Islam never accepts such acts. Fourthly: the media, which try to defame Islam and Muslims in order to rally against them the feelings of various nations, should immediately stop this unacceptable and unjustifiable practice, since all reasonable and just people know that such biased accusations have nothing to do with Islam.[30]

And again on February 11, 2003:

> The acts of shedding the blood of innocent people, the bombing of buildings and ships, and the destruction of public and private installations are criminal acts and against Islam. Those who carry out such acts have deviant beliefs and misguided ideologies and are to be

held responsible for their crimes. Islam and Muslims should not be accountable for the actions of such people. Islamic Law clearly prohibits leveling such charges against non-Muslims, warns against following those who carry such deviant beliefs, and stresses that it is the duty of all Muslims over the world to consult truthfully, share advice, and cooperate in piety and righteousness.[31]

Sheikh Muhammad Sayyid Tantawi, former Grand Mufti of Egypt and current Grand Sheikh of al-Azhar University and thus among the highest religious authorities globally, draws a sharp distinction between suicide bombings that constitute self-sacrifice and acts of self-defense versus killing noncombatants: "Attacking innocent people is not courageous; it is stupid and will be punished on the Day of Judgment. . . . It is not courageous to attack innocent children, women and civilians. It is courageous to protect freedom; it is courageous to defend oneself and not to attack."[32]

Qaradawi and Tantawi clashed as the "war of fatwas" among religious leaders played out in the Arab media. When Tantawi condemned the suicide attack killing twenty-six Israelis in December 2001, Qaradawi dismissively retorted:

> How can the head of Al-Azhar incriminate mujahedin (Islamic fighters) who fight against aggressors? How can he consider these aggressors as innocent civilians? . . . Has fighting colonisers become a criminal and terrorist act for some sheikhs? . . . I am astonished that some sheikhs deliver fatwas (religious rulings) that betray the mujahedin, instead of supporting them and urging them to sacrifice and martyrdom.[33]

However, Tantawi was not alone. On December 4, 2001, Sheikh Muhammad bin Abdullah al-Subail, imam of the Grand Mosque of Mecca, also declared that killing Israelis is not permissible:

> Any attack on innocent people is unlawful and contrary to Shariah [Islamic law]. . . . Muslims must safeguard the lives, honor and property of non-Muslims who are under their protection and with whom they have concluded peace agreements. Attacking them contradicts Shariah.[34]

Qaradawi countered al-Subail in an interview with Al Jazeera. He rejected al-Subail's position and the use of the term "suicide operations," maintaining "martyrdom" operations should not be condemned as suicide. Drawing a fine line between terrorism and "martyrdom," Qaradawi declared:

> The Palestinian who blows himself up is a person who is defending his homeland. When he attacks an occupier enemy, he is attacking a

> legitimate target. This is different from someone who leaves his country and goes to strike a target with which he has no dispute.[35]

Qaradawi reinforced his position by claiming that hundreds of other Islamic scholars also believe that suicide bombings against "usurping colonialism in Palestinian territories are a legitimate form of self defense for people who have no aircraft or tanks, a defense endorsed by the divine laws, international laws and human values."[36]

Qaradawi's stance on suicide bombing inside Israel resulted in the United States refusing to grant him a visitor's visa. Similar pressures initially failed to ban his visits to the United Kingdom, although this later changed. At the same time, it also brought Qaradawi into sharp conflict with religious scholars like Timothy Winter, who, as noted above, said:

> Targeting of civilians, for instance, the aberrant use of terrorist violence is something that really is very new. . . . It hasn't gained much inroad into the leadership of the religion, but in the masses on the streets, as it were, particularly in very tense, unnatural places like Gaza, the slums of Baghdad and other places, it does have a certain standing unfortunately. And this is the great challenge of the leadership of the religion—how to reassert orthodoxy in the face of a growing groundswell of fundamentalist revolt.[37]

Qaradawi also used his considerable religious authority to oppose the American-led invasion and occupation of Iraq. He issued a fatwa stating that it was not permissible for Arab and Muslim countries to let the United States use their airports, harbors, and territories as launching pads for strikes against Iraq. Qaradawi warned Arab leaders that they risked being cursed by both history and their peoples if they sided with the United States, and he urged Iraqis to stand united in the face of war: "If the enemies invaded a Muslim country, the people of that country should resist and expel them from their territories. . . . It is an individual duty on all Muslims, men and women." Despite his strong opposition to American foreign policy, Qaradawi distinguished between the American people, whom he described as "kind," and an American administration that, he says, sponsors an "aggressive and criminal policy against the Muslim world."[38]

THEOCRACY OR DEMOCRACY?

The role of religion in politics and society, and the separation of church and state, are critical and contentious issues globally. They are reflected in constitutional debates in America over prayer in the schools, government support for religious schools, and abortion, and in European concerns over Islam and national integration, support for Muslim religious institutions, immigration policies, and domestic terrorism. However, nowhere has the issue of the relationship of religion to state and society been more contested and at times more explosive than in the Muslim world. Is the separation of church and state possible in Islam?

Some say that Muslims cannot accept a secular state, that they are obliged by their religion to implement an Islamic state. Militant groups like Hizb al-Tahrir and violent terrorists like al-Qaeda are striving for the restoration of the caliphate and global Islamic governance. Saudi Arabia, Iran, Sudan, Pakistan, and the Taliban have implemented Islamic states or republics, with models ranging from the conservative monarchy of Saudi Arabia to Iran's clergy-led parliamentary government and Pakistan's militarily imposed Islamization policies under General Zia ul-Haq. Is Islam then incompatible with democracy? Today's reformers have a good deal to say about this question.

Those who charge that Islam and democracy are incompatible often point to the fact that few Muslim countries are democratic. Many are autocratic regimes whose legitimacy and stability are based on their military security forces rather than on electoral politics and the popular will. But such critics overlook or forget the role that European countries played in setting up or approving many authoritarian leaders and the continued role that Western powers have played in propping up regimes that prohibit or crush opposition. Moreover, some Muslim countries, from Turkey to Bangladesh, Pakistan, Malaysia, and Indonesia, do in fact represent a variety of "democracies," some "limited or guided" democracies, with elected heads of state. These facts need to be put into the mix of impressions about Islam and democracy.

But what about theocracies like the Islamic Republic of Iran and the rhetoric of militant groups that assert that Islam requires a clergy-governed state? Timothy Winter tackles this issue of Islam and theocracy head-on. Winter dismisses the concept of theocracy as a modern aberration, a departure from Islamic belief and tradition. No single model of an Islamic state exists, nor is there any basis for a theocracy:

> Another result of this rejection of traditional Islam has been the notion that political power should be in the hands of men of religion. When he came to power in 1979, Ayatollah Khomeini remarked that he had achieved something utterly without precedent in Islamic history. The Taliban, by ruling directly rather than advising hereditary

> rulers, have similarly combined the "sword" and the "pen." Far from being a traditionalist move, this is a new departure for Islam, and mainstream scholarship regards it with deep suspicion.[39]

Modern fundamentalism, Winter insists, has diminished or eliminated the traditional institutional separation between rulers and religious men. While historically the sultan or caliph claimed religious legitimacy in Islamic empires and sultanates, the ruler did not legislate or have any control over religion. And religious scholars had no formal control over the sultan. In contrast, today,

> what's happening in modern fundamentalism, is that the traditional Sultan or Caliph figure is being abolished, because the Royal Family has become too decadent, as in the case of pre-revolutionary Iran, for instance, and the "clergy" think that it's their responsibility now really for the first time in Islamic history, to step into the vacuum and try and put things right. So what we're seeing now, the sort of theocratic model, the Islamic republican model in many parts of the Islamic world, is something that's radically new and doesn't really represent our traditions.[40]

The net effect, says Winter, is that Muslims are rejecting Islam as a reaction to Islamic theocracies:

> If you force it down people's throats, then the danger is many of them will want to vomit it up again. . . . If you look at the Iranian experience, after 25 years of Islamic rule, their Ministry of Religious Guidance recently published figures that show that only 3% of Iranians now attend Friday prayers. Before the revolution, it was almost 50%. So what kind of Islamic reformation and revival has that actually delivered?[41]

As we have seen, in recent decades Islamic political activists (Islamists) have become major players in electoral politics and held significant positions in government. While rulers have sought to co-opt, contain, or ban them, they have enjoyed popular support and support from many major religious authorities like Yusuf Qaradawi. However, Ali Gomaa, Grand Mufti of Egypt, where political parties are strictly controlled and religious organizations like the Muslim Brotherhood are officially banned, insists that Islamic parties and organizations and Islamic investment houses are un-Islamic. He distinguishes sharply between two functions of politics: (1) looking after the internal and external affairs of the community, which is

Islamic, and (2) gaining power, which is the work of "modern" political parties and which he sees as totally unacceptable. The government-appointed Grand Mufti of Egypt, who critics charge reflects the Mubarak government's position, maintains that it is "unfair to raise the flag of religion" to acquire power in Parliament or in any professional association or organization. It is repugnant to Islam for one group to claim a monopoly on religion so that those outside their circle are not religious:

> Islam is concerned with all walks of life including political aspects, economic, social, intellectual, and others—where we refer to politics meaning to attend to the affairs of the community, participating in its construction, and accomplishing the interests of all—and our refusal that religion be used (Islam or any other religion) in politics that are limited to a political party and its constituency.[42]

DEMOCRACY AND RELIGIOUS PLURALISM

If some religious leaders and Islamic activists today call for Islamic states and criticize or condemn democracy, Mustafa Ceric, Grand Mufti of Bosnia-Herzegovina, regards democracy as one of the great benefits brought by the creation of the modern nation-state. As a European born in the former Yugoslavia, and trained in the Arab world and the West, Ceric is a Muslim religious leader who also possesses the skills of a politician. He is extraordinarily well equipped to be a bridge between the Muslim world and the West, and between diverse Muslims in Europe. Ceric earned his B.A. in theology at Egypt's al-Azhar University, sometimes referred to as the Vatican of the Muslim world, and his Ph.D. in Islamic studies at the University of Chicago. Like another of our reformers, Nurcholish Madjid, Ceric's mentor was Fazlur Rahman, who trained a generation of scholars of Islam.

A strong believer in Rousseau's social contract, Ceric emphasizes the importance of its four basic rights: protection of life, religion, property, and dignity.[43] Yet, while crediting Western civilization, especially Europe, for establishing democratic legal systems, Ceric insists these systems are not exclusively Western, stemming from "inherent" Western values, since they are now values that others accept and claim for themselves.

Ceric shares a sentiment common in many parts of the Muslim world that though the West espouses democratization, it has failed to adequately do so in the Muslim world. The West's support for authoritarian Muslim regimes, equation of the political status quo with stability and security, and fear of Islam reflect a double standard: "What is happening now," Ceric says, "actually represents a crisis of western civilization, which obviously does not want to share these values with others."[44]

Influenced by Bosnia-Herzegovina's multireligious societies, Ceric advocates a democracy incorporating a strong policy of religious pluralism and rejects proponents of "a clash":

> We don't believe in the clashes of civilizations, we don't believe in the clashes of religions, we believe in the clashes of civilization and non-civilization. . . . We believe in clashes between religion and non-religion, we believe in the clashes between good and evil, because it happens all the time.[45]

He denounces Muslims who oppose multicultural, multireligious, and multinational life, noting that the Quran states many times, "If God wanted, he could create you to be one nation, but he wanted you to be different nations."[46]

The views of Nurcholish Madjid, a proponent of democracy, reflect his personal experiences as an Islamic activist in the most populous Muslim country, Indonesia. Although in his youth he was an Islamic activist student leader, his experiences as an opponent of both the Sukarno and Suharto regimes convinced Nurcholish of the futility of opposing the power of the state. Moreover, the infighting and inability of Islamic political parties to work together led him to conclude that the mixing of state and religion was counterproductive. His well-known slogan is "Islam, yes; Islamic political parties, no."[47]

Insisting that there is no Quranic basis for the creation of an Islamic state, Nurcholish warns that modern constructions of an Islamic state reduce Islam to a profane ideology, easily manipulated by those who want to impose their own views in the name of religion. He equates it with "the sin of shirk or polytheism."[48] Thus he also rejects modern Islamists' contention that it is necessary to impose Shariah as the rule of law to make Indonesian society more Islamic. He insists instead that true spirituality and religiosity come from inner transformation (individual and national). Rather than the imposition of Islamic law, what is needed is a spiritual and cultural path that fosters ethics in society.[49] The primary means to this path are education, to transform individuals and society, and dialogue, an open exchange, to improve relations between Muslims and other religious communities as well as between the Muslim world and the West.[50]

Having rejected the notion of an "Islamic state," Madjid roots his advocacy of democratization in his belief that democracy has Quranic precedents, the

Quranic and traditional Islamic notions of deliberation and consultation (*musyawarah* and *shura*). However, no single model of government exists or is required; instead, different countries need to formulate models appropriate to their environment.[51]

Like Mustafa Ceric, Nurcholish was influenced by his country's multireligious and multicultural society. Religious pluralism and tolerance, he believes, are not simply theological issues but a mandate, rooted in Quranic passages (2:62; 5:69) that teach that God will judge and reward all believers, including Jews and Christians, in the next life. Therefore, all religions are on a par with Islam, and God gives salvation to anyone regardless of his or her religion.[52] So too, since each religion is committed to ethical values, all religions, not just Islam, have a role to play in the implementation of religious values such as social justice and democratic governance in politics and society.[53]

Perhaps no issue is more sensitive in interfaith relations than interreligious marriage. Although no official ban exists in Indonesia against interreligious marriages, in practice Indonesian couples face one of two choices: to wed in the Religious Court for Muslims or in the Civil Registration Office for non-Muslims. Some have chosen instead to circumvent this restriction by feigning religious conversion, while others travel to Singapore, Hong Kong, or Australia to get married.[54]

Nurcholish Madjid did not shrink from addressing this potentially explosive issue head-on. His Paramadina Foundation began in 2002 to facilitate interreligious marriages of thousands of Indonesian couples. Paramadina offers services for interfaith couples, including counseling reluctant parents on the religious grounds for interfaith marriages, or finding a priest or imam to officiate—a critical step since many churches refuse to sanctify a wedding involving a non-Christian.[55]

Not unexpectedly, Nurcholish's reformist initiative drew strong criticism from many religious scholars. Although he argued that no text in the Quran explicitly bans a Muslim from marrying a non-Muslim, most ulama in Indonesia as elsewhere continue to follow classical Islamic law and believe that interreligious marriages between Muslim women and non-Muslim men are un-Islamic.[56] This position and others led some to condemn Nurcholish as *kafir*, an unbeliever.

In Indonesia, Nurcholish Madjid's pluralistic Islam has been matched by what his longtime friend Abdurrahman Wahid calls cosmopolitan Islam. At first glance, Wahid appears to be something of an anomaly among religious reformers; he reflects his traditionalist roots, leadership, and charisma but also displays an Islamic modernist perspective. Although for a long time he led the more traditionalist Nahdlatul Ulama (Renaissance of Religious Scholars), with forty million members the biggest Islamic organization in the world's largest Muslim country, Wahid has long espoused a very modern and cosmopolitan interpretation of Islam. In 1999, he became the first president of Indonesia's emerging democracy.

Bridging the worlds of traditional Islam and "modern" thought, Wahid espouses an Islam responsive to the demands of modern life and reflecting Indonesian Islam's diverse religious and ethnic history and communities. It is an inclusive religious, democratic, pluralistic force.[57]

Wahid believes that contemporary Muslims are at a critical crossroad. He rejects both fundamentalism and the legal-formalism of many conservative Muslims as aberrations and major obstacles to Islamic reform and to Islam's response to global change. He sees two choices or paths confronting Muslims today: to pursue a traditional, static, legal-formalistic Islam or to reclaim and refashion a more dynamic cosmopolitan, universal, pluralistic worldview. He rejects the notion that Islam should form the basis for the nation-state's political or legal system, which he characterizes as a Middle Eastern tradition, alien to Indonesia. Indonesian Muslims should apply a moderate, tolerant brand of Islam to their daily lives in a society where "a Muslim and a non-Muslim are the same," a state in which religion and politics are separate.[58]

Reflecting the growing empowerment of the laity in Islam today, which many ulama see as a challenge to their authority, Wahid affirms the right of all Muslims, both laity and religious scholars (ulama), to "perpetual reinterpretation" (*ijtihad*) of the Quran and traditions of the Prophet in light of "ever changing human situations."[59]

But what about the future of Islam in the West? Having looked at Muslim challenges to creating democracy in Muslim states, now let's turn to the experiences of Muslims living in the democracies of Europe and America.

Muslims in the West: Can They Be Loyal Citizens?

The growing numbers of Muslims in the West have been seen as posing a dangerous demographic threat to Europe and America. Europeans who are witnessing a massive exit from Christian churches as a result of secularism's impact as well as falling birth rates are deeply threatened by significant increases in their Muslim populations from immigration and higher Muslim birth rates. Commentators echo Patrick Buchanan's "Rising Islam May Overwhelm the West."[60] The attacks on 9/11 and 7/7 have reinforced fears of a global threat. Anti-immigrant propaganda is reflected in warnings of a new Eurabia or Londonistan.

Some Muslims in the West have also questioned, though for different reasons, whether they can be both good Muslims and loyal citizens in the West. Can they live in and recognize the legitimacy of "foreign" non-Muslim states whose laws are based upon a Western secular or Judeo-Christian tradition? Can one be an American or European Muslim, or does Islam require them to be Muslims simply living in America or Europe?

Finding the road to integration, rather than choosing isolation or militancy, is a process that benefits from and greatly depends on reformist thought. A diverse group of Muslim scholars and religious leaders in Europe and America are effective voices in the process of integration, as they address questions of faith and identity, assimilation, religious pluralism, and tolerance. Important insights come from European Muslims like the British Winter and Swiss Ramadan as well as Ceric of Bosnia-Herzegovina. Rejecting a polarized view of the world that posits "Muslims" against the "West," they advocate a synthesis, a European or American Muslim identity based on common values. Though recognizing distinctive religious and cultural differences, they nevertheless affirm the essential compatibility of Islam and the West.

For Tariq Ramadan, Muslims in the West, like other Europeans and Americans, share an identity informed by multiple subcultures. Muslims are Muslim by religion and French, British, German, or American by culture. Mustafa Ceric concurs: "If Arabs use Islam to further their national goals, then we in Europe can do the same thing. If an Egyptian has the right to be a patriot for his country in the name of Islam, then we European Muslims can also be European patriots in the name of Islam. . . . As a European Muslim, I want to make my contribution to European civilization and be automatically recognized as such."[61]

Ceric believes that to be a British, German, or French patriot does not negate one's religion but is in fact a Muslim's religious duty: "I am proud that Islam defines my European patriotism."[62] There are many forms of Islam: Arab, Ottoman, Bosnian (European). Historically, Islam, like Christianity, was synthesized with indigenous cultures and in that way developed its unique traditions: "Just as differences can be found between Catholics in Poland, Austria or France, or between them and other Christian churches, there are different forms of Islam."[63]

But is there a clash of basic values between European or American Islam and Western values and secularism? Both Ramadan and Ceric speak of common values (Muslim and Western) as a basis for citizenship. An "ethics of citizenship" requires that decisions be made in the name of shared principles such as the rule of law, equal citizenship regardless of religion, universal suffrage, and the accountability of leaders, not solely based on religious identity.[64] Moreover, Ramadan chides Muslims that they must stop perceiving themselves as minorities and instead move from integration to contribution, "being proactive and offering something to the society."[65]

But what about Islam and Western secularism? Are they incompatible? Contrary to many Muslims, who have viewed secularism as antireligious or antithetical to religion, Ramadan believes that to embrace secularism and an open society is not a betrayal of Muslim principles; it enables all citizens to live together and is the necessary condition for religious freedom—for Muslims and others. Thus he calls upon Western Muslims to spread the message at home and abroad: "we live in democracy, we respect the state of law, we respect open political dialogue and we want this for all Muslims." Ramadan considers the question "Can you be a European Muslim?" passé. Nothing in the Quran, the Sunnah of the Prophet, or Western constitutions prevents a Muslim from being both a practicing Muslim and a loyal European, he argues. The millions of Muslims who live, work, and vote in Europe are a living testimony that one can be Muslim and European at the same time. There is no inherent conflict.

Ramadan reminds Europeans and Americans that Western civilization's overlooked component is Islamic civilization. He points out that Islamic civilization is in fact integral to Western civilization, having passed on its rich legacy and influenced the West in philosophy, medicine, the sciences, art, and architecture. To anti-immigrant Europeans who dream of a white, Christian Europe, Ramadan counters, "It is far too late."[66] Muslims have been in Europe for decades and have made it their home. While early immigrants may have believed that their presence in Europe or America was temporary, "new generations are more visible and engaging the wider society."[67]

However, Ramadan believes that integration does not mean wholesale assimilation. Muslims must be allowed to develop their own European Muslim identity and culture just as other faiths and ethnic groups have done before them.[68] Integral to that culture is Muslim acceptance of the constitution, laws, and framework of any European country in which a Muslim lives. Ramadan's position on Muslim girls wearing the hijab reflects this belief. He insists that "no one should be able to force a woman to wear hijab or not to wear it," and he thus opposes the French ban on the hijab. Nevertheless, he counsels Muslim schoolgirls to respect French law and, until the law can be changed, to replace their hijab with the more acceptable bandana: "But Muslims must be clear to their fellow citizens and Muslims around the world: We are respecting the law, even if we disagree with it."[69] But what then do Muslim rioting and other "Muslim issues" in France say about respect for French law?

Ramadan insists that many so-called Muslim problems (slums, crime, unemployment), often highlighted as examples of Islam's incompatibility with the West, are not in fact related to religion but reflect social, economic, and educational inequities faced by immigrant communities. Because European Muslims are often essentialized or defined simply in terms of their faith, these problems are incorrectly seen as "Muslim issues." In fact, given their nature and primary causes, they require social, not religious, solutions. An example is the so-called Muslim riots in France in 2005. The riots began October 27, triggered by the deaths of two teenagers in Clichy-sous-Bois, a poor banlieue (suburb) of Paris, and subsequently over a three-week period spread to other urban and some rural areas, impacting some 274 towns throughout the Paris region. The rioters, mostly unemployed teenagers from destitute suburban housing projects, torched nearly nine thousand cars and dozens of buildings, including daycare centers and schools. While most of the rioters were from North African Muslim backgrounds, and some in the press spoke of Islamic radicalism, the underlying issues proved to have nothing to do with Islam but rather with unemployment, poor housing, and social exclusion.

For Mustafa Ceric, as for Ramadan and others, the successful encounter of Europe and Islam has two interconnected prerequisites: Muslims must embrace their European identity, and European governments must facilitate Muslims' integration by accommodating and institutionalizing their religious needs.[70] A major challenge is the "environment of fear" in which many live. On the one hand is the broader society's fear of Muslims within; on the other, poverty perpetuates fear in Muslim communities and a sense of paralysis and isolation from the broader society that results in their being labeled as "outsiders" or alien to the local culture.

Like Ramadan, Ceric counsels Muslims to recognize that the West does not have a monopoly on values such as democracy and the rule of law, that these are universal values: "if European-born Muslims look inside their faith for what are presented as Western notions of human rights and individual freedom, they will find them."[71] He believes that European Muslims, freed from fear and poverty, will not only succeed but can also become an example to Muslims in the Middle East.

The role of government in guiding and facilitating Muslim integration through education and the training of imams is a contentious issue today in

Europe and America. Ceric takes a strong stand in favor of government support, a policy that some critics characterize as intervention or engineering. European governments, he believes, will only gain the trust of the Muslim community when they institutionalize Islam through state sponsorship of Muslim schools, state councils, and mosques. Ceric also emphasizes the importance of training European imams in Europe rather than in Muslim countries and advocates the creation of a unified European-wide Islamic authority, similar to Bosnia's model, with an elected head or president of the ulama. State institutionalization of Islam would acknowledge that Muslims are loyal citizens and contribute collectively to European culture and civilization.[72]

THE FUTURE OF AMERICAN AND EUROPEAN MUSLIMS

The traditional battle cry for the defense of Islam is "Islam in danger." Today, some Muslims speak and write of "Islam under siege" or of the rise of creeping Islamophobia or, like Timothy Winter, of the "incipient inquisition" Muslims face today. What are Muslims in the West to do?

Winter lays out a path of acculturation, self-criticism, and reform.

> Are we Americans, or Canadians, or Britons, simply by virtue of holding a passport and finding employment? Or is this our emotional home? Traditional Islam has been expert in adoption and adaptation. The new anti-semitism makes not the slightest headway against it. It is also manifestly the case that moderate reformists have produced many American Muslim communities that are sincerely American, and speak frankly against extremism. Yet it needs also to be recognised that a growing number of scriptural-literalist community leaders, particularly those funded by Middle Eastern states where the language of sermons is violently anti-American, are sceptical of the kind of versatility offered by traditional Islam or by the reformers.[73]

Winter sees the future in terms of the next generation.

> It is this new generation that is called upon to demonstrate Islam's ability to extend its traditional capacities for courteous acculturation to the new context of the West, and to reject the radical Manichean agenda, supported by the extremists on both sides, which presents Muslim minorities as nothing more than resentful, scheming archipelagos of Middle Eastern difference.[74]

The challenge for European Muslims, as for American Muslims, is, first, a firmly rooted Muslim identity:

> Unless American Muslims can locate for themselves, and populate, a spiritual and cultural space which can meaningfully be called American, and develop theological and social tools for identifying and thwarting local extremism, they will be increasingly in the firing line.[75]

Second, acculturation requires recognizing that the anti-Western writings of popular Islamist writers like Pakistan's Mawlana Mawdudi and Egypt's Sayyid Qutb were written in the mid-twentieth century for postcolonial societies in Muslim countries facing repression and corruption, not for Muslim minorities in the West.

Third, an authentic understanding of Islam's position toward the non-Muslim countries in which Muslim minorities live requires that Muslims de-ideologize recent militant, distorted interpretations of Islam and return to the Islamic tradition. Winter warns:

> An insulting guest will not be tolerated indefinitely even by the most courteous of hosts. . . . A measured, concerned critique of social dissolution, unacceptable beliefs, or destructive foreign policies will always be a required component of Muslim discourse, but wild denunciations of Great Satans or global Crusader Conspiracies are, for Muslims here, not only dangerous, but are also discourteous—scarcely a lesser sin. This must be made absolutely clear to organisations who visit communities with a view to offering funding from totalitarian [Muslim] states.[76]

Fourth, and most important, Winter insists that Islam's past heritage, the classical Islamic tradition, not Islamic fundamentalism or Islamic modernism, holds the key to the future of Islam and Muslims. The providential success story of Islamic civilization needs to be reappropriated and built on:

> Salafist and modernist agendas which present medieval Islam either as obscurantism or as deviation from scripture will leave us orphaned from the evolving and magnificent story of Muslim civilisation. If we accept that classical Islam was a deviant reading of our scriptures, we surrender to the claims of a certain type of Christian evangelical Orientalism, which claims that the glories of Muslim civilisation

arose despite, not because of, the Qur'an. We are called to be the continuation of a magnificent story, not a footnote to its first chapter.[77]

MUSLIMS AND THE WEST: COUNTERING AN IDEOLOGY OF FEAR

Mustafa Ceric warned in an interview in 2005, "We are, I am afraid, on the verge of seeing a situation develop whereby it would be a crime to be a Muslim in Europe. The events of 11 September, 2001, have made things worse. May Allah protect us."[78]

Not surprisingly, when asked how he felt about the future of Islam in Europe, Ceric responded, "Not very good," citing "the rise of fascism" and "an officially-sanctioned tendency to be unreasonable" about Islam as "bad omens." Yet he is not a pessimist. Ceric believes that it is pointless to obsess about "the end of time" or "apocalypse." Muslims must become educated and get organized. The strength and unity of Muslims in one country will strengthen the Muslim community in other countries. "This is because we live in a time in which all our actions and deeds have global implications. If you are strong, united and organized here we will naturally be strong, united and organized in Bosnia, Kashmir, Palestine, and the rest of the world. . . . It is useless if only parts of that body are functioning and others are not: we all need to get our acts together."[79]

As a realist and leading public voice against religious extremism and violence, Tariq Ramadan warns Muslims and non-Muslims alike: "The first tragic consequence of the ideology of fear is to transform all societies and their members into victims. . . . We must break the bonds of our fear. . . . We must once more become thinking 'subjects.' "[80]

Ramadan sees "victimhood" as a shared and dangerous fear: "The Muslim world's insistence that it is a perpetual victim at the hands of the West is the flip side of Western accusations that Muslims are bent upon destroying Western values and 'freedoms.'" A Muslim "victim" mentality that assumes that any action on the part of the West is driven by a deep-seated hatred of Islam has become as dangerous as the right-wing ideology of some in Europe and America who assume that Muslims' behavior is driven by hatred or rejection of the West. Failure to remain true to democratic principles in this climate of fear risks the loss of the most essential and integral aspects of Western democracy.

Mutual fear and victimhood reinforce an "us" and "them" vision of the world that inhibits understanding the reasons behind the actions of the "Other": "In the new regime of fear and suspicion, to understand the Other is to justify him; to seek out his reasons is to agree with him."[81]

Ramadan attributes today's ideology of fear and victimhood to a globalization of what he calls the "Israeli Syndrome": "Since the 1940s, the history of the state of Israel has been shaped by fear, by the imperative of self-protection and by mistrust of the Other." He believes that Israel's self-perception as a victim in a sea of hostile territory has been globalized to Europe and the United States in their war on terrorism. "The 'war' that has been unleashed to destroy terrorism is now founded on the same logical bases, but on a global scale."[82] American neo-conservatives and "their European imitators," according to Ramadan, have instigated and nurtured a permanent sense of fear. They use this ideological worldview to justify draconian domestic security policies that are hostile to freedom.

Ramadan sees this Israeli Syndrome producing a binary vision of the world, a perceived state of siege in which demonization occurs:

> The Other is no longer criticizing our policies, he is negating our existence; he detests our values, our very civilization. He must no longer be held responsible for his acts alone but for his hatred, his nihilism, his madness and "why not?" his beliefs and his religion.[83]

Toward a New Paradigm of Women's Empowerment

"Islam is misogynist." "Islam liberates women." "Muslim men oppress their women." "Women are the heart of the Muslim family." Few issues grab more headlines than gender, and none is more important as a lens through which many non-Muslims and Muslims alike see and judge Islam. Western perceptions of women in Islam are framed by images of veiled women, sexually segregated societies, violence against women, and denial of their human rights.

Men and women in Muslim societies and communities grapple with many gender issues, ranging from women's education, employment, and role in the family to their religious leadership and authority. Not surprisingly, influential ulama and Muslim scholars have weighed in on these issues, issuing diverse and sometimes conflicting fatwas and advice.

Today, greater participation of women in society can be seen on many fronts. Some Islamic movements, like the Muslim Brotherhoods of Egypt and Jordan and Tunisia's Ennahda, as well as movements in Morocco, Lebanon, Kuwait, Turkey, Malaysia, and Indonesia, have emphasized increased access to education and expanded employment opportunities for women. Women have also become more visible in the councils of Islamic organizations and as political candidates. Islamist women are increasingly found in the professions (physicians, journalists, lawyers, engineers, social workers, university professors) and as administrators and staff in schools, clinics, and social welfare agencies.

Perhaps most significant, Muslim women and Islamic scholars and activists, representing many ideological orientations, are increasingly speaking out. They are empowering themselves not just as defenders of women's rights but also as interpreters of the Islamic tradition. Many argue that patriarchy as much as religion, indeed patriarchy linked to religion, accounts for customs that became long-standing traditions affecting gender relations. The primary interpreters of Islam (of the Quran, traditions of the Prophet, and law) have been men, functioning in and reflecting the values of patriarchal societies. Religion was linked to patriarchy through its interpreter-scholars and their appeal to Islam to legitimate their formulations of doctrine and law.

In areas as diverse as the Arab world, Iran, and South and Southeast Asia, women have formed their own organizations, created their own magazines, and contributed to newspapers to set forth new religious and social interpretations on issues ranging from dress and education to employment and political participation. Organizations like Women Living Under Muslim Laws (Geneva) and Sisters in Islam (Malaysia) have become visible and vocal representatives within their own countries and internationally, writing, publishing, and participating in international conferences such as the Cairo conference on population and Beijing's conference on women. Increasing in number, these women may well prove to be an effective vanguard in a long-term process of Islamic reassessment, reform, and transformation.

Muslim reformers like the Egyptian Dr. Heba Raouf focus on the extent to which Quranic teachings about women—that they have the same religious duties and are promised the same rewards as men—were subverted by male religious scholars:

> In the centuries after the death of Prophet Muhammad religious scholars increasingly cited a variety of reasons, from moral degeneration in society to woman's imagined tendency to be a source of temptation and social discord, to restrict both their presence in public life and in the space of the mosque.[84]

Raouf stresses the long-overlooked role of women in Muslim history, their role in Sufism as poets and writers of literature, their role as hadith scholars, their work in trade and education, and especially their roles in raising and educating children. Muslim women have also established endowments (*waqf*), using their wealth to contribute to building mosques, hospitals, madrasas, and shelters for battered women.

A professor at Cairo University, social activist, and public intellectual, educated in Cairo and London, Raouf calls for a reconceptualization of Muslim women's history. In contrast to some, however, she insists that efforts to reformulate women's role in Islamic teachings have not been inspired by Western feminism but rather are rooted in Islamic culture and the liberating potential of Islam. She rejects the newly coined term "gender jihad" as a "Western feminist" perspective and prefers "tajdid [renewal] jihad," reflecting the struggle to redefine and renew the vision of an Islamic future.

Contemporary Muslim women, Raouf maintains, have "boldly struggled with balancing the Quran's eternal nature and the way to implement it in historical and cultural context." They do so, she points out, as distinguished scholars of Islam and members of Islamic social movements, as active muftis who reexamine dominant classic religious opinions and produce new interpretations. She emphasizes that it is women's right and duty to engage in this struggle, leading an Islamic renaissance, reconstructing the Muslim mind, "reforming our understanding of the Quran and the Prophet to understand Islam and practice it."

Raouf points out that in contrast to what one would expect in the Western world, namely that women's entrance into the workforce would naturally lead to increased suffrage in politics, in the Arab world women's growing access to executive positions and participation in civic associations has been paralleled by their simultaneous disengagement from political parties and trade unions. For example, in Egypt only 7.6 percent of a random sample of executive women in official bodies and private sector businesses were members of political parties.[85]

Thus, for Raouf, empowering women politically requires disempowering authoritarian regimes. She points out that while empowerment for women has focused on "bringing some women to power" to represent their sisters, what is needed is "empowering the majority of women." She questions whether appointment of women to senior positions in government really reflects democratic change when at the same time organizations like Amnesty International and Transparency International report continued violations against women's basic human and political rights in these same countries.[86]

Raouf advocates a paradigm shift from defining political participation as the "politics of representation" to the "politics of presence." Equating power with state power and political participation with representation is no longer the only way for women to become more powerful, more politically and socially active and visible.[87] Civil society and the private sector are also important avenues for grassroots empowerment of the majority of women, poor women, in the Arab world.[88] Civil society becomes political as well as social and civil, and local governance becomes the key to engaging more people in the public domain so that they can influence policies affecting their day-to-day lives.

> Women's movements engaged in formal politics may risk being co-opted by the state, or making concessions ... to guarantee the state support ... and access to power whereas empowering women in the local communities ... to step into the public sphere to defend their interests can foster democracy in all its ... complex dimensions.[89]

The role of religion as a force for progressive change is a question prominent religious officials and scholars address in debates on the direction of an Arab and Islamic vision of women's political and public participation in human development. The debate in countries like Egypt, Syria, Morocco, Tunisia, and Sudan seeks to avoid polarization between Islamists and secularists on the one hand and the religious officials and religious social movements on the other.[90] Their Contributions, Raouf believes, should be part of a new paradigm that reestablishes the connection between culture, religion, and human rights/women's rights discourse and activism.

GENDER JIHAD

On March 18, 2005, Amina Wadud, a scholar of the Quran and Islamic studies and a Muslim feminist, broke a centuries-old Islamic tradition requiring that only a male may lead the Friday communal prayer. Wadud took this role for herself at a mosque in New York City, with a congregation of over one hundred men and women. Some have recently argued that because Islam has no ordained clergy to lead prayer or officiate at weddings, nothing in revelation prohibits women from performing such roles. Although it is still uncommon, other women have led mixed-gender prayers in the United States, Canada, and elsewhere in the face of objections from other Muslims around the world and even some death threats; a small but growing minority has begun to support Wadud and others in their bold actions.

Leading Friday prayer as the imam was just a moment in Amina Wadud's decades-long struggle for women's equality and rights, which she has characterized as "gender jihad." The struggle is to liberate women from within the Islamic tradition, to counter the use of Islam to justify women's inequality, which Wadud believes has increased since she converted over three decades ago.

Wadud's Islamic feminist thought is based on a re-reading of the Quran to challenge literalist, misogynist laws and policies and achieve legal, political, and social reform. Central to her position is the idea that prejudice against women is attributable to the Quran's interpreters, not to the Quran itself. Those who believe that men are superior to women have interpreted the Quran based on those assumptions. The problem in modern times, Wadud argues, is not simply patriarchy and the fact that men formulated and developed Islamic law or customs but the continued influence of patriarchal structures and their hegemonic presumption of dominance and superiority. Male religious scholars today, she says, abuse their power. Thus, she urges, "the proactive inclusion of women's experiences and interpretations is crucial to transforming gender status toward its higher egalitarian potential."[91]

In the past, Muslim women dealt with the disjunction between the traditional teachings of Islam and misogynist patriarchal practices by dismissing them as isolated incidents or failure to uphold the true tenets of the faith. Rarely did they call for a reimagining of the tradition.

Wadud notes that Quranic interpreters have not distinguished between the Quranic text and their own subjective interpretations. No two readings of the Quran are the same, although individual understandings can converge on some or many points. To get at the "spirit of the Quran," a reader must first understand the implications of the passage for the particular time and context in which it was first revealed and then derive universal principles from that meaning.

Wadud's basic method is to interpret the Quran with the Quran. When interpreting a Quranic passage, she argues, one should look for similar or related Quranic passages as well as the context of the passage: the general and particular circumstances in which the verse was revealed. Texts must also be interpreted within the context of the Quran's worldview and in light of overriding Quranic principles.

Wadud believes that the Quran can and should be re-read to accommodate women's changing needs and circumstances. She attempts to re-read the Quran from within her female experience, free of the stereotypes that she believes plagued earlier exegetes.

The distinctiveness of Amina Wadud's approach is apparent if we contrast her methodology with that of a traditionalist like Timothy Winter. To assess the roles of men and women in Islam, Winter relies on classical or medieval Islam as his primary authoritative reference point. Islamic societies, he maintains, are simultaneously both matriarchal and patriarchal. Men dominate public space; private space is dominated by women, who, he says, consider their sphere to be of greater importance. Islam's emphasis on a woman's obedience to her husband is complemented or balanced, in Winter's view, by the traditional veneration of mothers. Like many other traditionalists, past and present, he buttresses his position by citing a reported statement of the Prophet Muhammad that "paradise is at the feet of the mother."

Wadud counters that, paradoxically, this Prophetic saying has been used not to honor women but to justify the suffering they experience in a patriarchal order. Women have been relegated to serving the needs of men and are identified solely in relation to what they offer men as wives and future generations as mothers, without any consideration of their own needs or the costs of their sacrifices.

At the heart of Winter's interpretation of Islam is not just respect for tradition but the "sacralization" of it that Nurcholish Madjid and other reformers have warned against. This approach, epitomized by Winter's belief in the "normative" status of the tradition for gender relations in Islam, has implications for many issues such as whether women have a right to lead Friday congregational (juma) prayer. Despite his admission that no Quranic or hadith text explicitly prohibits women from leading men in prayer, nevertheless Winter, like Qaradawi, Ali Gomaa, and many other traditionalist religious authorities and reformers, still uses the consensus of classical Sunni Islamic law to argue that the imam (leader of the prayer) must be male if men and women are praying together. Of course, this methodology is not unique to Islam. Conservative or traditionalist Christian and Jewish leaders and congregations opposed to the ordination of women also use a similar argument or retreat to tradition.

A champion of traditional scholarship, Winter opposes going back directly to the Quran and Prophetic traditions to derive a ruling that differs from the consensus of early Muslim scholars:

> Although those who reject the Four Schools [of Islamic jurisprudence], and attempt to derive the shari'a directly from the revelation, sometimes repudiate this consensus, only a few, such as Farid Esack [a South African- and British-trained Muslim scholar and reformer], have proposed it seriously. . . . One can be a religious leader without being imam of a mosque, the example of prominent theologians such as Bint al-Shati' in modern Egypt, and a host of medieval predecessors . . . , affording sufficient proof of this.[92]

Winter falls back on historical practice in Sunni Islam; what was understood as the Sunnah of the Prophet has controlled the understanding of the Quran, and consensus (*ijma*) of the ulama has controlled understanding of the

Sunnah. In other words, in Sunni Islam, *ijma* overrules everything. So even if someone argues that the Quran doesn't advocate hijab and that the relevant Prophetic reports/traditions (hadith) that require wearing of the hijab are false, the authority of past consensus continues to be critically important. One must not depart from tradition.

Like Winter, Dr. Muzammil H. Siddiqi, the American Muslim religious leader and mufti, former president of the Islamic Society of North America, and chairman of the Fiqh Council of North America (an organization of Islamic legal scholars), also exemplifies the views of many conservative religious leaders and scholars. Educated at traditional institutions, Aligarh Muslim University and Darul-uloom Nadwatul Ulama in India, and the Islamic University of Medina in Saudi Arabia, Siddiqi also earned an M.A. in theology from Birmingham University in England and a Ph.D. in comparative religion from Harvard University. In a fatwa Siddiqi declared:

> Islam places no restriction on women to teach, preach, and guide both women and men. The Qur'an says, "Men and women are supporters of each other. They command what is right and forbid what is wrong" (At-Tawbah 9:71). There are many women today who are fully qualified to be jurists (*faqihah*) and give religious opinions (fatwas). They do issue fatwas and teach Qur'an and Hadith in schools, colleges, and universities all over the world. . . . Muslims should give them more opportunities, allow them and encourage them to become full partners in Islamic work.
>
> Leading *salah* (Prayer), however, is restricted to male imams only when the congregation consists of men and women, whether . . . in the mosques or outside mosques, . . . daily Prayers or Friday and Eid Prayers. Women are not allowed to lead such Prayers.
>
> This has also been the practice of Muslims all over the world since the time of the Prophet (peace and blessings be upon him). This Shar'i ruling is not because of any notion of spiritual deficiency among women. Men and women both are equal in the sight of Allah and both of them must be fully respected and honored. Women are allowed to lead the Prayer when the congregation is all women. They are also allowed to lead the Prayer in their homes among their family members, if they are more knowledgeable of the Qur'an and Islamic rules.[93]

If women reformers are sometimes simply seen as liberals who are challenging tradition, the Quranic interpretations and conclusions of others like Dr. Farhat Hashmi reveal a far more complex profile.

FARHAT HASHMI: REFORMER OR FUNDAMENTALIST?

Farhat Hashmi, who fully veils her face and body, stands in sharp contrast to Amina Wadud or Heba Raouf. Trained in Islamic studies at the University of Glasgow, Hashmi insists that she is committed to the liberation, empowerment, and education of women, although her critics dismiss her as a fundamentalist rather than a reformer or an Islamic feminist. Ironically, Hashmi's greatest popularity is among "Westernized," English-speaking, educated women in Pakistan, who have traditionally been the torchbearers of the women's movement. Some have even credited her with spawning an Islamic resurgence among elite Pakistani women. Her influence and popularity in Pakistan and internationally can be seen in the crowds of up to ten thousand who attend her talks.

Modernists and feminists as well as conservative ulama have criticized Hashmi. She has been labeled both a modernist and a traditionalist, and her views characterized as feminist as well as patriarchal and even Taliban-like.

Hashmi focuses on the day-to-day practical aspects of Islam and attributes the popularity of her lectures to the fact that people are desperate for religion: "There is a search for direction, for guidance," she says.[94] She identifies her goal as reforming Islamic society by reviving authentic Islamic education. Her admirers come from across Toronto, where she now lives and works, and from as far away as Australia to take her twenty-month course Taleem-ul-Koran (Learning the Quran), held at her Al-Huda Islamic Centre of Canada for four days a week, five hours a day, all for the nominal fee of sixty dollars a month. Hashmi's courses on the Quran, exegesis, hadith, and Islamic jurisprudence feature research from surveys and interviews, as well as field work, and utilize multimedia presentations. The Al-Huda Institute, which serves full-time students as well as working women and homemakers, has graduated over ten thousand women. Al-Huda also reaches out to women in rural areas, staff and inmates in the prison system, and women in hospitals.[95]

Hashmi believes that Islam holds out a cure for social and personal ills and that the younger generation "will become better equipped to tackle life's problems in light of Islam."[96] Her approach is Quran-centric, emphasizing the importance of women understanding the Quran for themselves.[97] Through Al-Huda's online resources, men and women have been accessing Hashmi's word-for-word translation and interpretation of the Quran and downloading her lectures.[98]

Despite Hashmi's prominence, many traditionalist ulama maintain that she is not a qualified scholar, because she is not traditionally trained. They also criticize Hashmi's public profile and the fact that her lectures are available to men, as it is not appropriate for women to have a public role in *da'wa* (propagation of Islam), which they see as a radical departure from orthodoxy.

Hashmi responds:

> They do not recognize my Ph.D. [in Islamic studies] at all. According to them I am not qualified to be a religious scholar despite my years of study. They say until I go and study in their *madrassas* and adopt their way of thinking I am not qualified to be a scholar. . . . I do not fear the ulema. I do not fear anyone. All I am doing is spreading the message of the Quran. If somebody objects to that, then their fight is not with me, but with God.[99]

Unlike many other nonclerical modernist reformers, Hashmi asserts that only religious scholars (here she includes herself and other lay experts as well as the ulama) should reinterpret Islamic law and that the Quran should dictate the parameters of such reform. She walks a very fine, often blurred line between reform and tradition. She sounds like an Islamic modernist:

> I feel that there is a need for reinterpretation on all issues. But this should be done by a group of people who understand today's problems and . . . who understand religion. . . . An interpretation for a problem made a 1000 years ago was made in a different historical era and environment. . . . It has to be reinterpreted within the parameters of the Quran.[100]

She criticizes orthodox scholars (ulama) for their narrow-mindedness, which has stifled religious growth and turned many away from Islam.

> There is also too much rigidity. Whatever a scholar said a 1,000 years ago is the final word. . . . This has hurt and damaged the Muslims because there is a capacity within Islam to grow with changing times. . . . This view has turned the younger generation away from Islam. They regard it as a religion that instead of solving their problems will throw them back into the dark ages.[101]

Instead of legalism, Hashmi says, Muslims should focus on inculcating Islamic values in a gradual approach to implementing Shariah:

> I don't think that the Shariah should be artificially enforced. . . . Unfortunately this is what has been happening in Pakistan. The Prophet (PBUH) first won the hearts of the people by giving them laws to live by and for Him to explain and achieve this took many

> years. Take the case of alcohol: it was first touched upon lightly, then after a while more strongly and then the third time it was banned. The purpose behind it was gradually explained so when the final ban came, people were ready to accept it. I feel it is important to first explain the concept to people and give them time to understand, debate and accept it. Nothing should just be imposed arbitrarily.[102]

Islamic Feminist or Female Taliban?

Hashmi's critics at both ends of the spectrum criticize her views on women: the conservative ulama call her a "feminist," while secular Muslims dismiss her as the "female face of the Taliban." When asked if her teachings might encourage the talibanization of society and result in the loss of women's rights, Hashmi responds:

> When I myself have done my Ph.D. and gone to a foreign land to study, how can I tell others not to do the same? My point of view is that a woman's primary responsibility is her home, after she has fulfilled that it is up to her to go into whatever field suits her best. I have no agenda to take away women's rights. Al-Huda holds evening classes specially for working women. But, peace in the home depends on the woman and that aspect should not be ignored at the cost of working outside the home. A woman's role as a home-maker should not be sacrificed at the altar of ambition.[103]

Hashmi does not restrict the type of profession that a Muslim woman should pursue. Asked what career options she would suggest for women that would "suit" their "nature," she responded:

> You cannot make a law telling people what to do and what not to do. Everyone has different skills and an aptitude for different things. I would say that every woman must learn to recognize her own abilities and assess her own circumstances and at the same time understand the limits set by Islam. Whichever field fulfils both the requirements of the individual as well as Islam, then that would be the appropriate career.[104]

Despite Hashmi's seemingly "progressive" views on women's education, career opportunities, and right to be a religious authority, her choice of dress, preference for hijabs, and support of gender segregation have worked against her and drawn sharp criticism. Tarek Fatah, former communications director of the Muslim Canadian Congress, warned: "Her concept is a grave threat not only to Canadian values but also to Canadian Muslims. She's segregating society and encouraging the ghettoization of the South Asian Muslim community and making it very difficult for them to integrate into mainstream society. . . . She is completely brainwashing these educated, middle-class women to stay at home."[105]

Hashmi insists that she doesn't prescribe any specific form of dress to women, besides what God ordains in the Quran:

> I am not prescribing the design of what a woman should wear. . . . The Islamic code of dress is to hide your beauty, however you choose to do it. It is, however, clearly stated that there should be a head covering that also covers the upper part of one's body. It can be a scarf, a chador, a burqa.[106]

Hashmi has also been accused of "preaching" polygamy in countries like Canada where it is against the law, because she teaches that if a man has relations with a woman, he must marry her. She counters, "Islam gives women rights, so that a man cannot take advantage of her. If a man has relations with a woman outside of marriage, the Koran orders him to marry her."[107] Her followers leap to her defense: "Mrs. Hashmi may have talked about polygamy . . . but she does not encourage her students to find a second wife for their husbands. Under her tutelage, Muslim women from all walks of life became more knowledgeable about Islam, enabling them to become better Muslims."[108]

Despite her critics, few would deny Farhat Hashmi's international influence on the lives and spirituality of thousands of well-educated as well as less-educated women.

ULAMA REFORMERS FOR WOMEN

Despite the rigid conservatism of many ulama, there are prominent senior religious scholars and authorities like Yusuf Qaradawi who also espouse reform with regard to women's rights. Qaradawi's scripture-based paradigm of gender equality argues that the Quran places equal obligations on both sexes to maintain individual and collective morality (9:71). While affirming women's duties as wives and mothers and the need for Islamic dress, he also defends women's right to function in public space, to be educated and employed, and to vote and run for public office. Qaradawi argues that all of these roles are consistent with Shariah; since no revealed text prevents these rights and roles in society, women are able to fulfill their Quranic duty of guarding the well-being of the nation.

A strong and vocal critic of the Taliban, Qaradawi dismissed their treatment of women as due to a false understanding of Islam "that must be rejected." He condemns the fact that they "prevented women from working and locked them in their homes, including thousands of widows who had lost their husbands in the war and who needed their work to support their children." And he further noted, "Some of these women are intellectuals and others are university graduates."[109]

Qaradawi's theological views on women are reflected in his family. He often notes with great pride that he has four daughters. Three have Ph.D.'s from universities in England: in nuclear physics from the University of London; photochemistry from the University of Reading; and molecular biology from the University of Nottingham. The fourth finished a master's in genetics at the University of Texas at Austin. One of his daughters is the dean of Qatar University.

Because Qaradawi criticizes militant Salafis and defends women's rights, Salafis have charged that he is an "innovator" who leads Muslims astray. Salafi Web sites call him "the straying imam"; their hostility is expressed in such titles as *Refuting Qaradawi* and *Silencing the Hounding Dog*. They denounce him as the wicked mufti whose evil verdicts or fatwas oppose the Quran and Sunnah of the Prophet and encourage people to indulge in ignorance and novelties that are instruments of the devil.[110] Like Qaradawi, Egypt's Grand Mufti, Sheikh Gomaa, also stresses a woman's right to education and to a profession, as well as her unequivocal right to choose her spouse (rejecting the idea that a father has any prerogative over his daughter's choice). Qaradawi's fatwas have also argued that women have the right to become heads of state.

Ali Gomaa's February 2007 fatwa affirming women as leaders of nations reveals his neo-traditionalist methodology as well as his rationale for modern reform, both of which generate controversy. After the leading Egyptian newspaper *Al-Ahram* reported that Gomaa had prohibited female presidents, he charged that they had distorted his position. Distinguishing between a modern president and a "traditional ruler or caliph . . . the supreme leader of the Muslims," he maintained that the reasons given by the earliest Muslim jurists for why a woman was not capable of assuming the office of caliph "clearly show us that the office of caliph is very different to our present concept of a president."[111]

Gomaa has spoken out on other women's issues such as female circumcision and polygyny. Female circumcision is not a religious obligation in

Islam. But it has long been practiced by non-Muslims in Africa and elsewhere and has been supported by religious authorities in some Muslim countries. In June 2007, after an eleven-year-old Egyptian girl died following the operation, Gomaa issued a clear and decisive fatwa: "The harmful tradition of circumcision that is practiced in Egypt in our era is forbidden."[112] The fatwa has major implications for Egyptian society, where a 2005 UNICEF report found that 97 percent of Egyptian women between the ages of fifteen and forty-nine had been circumcised.

Ali Gomaa, like other reformers, bases his support for reforms to limit polygyny on the Quran's stipulation regarding justice toward wives: "if you fear that you will not be able to deal justly with the orphans, then marry only one " (4:3).[113] He argues that men were never ordered to marry more than one wife. Moreover, polygyny was not to be practiced for its own sake but for specified situations (the deaths of many men in battle and need to care for many widows and orphans) that existed at the time the Quran was revealed.

A striking characteristic of Ali Gomaa's fatwas on gender issues is their defensive tone. He often juxtaposes his Islamic ruling with a negative description of women's position in the West:

> The irony is that those who attack Islam for allowing polygyny are themselves suffering from the breakdown of families, the spread of illicit sex, and the permissibility of multiple lovers without limit, for the lover does not enjoy the rights that a spouse enjoys, and the wife is also betrayed. The female lover loses many of her rights. Neither she nor her children are acknowledged. She alone bears the burden of an abortion or the burden of living as a single mother to raise illegitimate children.[114]

Many of Ali Gomaa's positions on women's rights are seen as relatively progressive. However, he reflects a different perspective by equivocating when interpreting Quran 4:34, concerning a man's right to "beat" his wife. After identifying jurists who recommend that men completely avoid hitting their wives, citing a Prophetic tradition that prohibits beating women, and the Prophet's own example of never beating women, Gomaa himself proceeds to a more convoluted conclusion. His fatwa maintains that a man has the right to lightly hit his wife as a symbolic gesture if she is disobedient (*nashiza*), but only after he has fulfilled the first two requirements, admonishing her and if necessary leaving the marital bed. He defends his opinion by arguing that women in some cultural environments would expect a husband to hit his wife (lightly), as an indication of his manliness. He defensively concludes that, although the West is unfamiliar with such environments, the Quran came for all people and all times.

Farhat Hashmi offers her own challenge to interpretations of Quran 4:34 that allow men to physically chastise their wives for disobedience:

> Nowhere is it written that the husband has the right to chastise his wife if she does not obey him. That right has been given to him if she is unfaithful. I have been told that I have a feminist approach. I have elaborated this ayat {verse} in detail. The word used in the Quran for his is 'Nashoos' which does not mean not listening. It means a distortion of family life, when the wife shows she does not care for the husband and in doing that disturbs the harmony and peace in the home, and my interpretation of that is when she is unfaithful.[115]

Islam's "Billy Grahams": Muslim Televangelists

Until modern times, spreading "the Good News" required missionaries to travel great distances to reach their audiences. All this has been transformed by modern media, global communications, and the birth of televangelism. New technologies (television, cable religious networks, the Internet, audio, video, CD, and DVD) have transformed Christian theologians and preachers into religious media stars (Mother Angelica, Pat Robertson, Rick Warren, Joel Osteen). Without leaving their church or studio, they are able to reach in a single broadcast national and global audiences, far larger than Jesus, the apostles, and St. Paul reached directly in their entire lifetimes.

The globalization of communications has also produced a crop of Muslim media stars, both scholars like Yusuf Qardawi and Tariq Ramadan and a new breed of charismatic and enormously successful preachers like Amr Khaled and Abdullah Gymnastiar. These televangelists reach millions, sometimes hundreds of millions, filling huge auditoriums and sports stadiums and disseminating their message on DVDs, video and audio tapes, satellite television and radio, and the Internet. Amr Khalid's Web site is said to get more hits than Oprah Winfrey's.

Televangelists and their organizations provide a religious alternative to traditional clerics and mosques, muftis and fatwas. Prominent ulama may call for a greater centralization of religious authority, but these popular alternative outlets enable Muslim televangelism, like Christian televangelism, to move in the opposite direction, toward a decentralization of religious authority. Most preach a direct, down-to-earth message, dispensing advice on everyday problems, promoting a practical, concrete Islamic spirituality of empowerment and success in this life as well as the next. Their audiences are drawn not as much by their religious or scholarly credentials as by their personalities, preaching styles, and distinctive messages.

AMR KHALED: "ARAB WORLD'S FIRST ISLAMIC TELE-EVANGELIST"

Amr Khaled has been called "the Arab world's first Islamic tele-evangelist, a digital age Billy Graham who has fashioned himself into the anti-Bin Laden . . . to turn around a generation of lost Muslim youth."[116]

Clean-shaven and well-dressed in a fashionable Western suit, Khaled speaks in colloquial Arabic to millions of young Muslims, ages fifteen through thirty-five. He targets upper-middle-class Muslims in the Arab world and Arab immigrants living in the West, because he believes they are the ones most capable of changing the Islamic world for the better. He attracts a large following of young Muslim women, drawn to him by his warm, friendly, emotional, and humorous style and practical messages, which focus on the problems of everyday life.

Like evangelical Christian preachers, Khaled blends conservative religious belief with a charismatic personality and speaking style, Western self-help, management-training jargon, and an emotive crowd-pleasing performance full of stories, laughter, and tears. He doesn't talk politics, preferring to emphasize God's love and issues of personal piety, daily prayer, family relationships, veiling, dating, and community responsibility. Muslim youth, in particular, are drawn to his down-to-earth religious and spiritual messages, emphasizing values and a positive, proactive attitude toward life. He replaces the negative "No, No Islam" of many Muslim preachers and fundamentalists with an affirmative "Yes to life Islam."

Khaled's ability to relate Islam to everyday life has made him extraordinarily popular and effective. He encourages young people to focus not on the things they cannot change but rather on what they can change, like their attitude, behavior, and character. His message stresses making small changes in everyday life—how one prays, the little acts of kindness one can do—that can lead to more dramatic progress. His television series, *Life Makers* (*Sunaa' al-Hayat*), challenges Muslim youth to improve conditions in their countries by improving the conditions of their lives. The themes of the forty-six episodes range from "Say No to Drugs" and "Say No to Alcohol and *Qat*" (a leaf that is chewed like tobacco) to "Preserving Our Resources," "Setting Goals in Your Life," and "Utilizing Our Minds."[117] In the first episode of the series, Khaled describes his philosophy of life and his purpose in launching his program: "We will not change unless we wake up from this indefinite coma that we live in. We have reached rock bottom in all the domains of life. I cannot imagine that we can go anywhere beneath the level we have reached, simply because it is rock bottom."[118]

Amr Khaled's goal is a renaissance (*nahda*) or renewal of the Muslim community. In contrast to those who simply romanticize past glories or grapple with issues of Islamic jurisprudence or law, Khaled's approach is simple, clear, and direct. He retells stories from Islamic history but with a new spin that emphasizes the need to inculcate and follow the Islamic spirit and values today. His reformist message combines traditional Islam (he regards wearing hijab as a requirement) with a strong social message for young men and women.

Like many other Muslim televangelists, Khaled is particularly popular among young women, whom he addresses directly in his sermons and articles in women's magazines. He combines stories about women's central role in Islamic history (for instance, Khadija, the first convert to Islam and the first martyr to die in jihad) with criticism of the oppression of women today. The importance of women's rights is underscored by his condemnation as un-Islamic of abuses like "honour killings" and forced marriages.

Khaled describes many in the Arab world as "parasites," lagging behind most of the world. However, his message is one of hope, not despair. Citing statistics from Arab-world studies that compare its poverty, unemployment, literacy index, average family income, and number of published books with other regions in the world, he says, "Our problem is that we have gotten used to taking without ever giving. In other words, we are living as parasites on the rest of the world."[119] Young people must be proactive, breaking the four chains that hold them back: (1) passiveness, (2) lack of purpose in life, (3) lack of seriousness, and (4) ignorance. He uses the metaphor of a man who is shackled in his home when the world outside of him is full of light.

But what can individuals actually do to change themselves and their societies? Khaled's message is simple and direct, prescribing everyday acts that empower people and contribute to the betterment of society:

- The garbage in the streets. Get rid of it yourself.
- The pothole in front of your house. Fill it yourself.
- The broken glass at your house. Replace it.
- The leaky water tap. Learn how to fix it or call somebody who can.
- Give private lessons to your neighbors' children. Teach them languages or show them how to use computers, etc.
- At your college, if the laboratory is lacking some instruments, collect some money from your colleagues and buy those instruments.

- Clean the mosques; do not be ashamed to do it yourself; your proactive attitude will give you courage.
- Teach an illiterate person to help reduce the percentage of illiteracy.
- Housewives, join in to start a project to help women and widows by teaching them a skill that they can work with instead of waiting for financial support from others.[120]

Khaled uses his Web site interactively to mobilize as well as instruct. The number and enthusiasm of his followers are evident in the overwhelming response to his request for ideas and suggestions. He reported receiving 6,000 by fax, 140,000 by phone, and 215,000 over the Internet from thirty-five countries in the Arab world, Asia, Africa, Europe, and the United States. A call for clothing for the poor drew thousands of people in twenty-six countries who collected one and a half million bags of clothes that were distributed to those in need.

Islam and the West

In 2004, Amr Khaled moved to Birmingham, England, and expanded his message and mission to Europe and America. His primary audience here is second-generation European Muslims, and his goal, bridging the gap between East and West: "My interest in this issue (dialogue with the West) stems from my prime interest and goal in life—to act as a catalyst for a renaissance that cannot be obtained in the presence of conflicts. I think I'm heading toward that goal through my 'Life Makers' programme."[121]

Khaled's goal is a transformation of society, a process of empowerment through an emphasis on faith and identity, pride, and a positive, action-oriented attitude toward life.

> We want to change our painful reality from one of humiliation to one of great dignity; from economical devastation to economical prosperity; from unemployment to work and production; and from loss of identity to pride in being Muslims. We want to trigger a new age in success for universities and systems of education, non-profit organizations, social organizations, and in the field of translation. We want to turn our culture from a cheap and tasteless one to a leading, refined, culture.[122]

When the Danish cartoon crisis erupted, Khaled convened an interfaith conference, "Know the Prophet," in Copenhagen in March 2006. The dialogue between twenty-five Muslim youth and their Danish peers concluded with such recommendations as establishing a cultural center in Denmark, supplementing Danish textbooks with some information on Islam, and promoting dialogue with various parties. Endorsed by forty-two prominent preachers and Islamic scholars, Khaled was nevertheless also strongly criticized for dialoguing with the Danes at that time. Yusuf Qaradawi said it was not the right time for Muslims to go to Denmark, unless there was an apology from the government. Khaled responded:

> We found the cartoon crisis to be a golden opportunity that may not occur again to introduce a true picture of our prophet to the West, where at least five million Danes were eager, for the first time ever, to hear about Islam. We wanted to eliminate misconceptions and stereotypes about Islam and abort attempts by antagonists to Islam to attract neutral non-Muslims to their side and alienate Muslims. We also wanted to get to know the Danes and how they perceived the offensive drawings.[123]

Without directly dismissing critics like Qaradawi, Khaled held his ground:

> There are two schools of thought: one that confronts attacks and one that rather focuses on building the future. Both schools are respectable, but it is my right to focus on building the future. We have to ask ourselves what we want: co-existence or conflict? What is in Muslims' best interest? Can we have a renaissance in the presence of continued, non-stop, conflicts? Co-existence does not mean that we do not confront attacks. But the danger lies in the fact that the awakening of the Muslim nation does not occur except in the pattern of conflict. At the time of Prophet Mohamed those who adopted Islam in times of peace were many times the number of those adopting it in times of wars and conflicts. That is one proof that Islam flourishes in peace.[124]

ABDULLAH GYMNASTIAR

Like their Christian counterparts, Muslim televangelists come in all sizes, shapes, and personalities. For theater and drama, few can compete with Aa Gym. *Time* magazine profiled him

> in the spotlight as usual, wireless mike in hand, dry-ice smoke swirling over the stage, his backing quartet ready to jump in on cue.

His velvet baritone is caressing the crowd one moment with a few lines from a famous love song, dropping low to an intimate whisper the next, and then suddenly soaring, cracking with emotion to a near shout. All the while, his free hand is waving, gesturing, pointing and then is clasped to his chest in rapture. . . . By the time Aa Gym ("elder brother" Gym) finishes his hour-long sermon . . . scores of women and men are openly weeping, and the roar of applause continues long after the TV cameras have been switched off.[125]

Abdullah Gymnastiar is Indonesia's most popular televangelist. His fame nationally exceeds that of Indonesian film stars and cuts across the social spectrum: rich and poor, educated and uneducated, men and women, Muslims and many Christians have been drawn by his emphasis on religious pluralism and belief that all religions ultimately preach the same message.[126]

A household name, the flamboyant Aa Gym disseminates his message on a weekly television program and to a radio audience of sixty million people in addition to his books, cassettes, videos, management training seminars, and aphorisms displayed on the red cans of Qolbu Cola, the soft drink he markets.[127]

Like Amr Khaled, the forty-seven-year-old Aa Gym combines religious teaching with practical self-help advice. His message has been likened to American Protestant evangelism's emphasis on people's ability to take control of their lives and their fortunes. Spiritual success for Aa Gym does not preclude temporal success. His optimistic message is that you can succeed in the "here and now" if you follow religious values and work hard, and his message is embodied in his own lifestyle. Like Khaled's, Gymnastiar's credibility and appeal stem from his emphasis on Islam's relevance to the everyday life of Muslims and on his own example; he practices what he preaches. Solahuddin Wahid, vice chairman of Indonesia's largest Muslim organization, the forty-million-member Nahdlatul Ulama, commented that Aa Gym's "sincerity is his strength. He's creating a society based on his words and deeds."[128]

Aa combines religion, popular Western business motivational principles and techniques, entrepreneurship, marketing, and modern media to produce a model that joins modern principles of business organization with the teachings of Islam and Indonesian culture. He calls his teaching method "Management by Conscience."[129] Three-day management seminars for business executives and middle managers cost two hundred to three hundred dollars per person. Major firms in Indonesia send their top executives to his

Islamic training center, where they train to be better professionals in a program that includes ethics and Quranic studies. The program emphasizes three keys to success—honesty (to gain people's trust), professionalism, and innovation—and promotes the basic belief "A system with a good management, no matter how small its potential, will be blessed with optimal results."[130] Sounding like a business guru, he preaches the Seven Tips for Success ("Be calm, plan well, be skillful, be orderly, be diligent, be strong and be humble") and Five Tips for a Good Product ("It should be cheap, high quality, easy to use, up-to-date and useful for both the world and hereafter").

While Gymnastiar's message often focuses on the practical issues of everyday life, he links this with the bigger picture of Indonesia's future. Personal morality is the key to the success and development of Indonesia itself: "We will only advance if we follow our conscience. . . . No party or group will ever unify Indonesia. That must come from within us, our conscience." He attributes the failures of Indonesia's leaders to their hypocrisy: "Indonesian leaders fall because they wear masks to hide weaknesses in their characters." Thus Gymnastiar's goal is "to build their characters and prepare a generation of professional Muslims."[131]

Unlike some of Indonesia's firebrand clerics, Aa rarely talks about world politics in his sermons. Yet his popularity is such that both Indonesian presidential candidates and visiting world leaders often meet with him. Like many other Indonesians, he is attracted by the United States, borrows from American business gurus, and advocates a close relationship between the two countries: "I hope America and Indonesia will join together to build a civilization of the heart." Yet he also reflects the sentiments of many Indonesians who have grown distrustful of America's intentions and policies. Although Gymnastiar met with former U.S. secretary of state Colin Powell during his visit to Indonesia in the fall of 2003, he declined an invitation to meet with President George W. Bush and three other moderate Muslim leaders. In a pointed reference to Bush, he observed: "American people need a president with a good heart so that America will be loved in the world and that will make America safe. If America does not treat the world fairly, people will hate America, and that will make America insecure." Aa spoke out against U.S. policies in Iraq and other parts of the Muslim world. Days before the U.S. invasion of Iraq, Gymnastiar led an antiwar protest of five thousand Indonesians to the gates of the U.S. Embassy in Jakarta. In his arms he carried his young son, who was dressed in clothing stained as if with blood. He condemns the use of violence against the United States or any other country.

Like many other Indonesian leaders, Aa Gym is a critic of violence and religious extremism. But what makes him more effective than other moderate preachers is that his teaching is not just a rejection of extremism but a positive and motivating message.

Although he avoids conflicts and confrontation,[132] Gymnastiar has not been above criticism. He was publicly criticized by Indonesia's press when he went to prison to visit Abu Bakar Bashir, the spiritual leader of Jema'ah Islamiah, the group responsible for the Bali suicide bombings. Bashir had been accused of providing support to al-Qaeda, a charge he denied. The Indonesian government arrested Bashir in 2002 under pressure from the U.S. government and charged him in 2005. Nevertheless, Bashir remains extremely popular in Indonesia (he was released in 2006), and many people, including Gymnastiar, doubt his guilt. Reflecting this skepticism, Gymnastiar dismissed the charges that Bashir's Jema'ah Islamiah underground group was behind the bombings of two Bali nightclubs in 2002 and the J. W. Marriott Hotel in Jakarta in 2003, which together killed 224 people. "America has been saying so much about this, but they can't prove it. . . . America talks a lot. But they can't prove what happened in Iraq, either. When they attacked Iraq, they lied."[133]

An unexpected revelation in late 2006 dealt a severe blow to Aa Gym's seemingly charmed life and alienated many of his followers. Although regarded as a progressive and modern imam, in a surprise move, he took a second wife. Many, especially his female followers, were stunned and shocked. Disillusioned and outraged, many women dropped out of his weekly weekend meetings and other programs in Bandung. Enraged listeners openly confronted him during his broadcast talk shows, charging, "You have sold out your religion."[134]

Indonesia's 1974 marriage law does permit a man to take a second wife, although only with the approval of his first wife and the courts. But he must prove that his first wife is unable to bear a child or is disabled, or cannot fulfill her duty as a wife. Aa's first wife, Nini Muthmaninah—who often accompanies Aa Gym on his speaking engagements and TV shows and is mother of their seven children—said she had thought about this for five years and had agreed to his second marriage. Aa Gym's new bride, Alfarini Eridani, thirty-seven, a single mother of three and a former model, works for his business group in Bandung.[135]

Although Gymnastiar apologized publicly, he countered defensively that Islam allows polygamy because men are by nature more inclined to it: "Women tend to be monogamous, that's how their 'software' is. . . . But men, you know . . . their software is different." Stating that polygamy is better than extramarital sex, he nevertheless added, "What I did should not justify other men to do the same—I do not recommend it."[136]

Is There Light at the End of the Tunnel?

The policies of Muslim governments like the Taliban's Afghanistan, rigid fundamentalist theologies, the medieval orientation of ultraconservative religious leaders, and the slow pace of development in some Muslim societies attract charges that Islam is incompatible with modernity and development. In fact, since the late nineteenth century Muslims have struggled with Islamic reform. Today, prominent religious scholars, intellectuals, Islamic activists, and televangelists across the Muslim world, aided by modern technology and global communications, address critical issues of reform in dealing with twenty-first-century realities.

Like all religious traditions, Islam represents ideals that have taken many forms through the centuries. While the life of Muhammad and the Medinan state he created remain ideal paradigms, historically there has been no single, agreed-upon model for an Islamic state. Muslim empires, sultanates, and modern states have varied. Islamic law, the blueprint for an ideal society, was and continues to be conditioned by diverse historical and social contexts and the human interpretations of individual religious scholars and rulers.

If some romantically or legalistically retreat to the past, others seek to reinterpret sacred scriptures, to reevaluate past traditions, and to reconstruct Islamic religious thought and law to address more adequately and effectively the present and future of Islam. As we have seen, robust debates range widely from the question of who is qualified to interpret Islam and how to interpret sacred texts to the authority of tradition or classical Islam versus the sacralization of tradition. Key issues include the status and roles of women in Muslim society, the nature of jihad, the causes of religious extremism, the legitimacy of violence and suicide bombing, and, in the West in particular, the relationship of religion, identity, and culture.

Widespread desire for reform is evident at the grass roots. The Gallup World Poll has found that Muslims across the world want to see reforms and recognize the need to frame such reforms within an Islamic discourse and context. It reveals a broad-based Muslim belief in the importance of religion to their identity and future progress, the desire for their government and society to be informed by religious principles and values rather than secularism, and keen interest in gaining more respect from the West for their religion, themselves, and their countries. But while many wish to have some role for Shariah, religious principles and values, they do not want a theocracy, nor do they see the ulama determining the laws of the state.

Contrary to what some have charged, most Muslims are as concerned as the West about the dangers of religious extremism and terrorism. Indeed, Muslims have been the primary victims of Muslim extremism and terrorism. Majorities denounced violence and terrorism, including the 9/11 attacks, recognizing that they are un-Islamic and threaten the safety and security of the state and its citizens. However, Western and Israeli policies fuel deep anger and resentment not only in Palestine but globally. As a result, resistance to the occupation and Israeli oppression has spawned support for conventional warfare as well as support for suicide bombers. While majorities of Muslims reject suicide bombing in Palestine, prominent religious scholars and leaders like Qaradawi have been at loggerheads with religious authorities in Saudi Arabia and Egypt on this issue.

The struggle (jihad) for reform in Islam, as in Christianity and other faiths, has spawned heat as well as light, both dialogue and diatribe, coexistence and conflict. The result is a wide range of religious interpretations and orientations: from the mainstream majority to a militant extremist minority, from traditionalists to modernists to Western-oriented secularists. What will relations between the Muslim world and the West look like in coming decades?

In light of Western attitudes toward Islam and Muslims, and conditions in Muslim societies globally, what are the critical problems, issues, and challenges that loom in relations between the Muslim world and the West? Given a world in which anti-Americanism is so widespread and global terrorism a continued threat, and in which protagonists in both the West and the Muslim world proclaim and seek to provoke an inevitable clash, is there light at the end of the tunnel?

Islam and Muslims today often seem caught between forces that drive change and those that block it. Moderate Muslim majorities desire and are a potent potential force for religious, political, and social change. Muslims in the West, many of whom enjoy greater religious, intellectual, and political freedom and experience, have been a resource in the development and dissemination of models for reform, from fresh religious interpretations of the Quran and Islamic tradition to their applications on issues of democratization, gender equality, human rights, and religious pluralism. This potential and progress are often overshadowed by the rhetoric and acts of terrorists and by the growth of Islamophobia, the new anti-Semitism.

Western attitudes that demonize and foster discrimination against Islam and Muslims, instead of recognizing and drawing on the rich resources of the moderate majority, undermine and threaten the development of our multireligious mosaic societies in the West and hinder the struggle against the global terrorism that threatens us all.

Chapter Four

America and the Muslim World: Building a New Way Forward

To the Muslim world, we seek a new way forward, based on mutual interest and mutual respect.

President Barack Obama, *Inaugural Address*

After eight years of the Bush administration, Muslims, like many others around the world, greeted an Obama presidency with great expectations for a change in direction. Obama's inaugural address signaled a new beginning. Distancing himself from the Bush administration's failed policies, and from the sacrifice of principles and values in the name of a war on terrorism, Obama spoke of his desire that America reemerge as a principled global leader.

> As for our common defense, we reject as false the choice between our safety and our ideals. Our Founding Fathers, . . . faced with perils we can scarcely imagine, drafted a charter to assure the rule of law and the rights of man, a charter expanded by the blood of generations. Those ideals still light the world, and we will not give them up for expedience sake. And so to all the other peoples and governments who are watching today, from the grandest capitals to the small village where my father was born, know that America is a friend of each nation and every man, woman, and child who seeks a future of peace and dignity. And that we are ready to lead once more.[1]

Obama underscored the need to exercise America's power wisely and morally: "Our power alone cannot protect us, nor does it entitle us to do as we please. . . . Security emanates from the justness of our cause, the force of our example, the tempering qualities of humility and restraint." Finally, he called for a reappropriation of and return to America's legacy: "We are the keepers of this legacy. Guided by these principles once more, we can meet those new threats that demand even greater effort, even greater cooperation and understanding between nations."

The Missing Link

Policymakers tend to rely on the opinions of experts as well as their allies, Muslim rulers and entrenched elites. However, a critical question in the formulation of foreign policy ought to be "What do Muslims globally, the mainstream majority, really think?" To chart a new way forward, we need to know not what everyone else says about Muslim attitudes, beliefs, grievances, hopes, fears, and desires but what the silent majority say.

A question raised repeatedly over the years is "Why do they hate us?" A common answer has been "They hate our way of life, our freedom, democracy, and success." While many continue to believe anti-Americanism is tied to insurmountable religious and cultural differences, the facts undercut this simple and rather self-serving response.

Terrorists may hate America (and some European countries), but the rest of the world does not. We fail to distinguish between the hatred of extremists and a broad anti-Americanism among those who admire our accomplishments, principles, and values but denounce what they see as U.S. arrogance, unilateralism, and hegemonic designs. Terrorists want to kill us, but most Muslims want us to stop making the world an even more dangerous place. Polls of the beliefs and attitudes of a cross-section of Muslims around the world give us a good measure of their admiration as well as their resentment, which, left unaddressed, has the potential to increase radicalization. The future of Islam depends upon our moving beyond facile and failed paradigms like "They hate our way of life," which reduce relations between the Muslim world and the West to an inevitable "clash" of civilizations, values, or interests.

Gallup World Polls from 2001 to 2009 have shown that our Western way of life is not the source of hatred in the Muslim world. Every European and American knows that the West is not monolithic; so too there is no monolithic Muslim world. Muslims do not see all Western countries as the same. They distinguish between America and Europe and between specific

European nations depending on their policies, not their culture or religion. During the pivotal years in the deterioration of U.S.-Muslim relations, Muslims globally drew a sharp distinction between America and Britain, under the Bush and Blair administrations, and other European countries. The United States and the United Kingdom were viewed negatively, while views of France and Germany were neutral to positive. For example, while 74 percent of Egyptians had unfavorable views of the United States, and 69 percent said the same about Britain, only 21 percent had unfavorable views of France and 29 percent of Germany. Across all predominantly Muslim countries polled, an average of 75 percent of respondents associate the word "ruthless" with the United States (in contrast to only 13 percent for France and 13 percent for Germany).[2]

The importance of foreign policy emerges starkly when we compare Muslim views of the United States with views of Canada (America without its foreign policy, one might say). Sixty-six percent of Kuwaitis have unfavorable views of the United States, but only 3 percent see Canada unfavorably. Similarly, 64 percent of Malaysians say the United States is "aggressive"; yet only one in ten associates this quality with France and Germany.[3]

Reactions to the U.S./U.K.–led invasion of Iraq underscore the influence of foreign policy on Muslim attitudes toward the West. When people in ten predominantly Muslim countries were asked how they view a number of nations, the attributes they most associate with the United States are scientifically and technologically advanced (68 percent), aggressive (66 percent), conceited (65 percent), and morally decadent (64 percent).[4] Majorities in most countries who were asked about the invasion of Iraq, Muslim men and women alike, believe the invasion has done a great deal more harm than good. Muslims clearly have not seen the conflict as with the West or Western civilization as a whole but rather with specific Western powers' foreign policies.[5]

While admiring American democratic principles and values, they do not see those values applied in the treatment of Muslims. This gap between U.S. policy and U.S. principles results in the charge that the United States has pursued a double standard in its promotion of democracy and human rights. Significant percentages of Muslims believe the United States is not serious about democracy in their region. Ironically, this view is especially prominent in countries that are viewed as American allies and where the promotion of democracy has seemingly been the loudest, such as Egypt, where 63 percent doubt American promises of democratic support, and Pakistan, where 55 percent have this view.[6]

Is There a Future for Democracy in the Muslim World?

It doesn't require a great deal of familiarity with Arab or Muslim political history to know that many Muslim countries today are not democratic. Authoritarian regimes rely on their military and security forces rather than the ballot box to ensure their continued rule. They limit freedom of speech, press, media, and assembly. Many foster an authoritarian culture and values. Political parties, unions, and professional associations require government approval and may be regulated, repressed, or simply banned. Governments control educational and religious institutions, from curriculum and jobs to speeches and sermons. Dissent can result in arrest, imprisonment, and torture.

Does this lack of real power sharing mean that democracy is nonexistent in the Muslim world, or incompatible with Islam? In fact, Muslims around the world have tasted various democracies in different, often limited, forms. In recent years elections have been cautiously and sometimes reluctantly introduced by some governments, and Muslim public opinion clearly indicates a desire for greater political participation and government accountability. Turkey, Iraq, Bangladesh, Senegal, Nigeria, Mali, Malaysia, Indonesia, and Pakistan have democratically elected governments. Other countries have more limited or government-"guided" electorates. Iran has elections at the national and local levels, though senior religious leaders influence and can disqualify candidates. In recent years, elections have been introduced in other nations such as Jordan, Bahrain, Kuwait, Qatar, and Saudi Arabia, though in practice rulers still retain the bulk of the power.

Overshadowed by the ranting and threats of extremists and the dire warnings of authoritarian regimes, a quiet revolution in some power sharing has occurred. As discussed in chapter 2, today, many examples exist of Islamically oriented candidates and parties participating in elections and serving in government at local, provincial, and national levels: serving in parliaments and cabinets and as prime ministers. Like other politicians, they have learned from their experiences of the realities of governance. Though many of its key founders were former members of an Islamist (Welfare) party, for example, Turkey's AKP is far more open, diverse, pluralistic, and inclusive, committed to a blend of Turkish nationalism, culture, and secularism.

What do Muslims want? Large numbers of Muslims throughout the world are unhappy with the status quo and clearly want broader democratization. When asked what they admired most about the West, among the top responses of both the mainstream majority (those who believe that the 9/11 attacks were not justified) and political radicals (those who may not be violent themselves but believe the 9/11 attacks were justified) were the

West's rule of law, fair political systems, democracy, respect for human rights, freedom of speech, and gender equality. Majorities of Muslims, more than 90 percent in Egypt and in Iran, said that if drafting a constitution for a new country they would include "free speech" as a fundamental guarantee. Freedom of assembly and religion were also cited as important.[7]

Admiration for Western democratic values does not, however, translate into support for a Western secular model of government. Most Muslims believe their own religion and values are essential to their progress. Thus, while some reformers dismiss the relationship of religion to the state, arguing for a secular state, majorities of Muslims expressed a desire for Shariah, the basis for religious values, as "a" source of law. Although perceptions of what the Shariah represents and the degree to which it is possible to implement its rulings in society vary enormously, most want democratic and religious principles and values to coexist in their government and thus see a role for religious principles in the formulation of state legislation.

However, most do not want Shariah as "the" source of law; nor do they want a theocracy (a clergy-governed state). Significant majorities in many countries say religious leaders should play no direct role in drafting a country's constitution, writing national legislation, drafting new laws, determining foreign policy and international relations, or deciding how women should dress in public or what should be televised or published in newspapers.[8] Thus many Muslims want neither a Western secular nor a theocratic state but rather one that combines religious values with broader political participation, political freedoms, and rule of law.

Does the rejection of a Western-style secular state entail ambivalence toward relations with the West? Among the most commonly expressed sentiments Muslims associate with their societies is "Eager to have better relations with the West."

The wish for better relations includes a strong desire for Western, in particular American, technology and economic aid. Like most people the world over, asked to describe their dreams for the future, Muslim majorities cited better jobs, increased economic well-being and prosperity, and a better future for their children. At the same time, democracy is among the factors most frequently cited as necessary for a more just society.

Islamist parties are an integral part of society, and they are not going away. The promotion of democracy should include overtures to moderate Islamist parties that have embraced democratic principles and participate in elections. They act as an effective bulwark against extremists and contribute to democratization in the region. Engagement strengthens the more moderate streams within these movements.

While the desire for democratization is strong in many Muslim countries, popular demand for broader power sharing remains a challenge for parties on every side. Islam and democracy may well be characterized as under siege for the foreseeable future for a number of reasons.

Militant movements as well as some conservative Muslims reject democracy as incompatible with Islam and its traditions. They contend that democracy is a Western institution that seeks to divide the Islamic community and that its values (popular sovereignty, individual rights and freedoms) contradict Islamic values and are a threat to society.

In light of the examples of Iran, Sudan, and the Taliban and the agendas of extremist groups, Islamic movements that have participated or wish to participate in electoral politics will continue to be challenged to prove that, when elected, they will respect the very rights of minorities and opposition groups that they demand for themselves. They must acknowledge that religious authoritarianism is as objectionable and dangerous as secular forms of authoritarianism.

Muslim regimes now use the specter of a global terrorism, as they did the threat of Communism during the Cold War, to elicit support from the West and excuse their authoritarianism or tepid approach to political liberalization. The credibility of Egypt's electoral reforms has been greatly undermined by the propensity of the Mubarak government in national elections to arrest and imprison its critics, secular and religious. The nationwide referendum on multiparty elections was discredited when military courts were used to circumvent Egypt's judiciary and its decisions, and progovernment mobs were allowed to violently attack demonstrators in the streets of Cairo. As Human Rights Watch reported, "Plainclothes security agents beat demonstrators, and riot police allowed—and sometimes encouraged—mobs of Mubarak supporters to beat and sexually assault protestors and journalists."[9] Similarly, the potential and impact of Saudi Arabia's reforms and limited elections have been vitiated by episodes of suppression and imprisonment of reformers and harassment of Shii as well as Christian workers.

Western governments, driven by self-interest (access to oil and strategically important locations) worsen the problem by continuing to support and perpetuate friendly authoritarian regimes. Governments in the Muslim world, particularly autocrats, must be challenged to demonstrate their commitment to political liberalization, civil society, and human rights by fostering the development of those civil institutions and values that support democratization. Policies must discriminate between organizations, secular or Islamic, that threaten the freedom and stability of society and those that are willing to participate in a process of gradual change from within the system.

Western governments that advocate self-determination and democracy need to demonstrate by their policies as well as statements that they respect the right of any and all movements and political parties, religious as well as secular, to participate in the political process. Promoting democracy, by actions, not just words, can overcome the "democratic exceptionalism" acknowledged by Richard Haass. Western hypocrisy, demonstrated by the failure to respond to the subversion of the electoral process in Algeria, Tunisia, and Musharraf's Pakistan, the attempt "to manage" the process of democratization in post-Saddam Iraq, and the refusal to recognize the democratically elected Hamas government in Palestine, must be avoided if the West, America in particular, is to avoid the charge that it operates on a clear double standard. Respect and support for the democratic process and human rights have to be seen as truly universal.

The perspectives and policies of experts and policymakers are often distorted by a "secular fundamentalism," a worldview whose principles are regarded as self-evident norms or absolutes. Modern notions of religion as a system of belief for personal life and strict separation of church and state in a secular state have become so accepted and internalized that they have become a new absolute, a necessary pillar of democracy, which for some also requires separation of religion and politics. Those who differ are regarded as abnormal (departing from the norm), irrational, dangerous, and extremist and are sometimes dubbed religious fanatics. Lost in the discussion is the fact that religion's relationship to the state varies in Western secular democracies. The so-called wall of separation between church and state is not found in many European countries. The United Kingdom as well as Norway, Sweden, and Denmark have state religions. In the U.K., Germany, Norway, and other countries, the state provides funding for a variety of religious activities, including religious schools and the salaries of ministers and priests.

When many secular-minded government officials, political analysts, and journalists in the West hear Muslims speak of the role of religion in politics and society, they label these Muslims as "fundamentalist," connoting that they are all rigid, antimodern, backward zealots who only want to implement an Islamic state. This attitude is utilized and reinforced by some authoritarian governments and secular elites in the Muslim world not only because of their concern about security and stability but also because open elections and political alternatives, including Islamist parties, threaten their power and privilege. These fears have so influenced some quite rational and liberal thinkers that they fail to distinguish between extremist Islamic movements and mainstream Muslims who believe democratization is compatible with their religious principles and values.

At the same time, it remains important to remember that broader political participation in elections and the greater role of political parties do not in themselves guarantee the development of a culture and values of power sharing. Muslim democrats in many countries need to demonstrate that when in power they too will value political pluralism, that their aspiration is not to come to power democratically in order to impose their new "enlightened" government. The litmus test for their internalization of democratic principles and values will be the extent to which their policies and actions reflect an acceptance of basic freedoms and diversity of opinion reflected in independent political parties and civil society organizations. Can they demonstrate an appreciation for the concept of a "loyal opposition," or will they only see alternative voices and political visions as a threat to their political system?

We forget that democratization is an erratic and potentially dangerous process. The Western experience was a process of trial and error, accompanied by civil wars and intellectual and religious conflicts. America's democracy was the product of an armed revolution and an even bloodier civil war. Almost two centuries passed before the equal rights of women and African Americans were recognized. So too in the Middle East, societies that attempt to reevaluate and redefine the nature of government and of political participation as well as the role of religious identity and values will in many cases undergo a fragile process of trial and error in which short-term risks will be the price for potential long-term gains. Autocratic governments may be able to derail or stifle the process of change; however, they will merely delay the inevitable.

WHAT ABOUT WOMEN'S RIGHTS IN ISLAM?

Few issues are more contentious than the debate and conflict over women's status and role in Muslim society. In a scene in the Hollywood movie *Baby Boom*, about a high-powered career woman who is a single mother, the heroine interviews prospective nannies for her new baby girl. One of the interviewees, dressed in a long black veil, speaks in a thick Arabic accent. She promotes her special qualifications by emphasizing, "I will teach your daughter to properly respect a man. I speak only when spoken to. I do not need a bed; I prefer to sleep on the floor." Such a radical stereotype is reinforced in news articles that often portray Muslim women as silent and submissive, relegated to the home while men monopolize the active roles in society.[10] A survey of all Muslim photographs in the American press indicates that three-quarters (73 percent) of the women versus-one fifth (15 percent) of the men were illustrated in passive roles. In American photographs of the Middle East, women were five times (42 percent) more likely to be portrayed as victims than were men (7 percent).[11]

This kind of media coverage, coupled with no other contrasting images, has a powerful effect on Western attitudes. If many Muslims try to counter negative images by emphasizing that Islam actually liberates women, others in Muslim countries, as well as the West, decry women's oppression in the name of Islam. So it is not surprising that when American women are asked the open-ended question "What do you admire least about the Muslim or Islamic world?" among the top responses is "gender inequality," associated with veiling, female segregation, illiteracy, and powerlessness.[12]

The realities of women in the Arab and Muslim worlds present a more complex picture of individuals in different situations and varied social contexts. Many are unfairly subject to powerful forces of patriarchy and religion, but many others are far more empowered and respected in their own cultures than blanket stereotypes might lead us to believe.

Today, the status and roles of women vary considerably, influenced as much by literacy, education, and economic development as by religion. Some women wear stylish Islamic dress, some are veiled, and others wear Western fashions. While in some sex-segregated countries educated Muslim women are not visible in the workplace, in other countries many women work as engineers, doctors, scientists, teachers, and lawyers alongside their male colleagues. The veil has become a particularly charged symbol; yet even the wearing of the veil has diverse meanings for wearers and observers. A modern Muslim woman isn't necessarily wearing Western clothes, and a veiled woman isn't necessarily oppressed.

The complexity of women's status is illustrated by many country-specific contradictions. Women in Egypt today have access to the best education and hold responsible professional positions in virtually every sector. Yet, like women in most other Muslim societies, they need a male family member's permission to travel. While women cannot vote in Saudi Arabia and Afghanistan, in almost every other Muslim country, they do vote and run for political office, serving in parliaments and as head of state or vice president in Iran, Pakistan, Turkey, Indonesia, and Bangladesh. Saudi women own 70 percent of the savings in Saudi banks and own 61 percent of private firms in the kingdom; they own much of the real estate in Riyadh and Jeddah, and can own and manage their own businesses, but they are sexually segregated, restricted to "appropriate" professions, and forbidden to drive a car. In modern-day Egypt women could not until recently serve as judges, but in Morocco more than 20 percent of judges are women. In Afghanistan and in some areas of Pakistan, the Taliban, in the name of Islam, have forced professional women to give up their jobs and prohibited girls from attending school. In Iran, where women must cover their hair and wear long-sleeved, ankle-length outfits in public, they hold professional positions and serve in Parliament. A woman is vice president in this Islamic republic.

In some parts of the world, women's basic literacy and education reflects serious inequality: in Yemen, women's literacy is only 28 percent versus 70 percent for men; in Pakistan, it is 28 percent versus 53 percent for men. Percentages of women pursuing postsecondary educations dip as low as 8 percent and 13 percent in Morocco and Pakistan, respectively (comparable to 3.7 percent in Brazil, or 11 percent in the Czech Republic).[13]

But these figures do not represent the entire Muslim world; women's literacy rates are 70 percent in Iran and Saudi Arabia and as high as 85 percent in Jordan and Malaysia. In education, significant percentages of women in Iran (52 percent), Egypt (34 percent), Saudi Arabia (32 percent), and Lebanon (37 percent) have postsecondary educations. In the United Arab Emirates, as in Iran, the majority of university students are women.

None of these examples should make anyone complacent about the condition of many women in Muslim (or Western) societies. Patriarchy with its legacy, legitimated in the name of religion, remains alive in many, although it is also progressively challenged in the name of religion.

Today, Muslim women are increasingly leading the struggle for equality in their societies. As Zainah Anwar, a founder of Malaysia's Sisters in Islam, has observed:

> For too long, Muslim women who demanded reform to discriminatory laws and practices have been told, "this is God's law" and therefore not open to negotiation and change. . . . Evidently, the problem is not with Islam. It is with the position that men in authority take in order to preserve their privilege. Naturally, the easiest and most effective way to safeguard this position is to employ the divine sanctity of God's will. To conflate patriarchal laws and practices with Islam is nothing more than tactical power play.[14]

Anwar was an organizer of a new global movement for "equality and justice in the Muslim family" launched in February 2009. Two hundred and fifty activists and scholars from forty-seven countries gathered in Kuala Lumpur to create Musawah ("equality" in Arabic). Its mission is

> to break the theological stranglehold of the patriarchs that prevents Muslim women from enjoying equal rights . . . at a time when democracy, human rights and women's rights constitute the modern ethical paradigm of today's world. . . . The reform movement is hardly alien to the Muslim tradition, in which family laws have long been adapted to social standards of the time. This time, however, the leading bearers of much-needed change will be Muslim feminists, working with progressive Islamic scholars.[15]

Social and cultural changes are happening in many countries, perhaps made slower by the fact that in these countries Muslims see themselves as marginalized outsiders lagging far behind the West in power and development. During the glorious past of Islamic history, Muslims were "in charge" and could confidently borrow from other cultures. Assimilation today, however, is often perceived as a threat to Muslim identities and values that intensifies the danger of Western religious and cultural penetration and even greater dependence on the West.

Women are at the center of the religious and cultural wars raging in many Muslim countries today, where they are viewed as "culture bearers," "maintainers of the tradition and family values," "the last bastion" against Western cultural penetration and dominance. Wearing the veil has become not only a sign of modesty but also a symbol defending Islam. Religious leaders and activists claim that the most dangerous threat from the West is not political, military, or economic but rather Westernization. Muslim women are seen as playing a central role in preserving the family and thus the Islamic identity of Muslim societies.

The veil has been regarded as a powerful negative symbol by secular governments like Turkey and France, which have banned the headscarf, claiming it violates state secularism. Islamic regimes in Iran, the Taliban's Afghanistan, and Sudan have used mandatory veiling to prove their Islamic credentials.

In the twenty-first century Islamic dress will continue to occupy a central role, but as an entirely new symbol, adopted voluntarily by young, well-educated, middle-class women to signal their empowerment and liberation from a male-dominated religious establishment and society. Their Islamic dress is both modest and distinctly modern. It features new styles and fashions that, contrasted with Western dress, represent a source of identity, protest, and liberation. The dress has multiple meanings: it asserts a new public morality rooted in Islamic rather than Western values, commands respect from men, encouraging them not to focus on physical attraction and to treat women as persons and professionals rather than sex objects, and communicates national pride and resistance to Western cultural dominance as well as resistance to authoritarian regimes.

WHAT DO MUSLIM WOMEN AND MEN THINK ABOUT WOMEN'S RIGHTS?

The gap between American and Muslim perceptions regarding women's rights parallels much of the misunderstanding that exists in the Western world today. Western misperceptions about Muslim attitudes emerged clearly in Gallup polling. A large majority (72 percent) of Americans polled disagreed with the statement "The majority of those living in Muslim countries thought men and women should have equal rights."

In fact, however, majorities in some of the most conservative Muslim societies do support equal rights. In sharp contrast to their popular image as silently submissive, socially conditioned women who readily accept second-class status, majorities of Muslim women in virtually every country surveyed say women should have the same legal rights as men: to vote without influence from family members, to work at any job for which they qualify, and to serve in the highest levels of government. In fact, majorities of both men and women in dozens of Muslim countries around the world believe women should have:

- the same legal rights as men (61 percent of Saudis, 85 percent of Iranians, and in the 90 percent range in Indonesia, Turkey, Bangladesh, and Lebanon).
- the right to work outside the home in any job for which they qualify (90 percent in Malaysia, 86 percent in Turkey, 85 percent in Egypt, and 69 percent in Saudi Arabia).
- the right to vote without interference from family members (80 percent in Indonesia, 89 percent in Iran, 67 percent in Pakistan, 90 percent in Bangladesh, 76 percent in Jordan, 93 percent in Turkey, and 56 percent in Saudi Arabia).[16]

As might be expected, Muslim men differ, with some less supportive of women's rights than others. For example, in Indonesia, Malaysia, Lebanon, and Turkey, there were virtually no gaps between men and women. In Turkey, 92 percent of men and women agreed that women should have the same legal rights as men. In contrast, in Morocco 55 percent of men and 87 percent of women said both should have the same legal rights. And in Saudi Arabia, the only country surveyed in which women are not allowed to vote, 41 percent of men said that women should be allowed to drive a car, compared with 61 percent of Saudi women.[17]

Women in the West often link what they believe is the unequal status of Muslim women to the Shariah, and with good cause. While Islamic law served as an idealized blueprint and moral compass for early Muslim communities, today it is used as an instrument of patriarchal and tribal repression by retrogressive ulama and fundamentalists, most recently in Iran, Saudi Arabia, Sudan, Pakistan, and the Taliban's Afghanistan, drawing widespread international criticism and condemnation. However, this is not the whole Shariah story.

Surprising as it may seem, majorities of Muslims, women as well as men, who believe that women should have equal rights also want Shariah as a source of law. Muslim women who favor Islam's role in their lives see a gap between this ideal and the Muslim world's reality. Gallup World Poll data reveal a strong desire in many Muslim countries for a new indigenously rooted model of government—one that is democratic yet also embraces religious values. Thus respondents want Shariah as "a" source of law: 96 percent of Egyptians and 89 percent of Palestinians think Shariah is a fair judicial system. In only a few countries (Jordan, Egypt, Pakistan, Afghanistan, and Bangladesh) did a majority say they want Shariah as the "only" source of law: in Jordan, the percentages were 54 percent of men and 55 percent of women; in Egypt, 70 percent of men and 62 percent of women. In Turkey and Kazakhstan a majority said that Shariah should have no role in society.[18] However, concerns about women's rights as women are inseparable from broader concerns about their political rights and the conditions of their societies.

Muslim women indicate that the need to improve women's status globally is inseparable from other essential needs such as stability, economic improvement, and political rights. Their stated priorities should be the guidepost for Western advocates who have Muslim women's interests at heart.

Azizah al-Hibri, an American law professor at the University of Richmond and founder of Karamah, an organization of Muslim women lawyers dedicated to defending women's human rights, describes the frustration of "Third World" women at what they see as "First World" women's desire to dictate what their priorities should be. In the context of international conferences on human rights, says al-Hibri:

> In Copenhagen, Third World women were told that their highest priorities related to the veil and clitoridectomy (female genital mutilation). In Cairo, they were told that their highest priorities related to contraception and abortion. In both cases, Third World women begged to differ. They repeatedly announced that their highest priorities were peace and development. They noted that they could not very well worry about other matters when their children were dying from thirst, hunger or war.[19]

The challenges to greater equality and fuller participation in politics for women cannot be overcome without addressing the more intractable problem of economic development and authoritarianism in much of the Muslim world. While U.S. policy has made the issue of women a concern in its foreign policy, it is equally important to focus as much effort and attention toward promoting education, economic development, and more democratic infrastructure. But in the modern global economy there can be no real progress in a country that does not recognize and include women as full and equal participants in all spheres of life.

Without political liberalization, the realities of most Muslim societies and the aspirations of their citizens, as suggested by examples of the struggle for democracy in other parts of the world, will continue to contribute to conditions that feed radicalization, political instability, and global terrorism. At the same time, to limit the growth of terrorism we must identify and understand the concerns of potential extremists, those who can be attracted to or recruited by extremists.

Targeting Potential Extremists and Terrorists

The good news is that Gallup's polling of Muslims worldwide determined that the vast majority of respondents (93 percent) belong to the mainstream who believe the 9/11 attacks were not justified. Still, many in this group do hold critical views of U.S. policy; while 40 percent are considered pro-U.S., 60 percent view the United States' policies unfavorably. This mainstream 93 percent, who comprise both critical and supportive people, represents our potential partners in improving relations and fighting radicalism. Controlling the growth of terrorism requires that we also pay attention to the other 7 percent, the politically radicalized who represent some 91 million Muslims. People in this group believe that 9/11 was completely justified and view the United States unfavorably. They are so concerned about American intervention, invasion, and domination that they are more likely to see civilian attacks as justifiable. (Thirteen percent say attacks on civilians are completely justified versus only 1 percent of the mainstream group).[20] If they continue to be alienated and marginalized, they may represent a recruiting ground for tomorrow's extremists and terrorists.

Much of the demographic information about this politically radicalized group contradicts "conventional wisdom." Although potential extremists are expected to be male, 37 percent are female. As we know, a minority of suicide bombers have been women.[21] On average, the politically radicalized are more educated and affluent than the mainstream majority, and they are also more internationally aware. They are surprisingly more optimistic about their personal futures but, as one might expect, more pessimistic about the political future of their country and region. Though more critical of the West, they believe better relations with the West are important. Even more than mainstream respondents (58 percent versus 44 percent), the politically radicalized believe Arab and Muslim nations are eager for better relations with the West. However, they are considerably more cynical about whether improved relations will ever occur.[22]

Those with more radical views are not necessarily antidemocratic. A significantly higher percentage (50 percent versus 35 percent of the mainstream) say that moving toward democracy will foster progress in the Muslim world. However, they are much more skeptical about whether democracy will come to the region. While half (52 percent) of the mainstream disagree that the United States is serious about promoting democracy, that percentage jumps to 72 percent among the radicalized, who also convey a strong concern about being "dominated" or even "occupied" by the West. In an open-ended question, they cite "occupation/U.S. domination" as among their greatest fears.[23]

BEYOND THE CLASH OF CIVILIZATIONS?

The tendency toward radicalization and terrorism has been linked by many commentators to the religion of Islam, "a militant, violent religion." Contrary to this common idea, in the Gallup World Poll those who belong to the politically radicalized group proved to be no more religious than the mainstream. Large majorities of all groups report that religion is an important part of their daily lives, and there is no significant difference in mosque attendance.

The relationship of religion to extremism and terrorism, at home and abroad, will remain critical in the twenty-first century. It will be important to recognize that the primary causes of global terrorism, political and economic grievances, are often obscured by extremists' use of religious language and symbolism. In recent decades, religion has proven a potent force, used by Jewish, Christian, Hindu, and Buddhist as well as Muslim terrorists to legitimate and mobilize popular support. Therefore, politics, not religious piety, drives the 7 percent of Muslims who condone the 9/11 attacks and distrust the West, particularly America. Looking at the majority of respondents who were asked in an open-ended question to explain their views of 9/11, those who condemned terrorism cited religious as well as humanitarian reasons. For example, 20 percent of Kuwaitis who called the attacks "completely unjustified" explained this by saying that terrorism was against the teachings of Islam. A respondent in Indonesia went so far as to quote a direct verse from the Quran that prohibits the killing of innocents. By contrast, not a single respondent who condoned the attacks used the Quran or Islam as justification. Instead, they relied on political rationalizations, calling the United States an imperialist power or accusing it of wanting to control the world.[24]

Beyond the "clash of civilizations" theory that is often promoted by terrorist organizations, we need to view both "the West" and "the Muslim world" in terms of conflicts or confrontations among specific countries, and policies of specific leaders. When asked to cite the most important thing the United States could do to improve the quality of life of people like them, the most common responses in the Muslim world, after "reduce unemployment and improve the economic infrastructure," were "stop interfering in the internal affairs of Arab states," "stop imposing your beliefs and policies," "respect our political rights and stop controlling us," and "give us our own freedom."[25] Failure to respond effectively to the hopes and fears of the mainstream, and even more importantly to the politically radicalized, will result in serious future consequences.

The voices of majorities of populations should not be ignored or overlooked because of the threat from an extremist minority or because Western countries have had established ties to authoritarian rulers in, for example, Tunisia, Algeria, Egypt, and Saudi Arabia. Supporting the growing authoritarianism of regimes because we view them as allies in the so-called war on terror or because they warn that Islamists could come to power in elections would be seriously shortsighted.

Supporting self-determination in the Muslim world requires that we make a crucial distinction: separating out violent extremists from mainstream Islamic activists, organizations, and political parties with proven track records of participation in electoral politics and government. Perpetuating the culture and values of authoritarianism and repression will only contribute to long-term instability and anti-Americanism that empower the terrorists.

We can best counter our concerns about mainstream Islamists coming to power by supporting a strong civil society rather than by strengthening regimes that crush all opposition. Multiple political parties and professional associations, and a free press and media, offer Muslim populations broader political choices. If Islamists are the "only game in town," as we have seen, their electoral support will come not only from their own followers but also from those who want to cast the only vote they can against incumbent governments and for the critical changes needed to improve their future.

WHAT ABOUT THE MILITANTS IN THE WEST?

As in the Muslim world, in many Western societies, pockets of extremism exist and remain a threat, especially in Europe with its greater proximity to the Middle East and South Asia, immigration of some radical political exiles and radical preachers, and depressed, alienated social classes. The most vulnerable countries remain Great Britain, France, Germany, the Netherlands, and Spain. While efforts to capture and contain potential terrorists and to monitor immigration more closely are obviously important, Muslim leaders and the Muslim majority, if seen and treated as partners against extremism rather than as suspect communities, will be the best allies in limiting and countering the growth of religious extremism and terrorism. Learning to "listen" more, not just talk, taking more seriously and better understanding grievances and needs, and building relationships of trust and cooperation with Muslim organizations, schools, and mosques are critical. Equally important, religious authorities and popular preachers as well as scholars, athletes, and media stars that younger people admire can play an important role in preventive and deradicalizaion efforts.

However, current attitudes in European countries present significant challenges in establishing such partnerships. Majorities do not see religious and ethnic diversity as a strength that can enrich societies. While in the United States (70 percent) and Canada (72 percent) majorities say that greater interaction with the Muslim world is desirable, in contrast, clear majorities in all European countries surveyed see greater interaction between the West and Muslim worlds as a threat: 79 percent of the population in Denmark, 67 percent in Italy, 67 percent in the Netherlands, 68 percent in Spain, 65 percent in Sweden, and 59 percent in Belgium. These responses correspond to the growing fear among Europeans of an "Islamic threat" to their cultural identities, driven by immigration from predominantly Muslim regions, high Muslim birth rates, and the impact of terrorist attacks. Not surprisingly, in a major poll only 21 percent of Europeans supported Turkey's bid for EU membership. Nicolas Sarkozy's successful presidential campaign in France included strong opposition to Turkish membership. A 2006 poll found that the main reason Germans opposed Turkey's membership was "fear of a growing influence of Islam in Europe."[26]

These fears tend to obscure the extent to which European Muslims see themselves as permanent and loyal citizens who are at least as concerned about terrorism as their fellow citizens, or sometimes even more. When asked to use a five-point scale to rate the moral acceptability of using violence in the name of a noble cause, "the proportion of Muslims in London who chose a low rating of 1 or 2 was 81%, compared with 72% of the British public overall. In France, the corresponding numbers were 77% of Parisian Muslims vs. 79% of the French public. In Germany, they were 94% of Muslims in Berlin vs. 75% of the German public."[27]

Another striking contrast is seen in European Muslims' attitudes toward other religions. Muslim integration is reflected in positive attitudes toward Christianity (which sharply contrast with attitudes in many Muslim countries)—91 percent favorable toward Christianity among French Muslims, 82 percent in Spain, 71 percent in Britain, and 69 percent in Germany. As for Jews, however, a majority favorable percentage exists only among French Muslims (71 percent). In contrast, significant percentages of Europeans and Americans held much more negative attitudes toward Islam. In Spain (83 percent), Germany (78 percent), and Russia (72 percent) as well as large numbers in France (50 percent), Britain (48 percent), and the United States (43 percent) associated Muslims with being fanatical.[28]

Most will agree that Europe as well as America will inevitably become more and more multicultural. Therefore focusing on marginalized, alienated younger Muslims most susceptible to recruitment and radicalization especially in Europe must be a priority. Key strategies include economic and educational reforms, employment opportunities, and housing. Equally important are antiterrorism legislation that does not compromise civil liberties of Muslim citizens and balanced foreign policies on contentious issues like Palestine-Israel, Iraq, Afghanistan, Kashmir, and elsewhere.

A few years ago when I visited Muslim areas in Bradford and Leeds in Britain, young Muslim professional and community leaders told me about their frustration with government officials who had come from London to investigate conditions that led to an outbreak of violence. When the Muslims mentioned that not only issues of identity and poor education but also foreign policies like Britain's role in the invasion and occupation of Iraq had had a strong negative impact, the investigators, dutifully supporting then prime minister Tony Blair, said that such reports were clearly wrong. Ironically, at the same time, the British media published a government-sponsored report that underscored the negative influence of Britain's Iraq policy on radicals.

Well-meaning initiatives to "win the hearts and minds" that have not included a representative number of well-qualified Muslim professionals reinforces their sense of second-class citizenship, and an "us" and "them" mentality. Equally important, European and American governments need to better integrate qualified Muslims into responsible positions in government agencies and as ambassadors to Muslim countries. Surprisingly, despite the significant number of well-educated American Muslim (and Arab Christian) professionals, they were virtually absent from government during the Clinton and Bush years, and have been even thus far in the Obama administration. This is especially true in controversial areas like Israeli-Palestinian relations. In the second Clinton term, many key positions that dealt with the issue in the State Department and National Security Council were held by American Jews, with virtually no American Arab or Muslim representation.

At the same time, Muslim communities through their schools, mosques, community centers, and nongovernment organizations must continue to blend their religious identity and values with a healthy sense of nationality, integration, citizenship, and active participation in politics and the public square. Muslim participation in government is increasing. In Great Britain Muslims serve in the House of Lords and House of Commons and in Prime Minister Gordon Brown's cabinet and have been elected to municipal positions. The U.S. House of Representatives has two American Muslim members, and a limited number serve in state and local government. Muslims played prominent roles as a growing, dynamic social and political force in the 2004 and 2008 American presidential elections in states like Florida and Michigan. Muslims' overwhelming (eight to one) support for Barack Obama and their positive response around the world to his election present a unique opportunity to rebuild bridges of trust and cooperation.[29]

Muslim Civil Liberties

The atmosphere of fear gripping Europe and America that terrorist attacks will continue has led to a proliferation of antiterrorism policies and legislation in the past decade. Some European countries have looked to American antiterrorism legislation and policies. While Western countries have responded to legitimate security concerns, they have also caused serious civil liberties problems.

European Muslim leaders have warned that policies impact not only terrorists or potential terrorists but also the peaceful Muslim citizen. Major civil liberties organizations have identified a host of serious abuses including racial profiling; overzealous and illegal arrests and detentions, surveillance, and wiretapping of Muslims as well as indiscriminate monitoring of mosques; and undercover law enforcement infiltration of Muslim civic and volunteer organizations. Growing Islamophobia and with it anti-Muslim rhetoric have impacted daily life, increasing hate crimes and workplace and housing discrimination.

In many countries government policies designed to control the Muslim community, to "domesticate" Islam, have put pressure on Muslims not simply to integrate into a multicultural society but to assimilate by abandoning elements of their Muslim belief and culture in order to enjoy full participation in their new country.

France's banning of the hijab in schools is seen as an outgrowth of an assimilation policy. After the 7/7 attacks in London, Britain, long an advocate of integration and multiculturalism, has followed many other European countries. This approach is embodied in phrases like "British values" (or French or German or Danish or Dutch) that recall Europe's white pre-immigration period and privilege "enlightened" Western secular (some would also add Christian) values.

The majority of Muslims in Germany, approximately 80 percent or 3.5 million Muslims, have no German citizenship and are therefore excluded from the right to vote and actively participate in the political sphere—the basis of real integration into German society. The government also introduced what some have described as a "loyalty test," required only for Muslims seeking German citizenship, on their attitudes toward Western clothing for women, whether parents should allow their children to participate in school sports, homosexuality, and whether husbands should be allowed to beat their wives. The state interior ministry said the test would be used to filter out Muslims who were unsuited for life in Germany.[30]

Given the number and diversity of Western countries representing different community problems, as well as limitations of space, we will look more closely at the American experience.

HOW MANY SLEEPER CELLS ARE THERE? CIVIL LIBERTIES AND THE AMERICAN MUSLIM COMMUNITY

I was on a flight returning to Washington from the Midwest. The woman in the seat next to me saw me reading something about Islam. When she learned what I did for a living, this educated, upper-middle-class professional leaned closer and asked, "How many sleeper cells are there in America?"

Her question was not surprising when you consider both the trauma of the 9/11 attacks and the influence of hardline Far Right political commentators like Daniel Pipes, who warned Americans:

> The Muslim population in this country is not like any other group, for it includes within it a substantial body of people—many times more numerous than the agents of Osama bin Ladin—who share with the suicide hijackers a hatred of the United States and the desire, ultimately, to transform it into a nation living under the strictures of militant Islam.[31]

Threats to America's national security are not new; nor is using or misusing "national security" as a pretext for violating civil liberties. The detention of Japanese Americans during World War II is a textbook example. The "war" against global terrorism sparked a wave of "antiterrorist" legislation and regulations whose application has resulted in one of the most serious civil liberties crises in modern American history.

Acting on what Attorney General John Ashcroft described as a new paradigm for prevention, the administration, according to David Cole, prominent civil liberties expert,

> subjected 80,000 Arab and Muslim immigrants to fingerprinting and registration, sought out 8,000 Arab and Muslim men for FBI interviews, and imprisoned over 5,000 foreign nationals in antiterrorism preventive detention initiatives. As part of this program, the government adopted an aggressive strategy of arrest and prosecution, holding people on minor charges—in fact pretexts—such as immigration violations, credit card fraud, or false statements, or, when it had no charges at all, as "material witnesses."[32]

The manipulation of domestic antiterrorism legislation and policies like the Patriot Act and the use of "secret evidence" by some agencies and prosecutors has led to extrajudicial procedures and the erosion of civil liberties. Muslims have been profiled, wiretapped, arrested, and imprisoned without due process: they have been detained without charges and denied access to lawyers and to bail, and evidence has been withheld from them and their lawyers. The circumvention of international law by designating prisoners "enemy combatants" has meant indefinite detention with limited access to lawyers as well as trials before military tribunals not subject to judicial review.[33]

In their book *Less Safe, Less Free,* a study of the Bush administration's anti-terrorism policies, co-authors Cole and Jules Lobel concluded:

> In the name of preventing terrorism, the administration has locked up thousands of individuals without trial—within the United States and abroad—the vast majority of whom have never even been accused, much less convicted, of any terrorist act. President Bush invoked the "preventive" rationale to defend his secret order authorizing the National Security Agency to spy on Americans without probable cause that they had engaged in any wrongdoing, without a court order, and contrary to a criminal prohibition on warrant-less wiretapping.[34]

In the five years after 9/11, the Bush administration held 6,472 individuals, the bulk of them during the two years after the 9/11 attacks, under "terrorist" or "antiterrorist" programs. The politicization of terrorism cases is reflected by the fact that some alleged to have been "terrorists" were not charged with anything more than a violation of disability insurance law, failure to file a tax return, or providing false statements. By 2006, the government had decided that nearly two out of three (64 percent) of them were not worth prosecuting; 9 percent more were dismissed or found not guilty, and only one out of five was actually convicted of any crime, with less than 1 percent receiving a substantial prison sentence. The vast majority received no prison time at all, and most who did received a sentence of one year or less.[35]

The administration's policies fostered a climate of fear and led to a proliferation of unsubstantiated claims: significant numbers of Muslims in America are terrorists; 80 percent or more of America's mosques are radicalized.[36] As for embedded cells, a leaked February 2005 FBI internal memo admitted that it had yet to identify a single al-Qaeda sleeper cell in the entire United States.[37]

Moreover, the Justice Department's high-profile terrorist cases have fallen apart: the case against Captain James Yee, a Muslim chaplain at Guantanamo accused of being a spy; Dr. Sami al-Arian, a computer science professor acquitted on charges of conspiracy to kill Americans; Sami al-Hussayen, a Saudi student acquitted of aiding terrorists by posting links on a Web site.

The vast majority of Americans have no idea what has transpired. In many of my talks across the country, I pointedly ask how many are aware that thousands of Muslims were rounded up after 9/11; how many know whether these people were accused or convicted of any terrorist act. Virtually no one is able to respond.

The excessive zeal of government officials was also evident in the cases of Yusuf Islam (the British singer and former superstar Cat Stevens) and Shahid Malik, a U.K. Muslim and a minister in Prime Minister Gordon Brown's cabinet. Yusuf Islam, honored internationally for his philanthropic contributions and commitment to peace, had visited America often post 9/11, but on September 21, 2004, he was en route to Washington, D.C., from London when his flight was diverted to Maine's Bangor International Airport because his name appeared on a "national watch list." After questioning by the FBI and Immigration and Customs Enforcement officials, he was refused entrance, detained for over twenty-four hours, and finally released the next day. On two occasions, government minister Shahid Malik was invited by the Bush administration to speak on terrorism in the United States. When exiting the country he was nevertheless detained, questioned, and subjected to rigorous search, despite his diplomatic status.

Furthermore, in fostering a climate in which acts like torture, waterboarding, and rendition of prisoners are justified, we have undermined the very principles and values that underlie our identity and seriously weakened America's moral status and authority in the international community. Coupled with the compromising of Muslim civil liberties by overzealous prosecutors and government officials, these violations of international law reinforce the sense that Muslims are regarded as inferior and are victims of a double standard.

By 2009, lawsuits that challenge illegal surveillance of political activists and organizers and discriminatory policing targeting Muslims, Arabs, and South Asians were pending against the FBI and the Justice Department. Moreover, President Bush's NSA warrantless wiretapping program has been criticized by FBI agents themselves who protested that it generated hundreds of bad leads, wasting significant time and resources.[38]

In the end, it is useful to recall the warning of Benjamin Franklin, one of America's most prominent Founding Fathers: "He who sacrifices freedom for security is neither free nor secure."

Preachers of Hate—Christian and Muslim

The fallout from the demonization of Islam and Muslims by hard-line Christian Zionist and by preachers like Jerry Falwell, Pat Robertson, Rod Parsley, and John Hagee is difficult to overestimate. Their importance stems not only from the number of their followers but from their close relationships with President George W. Bush and members of his administration and

Congress. Franklin Graham, who gave the invocation at George W. Bush's first inauguration, declared, "Islam has attacked us. The God of Islam is not the same God. . . . [Islam] is a very evil and wicked religion."[39] Pat Robertson, a longtime leader of the Religious Right, was equally provocative: "This man [Muhammad] was an absolute wild-eyed fanatic . . . a robber . . . a brigand . . . a killer."[40]

In an interview on *60 Minutes*, Jerry Falwell, founder of the Moral Majority and president of Liberty University, showed that the lines were clearly drawn. Responding to Bob Simon's observation "A lot of Muslims feel these days that Christians and Jews are getting together and ganging up on them," Falwell replied, "That's true. I'm sorry, that's true. I hope it will cease to be so. But I think that is the fact right now."[41] Most provocatively, Falwell called the Prophet Muhammad a "terrorist" on national prime-time TV. Prominent televangelist Benny Hinn at a pro-Israel rally was more incendiary: "This is not a war between Arabs and Jews. It's between God and the devil."[42]

In 2008, presidential electoral politics underscored the continued importance of religion and in particular the influence of the Christian Right. Many in the Muslim world (and in Europe) became convinced that religion, in the form of Christian fundamentalism, was a significant factor in American foreign policy. Like the majority of Muslims, who are sometimes identified with a minority of religious extremists, mainstream evangelical Christians have increasingly been brushstroked by the anti-Muslim pronouncements of hard-line Christian Zionists.

The Christian preachers of hate, however, receive a disproportionate amount of media attention and therefore obscure many other Christian leaders, churches, and organizations that have rejected their hard-line Christian Zionism and spoken out for a more pluralistic and balanced approach.

In 2006, the Latin Patriarchate of Jerusalem (Catholic), the Syrian Orthodox Patriarchate of Jerusalem, the Episcopal Church of Jerusalem and the Middle East, and the Evangelical Lutheran Church in Jordan and the Holy Land issued the Jerusalem Declaration on Christian Zionism, calling it a "false teaching that corrupts the biblical message of love, justice and reconciliation." They criticized its promotion of "a worldview where the Gospel is identified with the ideology of empire, colonialism and militarism. In its extreme form, it places an emphasis on apocalyptic events leading to the end of history rather than living Christ's love and justice today. . . . We call upon Christians in Churches on every continent to pray for the Palestinian and Israeli people."[43]

The National Council of Churches, the Reformed Church in America, the Mennonite Church, the United Methodist Church, the Presbyterian Church

(USA), and the United Church of Christ are among those churches that have denounced Christian Zionism. At its 2004 General Synod, the Reformed Church declared that Christian Zionism distorts the biblical message and is an impediment to achieving a just peace in Israel-Palestine.[44]

Hard-line Christian Zionist support is by no means welcomed by all Israelis. Gershom Gorenberg, author of *End of Days*, a book about Christian Zionists who read the Bible literally, commented in the *60 Minutes* feature entitled "Zion's Christian Soldiers": "The Jews die or convert. As a Jew, I can't feel very comfortable with the affections of somebody who looks forward to that scenario." Gorenberg argued that these Christians "don't love real Jewish people. They love us as characters in their story, in their play. . . . If you listen to the drama they're describing, essentially it's a five-act play in which the Jews disappear in the fourth act."[45]

On the political front, Yossi Alfer, a political analyst who served for twelve years in the Mossad, Israel's intelligence agency, thinks Christian Zionist support does more harm than good. Alfer, who later became Israel Director of the American Jewish Committee, said in that same *60 Minutes* segment, "God save us from these people. . . . What these people are encouraging Israel and the U.S. Administration to do, that is, ignore the Palestinians, if not worse, if not kick them out, expand the settlements to the greatest extent possible, they are leading us into a scenario of out and out disaster."[46]

Not only do hard-line Christian Zionists make real peace initiatives more difficult by demonizing "the other," but they also eliminate incentives for mutual religious understanding. In this, they mirror their counterparts, ultraconservative or hardcore Muslim fundamentalists and Muslim preachers of hate.

All believers are called to challenge hard-line interpretations of scriptures and exclusivist theologies that breed intolerance and impede healthy religious pluralism, as well as to confront the preachers of hate, Christian and Muslim, whose religious ideologies justify acts of terrorism.

MUSLIM PREACHERS OF HATE

The challenge today in assessing and responding to Muslim preachers of hate is to distinguish between those who preach and propagate an ultraconservative, exclusivist intolerant theology but remain nonviolent and those who promote the radical theologies and acts of terrorist organizations. Moreover, the terrorist minority must be distinguished from mainstream Muslims in the way that we separate Christian or Jewish terrorists from mainstream or even fundamentalist Christians and Jews. Exclusivist theologies may be intellectually repugnant and socially undesirable in our multireligious societies, but, as we see with many ultraconservative and fundamentalist forms of Christianity and Judaism, they do not necessarily lead to advocacy of violence and terror. Wahhabi and Salafi Muslims espouse an ultraorthodox brand of Islam: literalist, rigid, puritanical, exclusivist, and intolerant, believing that they are right and therefore all others (Muslims and non-Muslim) are wrong and damned as a consequence. Like Christian fundamentalists or Christian Zionists, they aggressively seek to convert the world and can be intolerant of other faiths as well as other Sunni, Shia, and Sufi Muslims.

While many religious fundamentalists or ultrareligious nationalists may not themselves be violent, their theologies and worldviews can have dangerous consequences. Religious extremists have appropriated their theological worldview to demonize "the other" as the "enemy of God," and to justify acts of terrorism: Christian extremist destruction of abortion clinics and killing of physicians, Jewish extremist assassinations of Israeli prime minister Rabin and massacre of Muslims at prayer in the Hebron mosque, and Muslim extremist attacks on the World Trade Center and Pentagon and bombings from Madrid to Mindanao.

Although exclusivist theologies are not in themselves violent, in the hands of Muslim militants globally, they are easily transformed into theologies of hate and violence. Such messages are not only beamed to the West but found in Muslim countries as well. In a documentary, *Undercover Mosque*, British filmmakers exposed sermons preaching bigotry and extremism in some of that nation's mosques. Saudi-trained preachers were filmed condemning British democracy as un-Islamic and praising the Taliban for killing British soldiers. Following the program, Shahid Malik, an MP and Muslim member of Gordon Brown's cabinet, condemned the preachers, calling upon the head of Scotland Yard to bring them to justice, saying:

> We're fortunate to live in a free society but that does not give people the freedom to incite racial hatred, to inflame discord and promote division. Those who do so should know that they will be dealt with swiftly and with the full force of the law irrespective of whether they do so in the name of Islam or as white supremacists. . . . Decent people have a duty to root out extremism in their communities and mosque committees must begin to take greater responsibility for those speaking in their mosques. We can't afford to allow the evil voices of a small yet vocal minority reinforce negative images and fuel community strife and division. I am pleased with the outcry from my

> Muslim constituents who were horrified at the preachers of hatred in the Dispatches programme and all the mosques have condemned outright the behaviour of these preachers of hatred.[47]

Muslim rejection of militant forms of Wahhabi and Salafi Islam, and a more robust critique and condemnation of violent excesses committed not only by terrorists but also by Muslims engaged in legitimate resistance or liberation movements, remain critical to the future perceptions of Islam and Muslims in the twenty-first century.

Muslims in the West—Where are the Moderates?

After 9/11, I received a call from a congressional staffer on the Hill. A group of members of Congress wanted to meet with Muslim leaders but were concerned that they be "moderate Muslims." I was asked if I could come up with a list of such leaders and then meet with the staffer to discuss (vet) my candidates. Obviously, this request raised many questions for me. I wondered, "Why is the term 'moderate' rather than 'mainstream' Muslim used?" and "When they speak of Jewish and Christian leaders, do they ask for moderate Jews or Christians?" I thought to myself, "Treating Jews or Christians in this way would create a public outcry!" Most important, I wondered what asking about "moderate Muslims" says about our government's failure over the years to get to know and work with the sizeable American Muslim community and its leaders.

Lack of direct, personal interaction with real individuals who happen to be Muslim can lead to a more facile use of terms like "moderate" and "fundamentalist," and these terms stand in the way of understanding Islam. As Martin Marty, director of the Fundamentalism Project, has noted, many have stretched the meaning of the word "fundamentalism," applying it "wherever staunch conservatism links with political power and threatens liberal polities and policies."[48] Governments, religious leaders, or movements that advocate a role for religion in society or, in the name of God, oppose homosexuals' right to marry or women's rights to be ordained are commonly labeled "fundamentalist."

Too often, for non-Muslims and Muslims alike, "moderate" Muslims are played off against "fundamentalist" Muslims; fundamentalism is simply equated with religious extremism and terrorism. In an even more restrictive usage, a "moderate" Muslim is defined as someone "just like us." Thus, for many Western secularists, moderate Muslims are those who advocate secular liberalism. Conservative or traditionalist Muslims are regarded as fundamentalists: theologically closed-minded, suspicious, or extreme. Liberal or self-styled progressive Muslims often fall into the same trap, appropriating the term "moderate" solely for themselves and using the term "fundamentalist" to dismiss or ridicule those espousing more conservative theological positions. A few years ago, a published discussion/debate on moderate versus extremist Islam showed the misunderstandings that this simplistic dichotomy can foster. An American think-tank "expert" discussing the need for Islamic reform identified Islamic scholar Amina Wadud as (his kind of) a moderate Muslim. His criterion? She had led a mixed-gender Friday congregational prayer. While many of us, Muslims, Christians, and Jews, may believe that women should be able to be priests, rabbis, or imams, many other "mainstream" believers do not. By this criterion, would the pope and conservative Catholics, Anglicans, Baptists, Evangelicals, Lutherans, and many Orthodox Christians and Jews who do not believe women can be ordained as clergy pass the litmus test for "moderation"? Are they "fundamentalists" or religious "extremists" if they oppose the ordination of women, gay marriage, abortion, or euthanasia?

What, then, are the criteria for qualifying as a moderate American or European Muslim? Are moderates those who accept integration while preserving some of their own identity and values, or must they opt for total assimilation? Can a woman be a moderate Muslim if she wears a hijab, prays five times a day, avoids alcohol, and refuses to dance with men? For some, the litmus test involves whether a Muslim accepts and approves American foreign policy in Palestine-Israel, Iraq, Afghanistan, Pakistan, Kashmir, or Chechnya.

The caricatures of Islam and Muslims and the equation of the word "moderate" with Western liberalism lead many to see more conservative believers and the entire religion of Islam as a threat. As previously noted, a 2006 *USA Today*/Gallup poll found that 44 percent of Americans said Muslims are too extreme in their religious beliefs. Nearly one-quarter of Americans, 22 percent, said they would not want a Muslim as a neighbor; fewer than half believe Muslims are loyal to the United States and therefore favor heightened security measures to prevent Muslim terrorism.[49]

As we have seen throughout this book, the war on terror has raised difficult questions and choices for American and European Muslims. Changing political and legal environments in Western countries threaten and undermine Muslims' acceptance by others, their quality of life, and their security. Many face workplace discrimination, racial and religious profiling, and overzealous security measures. The situation has become especially difficult for Islamic institutions: mosques, Islamic charities, and NGOs that face harassment, unwarranted scrutiny, and indictment without prompt adjudication.

If things get worse, if there are other Muslim terrorist attacks in the West, what will happen? Will governments heed the rhetoric and recommendations of Islamophobic political commentators, who question the patriotism of all Muslim communities in the West, support draconian antiterrorism measures that violate international law, and even cite approvingly the example of the internment of Japanese Americans during World War II?

WESTERN MUSLIMS: CITIZENS AND PARTNERS

Ironically, even in the face of civil liberties abuses post 9/11, major polling of American Muslims by Gallup, Pew, and others nevertheless reveals a community that is integrating into American society. As a Pew/*USA Today* poll found, America's Muslims hold more moderate political views than Muslims elsewhere in the world. Mostly middle class, they have adapted to life in America. Luis Lugo, director of the Pew Forum on Religion and Public Life, concludes, "Muslim Americans are very much like the rest of the country. . . . They do not see a conflict between being a devout Muslim and living in a modern society."[50]

The future will be greatly affected by the generation of young Muslim men and women born, raised, and socialized in America, many of them educated at our top universities and medical, law, and business schools. Their American Muslim upbringing and experience have equipped them with a more integrated American Muslim identity. They possess the skills to compete and function more effectively not only in the professions but also in the public square. Congressman Keith Ellison, the first Muslim elected to the U.S. House of representatives, addressed this agenda:

> It is time we assume our place at the table. . . . However defined we are by our religion, we are equally defined by our nationalism; we are Americans. As Americans, we share the pride and suffer the sorrows of all Americans. We grieved with the nation on 9/11, and we cheered with many Americans at the election of Barack Hussein Obama as president.
>
> We must become participatory citizens in the American experiment. I want to see our community give back to their country—not make the mistake that so many insular and immigrant communities make. I want to see many more Muslims serving in the U.S. Congress—instead of the two there are now. I want to see hundreds of

> thousands of teachers who "happen" to be Muslim. There should be senators and mayors, state legislators, and city council members who "happen" to be Muslim. And each of you should wear a hijab or a jilbab if you so choose; pray when you pray—and have it perceived as a demonstration of your faith, and not a threat to your country. I want to see an America that embraces our faith as its own—if we step out of the shadows.[51]

At the same time, in matters of religion and foreign policy, the advice of Sherman Jackson, a professor of Arabic and Islamic Studies at the University of Michigan and a prominent Muslim leader, rings true for both American and European Muslims:

> Islam in America must acquire the necessary learning and intellectual autonomy to confer upon Muslim Americans the ability to self-authenticate. . . . We cannot continue to rely on the Muslim world's understanding of America as the basis of what is accepted as Islamically authentic in America. Nor can we make the mistake of following the Muslim world in its tendency to judge America *solely* on the basis of foreign policy (though again, we speak truth to power). Nor can we afford to squander our moral capital in America through sheepish analyses of some of the more unfortunate occurrences that take place in the Muslim world.[52]

The near-term challenges and priorities for Muslim communities will continue to include addressing internal religious and social problems on the one hand and the fact that their faith and community are often suspect, their rights as citizens threatened by an erosion of civil liberties on the other. Muslim religious and community leaders must continue to condemn instances of extremist rhetoric in sermons and public statements by militants and to counter the radical theology of a vocal minority of extremists. All Muslims can play a role in addressing foreign and domestic extremist rhetoric that feeds fears of Islam, paints with broad and inaccurate brushstrokes the mainstream majority, and provides ammunition for attacks from the Christian Right and anti-immigrant politicians.

WESTERN ISLAMIC REFORM: THE INTERNATIONAL SUPERHIGHWAY

The emergence of Islam as a major faith in America and Europe is slowly transforming relations between Muslims in the West and Muslims in predominantly Muslim countries.

For centuries, the source of religious authority resided in the Muslim world's religious centers, in the writings and interpretations of its ulama, intellectuals, and activists. Transmission and communication of knowledge and opinions were one-way. Today, as the Islamic community itself has become global geographically, information, ideas, financial resources, and influence flow in both directions on a multilane superhighway. It is a movement encompassing diverse theologies, ideologies, institutions, and modes of communication. The process involves individuals (scholars, preachers, and activists), movements (mainstream and extremist), and multiple countries. This two-way communication and exchange between the heartland and the periphery occur through travel, publications, speaking engagements, and a global communications network of TV, radio, video and audio tapes, DVDs, and increasingly the World Wide Web.

The more open religious, political, and intellectual climate in the West has produced a broad range of American- and European-educated religious and lay scholars, activists, and leaders whose writings and training of a new generation have become increasingly important and influential in the West and abroad.

Many have pursued reformist methodologies in Quranic and hadith (Prophetic traditions) criticism as well as legal reform. Muslim experiences of the West have produced serious reflection about the need for thoroughgoing reinterpretation and reform. Reformers have addressed issues of faith and practice, religious leadership and authority, religious and political pluralism, minority rights (Muslim and non-Muslim) and tolerance, women's status and rights, and gender relations, and have engaged in interreligious dialogue nationally and internationally.

Muslims were initially suspicious of interfaith dialogue because it was initiated by Christians, just as Catholics were vis-à-vis dialogue with Protestants. Memories of European colonizers and missionaries as well as the continued political and economic dominance of the Western world led some to wonder whether talk of religious pluralism and interfaith dialogue was cultural imperialism in disguise. Nevertheless, in a matter of decades, Muslims have become partners in dialogue, locally and globally, with the Vatican, the World Council of Churches, the National Council of Churches, and the United States Conference of Catholic Bishops, as well as participants in local interreligious sessions in many cities and towns around the world. Interfaith dialogue and issues of pluralism, religious and political, and human rights have become an important part of contemporary Islamic discourse.

Perhaps the most enduring influence of the Muslim diaspora will come out of the networks of European- and American-trained scholars and activists who have studied with specific Muslim and non-Muslim scholars or in certain Islamic studies programs at St. Antony's College or the Oxford Centre for Islamic Studies at Oxford University, SOAS at London University, the London School of Economics, Edinburgh, Birmingham University/Selly Oak, the Sorbonne, Amsterdam, Leiden, Temple University, Georgetown, Harvard, or the University of Chicago. Some speak of the "Temple mafia" in Southeast Asia, referring to the many former students of Temple University professors Ismail al-Faruqi, Seyyed Hossein Nasr, and Mahmoud Ayoub.

The influence of European and American Muslim scholarship and ideas can be found from Egypt and Sudan to Malaysia and Indonesia among university vice chancellors and presidents, distinguished professors, religious scholars, government officials (parliamentarians and cabinet ministers), and leaders of major Islamic organizations like the thirty-million-strong Muhammadiya in Indonesia. The experience of Western Muslims as a minority has affected both contemporary Muslim thought and popular attitudes. If some have become more isolationist, many others have embraced a more pluralistic outlook.

Religious Pluralism in the Twenty-first Century: Who's Going to Hell?

A number of years ago, I was invited to lunch by a young undergraduate who was a born-again Christian. We had a great time talking about his studies, his parents, mainline Christians who were my friends, and his own conversion or born-again experience. After lunch, I asked him if he wanted to get together again. He beamed and said, "Yes!" Putting my arm around his shoulder, I said, "Even if I, like your parents, am going to hell?" Chagrined and a bit embarrassed, he replied, "Yes."

A few years later, I keynoted a conference on Islam and civil society in South Africa. After my talk a young South African Muslim scholar, trained in Islamic studies in South Africa, Pakistan, and the West, went to the podium and profusely praised and thanked me for my presentation. His remarks were so prolonged and exaggerated that I soon realized the shoe was about to fall. Looking at the audience, he summarized his comments: "And so, Professor Esposito, we applaud your stellar role as a scholar of Islam; we appreciate your understanding of Islam and work to enhance its understanding in the West, but of course this doesn't change the fact that as a non-Muslim, you are still going to hell!" Half the audience smiled, acknowledging the point he was making; the other half looked embarrassed that he had articulated their position to my face.

One of the great ironies of religion is that throughout the ages, many Christians and Muslims, who believe in a God of mercy and compassion and a just judge, and who acknowledge that they are imperfect human beings, nevertheless feel comfortable passing harsh judgment on their neighbors: "My faith is right and therefore yours is wrong; you are going to hell." Even if you are a good person, they say, unless you are "born again in Jesus" or "embrace Islam," you will go to hell. Many will insist that if you are no longer a good Catholic, or Protestant, or Muslim, if you don't believe in this doctrine or obey this rule, you are going to hell.

We tend to think of ourselves, we Jews, Christians, nonbelievers, as thoroughly modern and pluralistic. We dismiss religious fundamentalists within our communities as marginal, as an aberrant nonrepresentative minority. However, Americans' pride in our separation of church and state belies the fact that in the twenty-first century almost 50 percent of our population believes that our legislation should be based on the Bible and that members of the Christian Right (both Protestant and Catholic) have brought their faith positions to bear in the selection of Supreme Court justices and in recent presidential elections.

WHAT ABOUT MUSLIM INTOLERANCE?

Anyone who reads the newspapers or follows human rights and religious freedom reports is aware of problems with religious pluralism and tolerance in the Muslim world. On Saturday, August 1, 2009, after several days of rioting and violence over allegations that Christians had desecrated the Quran, an estimated crowd of one thousand stormed a Christian neighborhood in Gojra, Pakistan. The mob killed eight, including six women, and burned and looted dozens of houses. This was not an isolated incident in Pakistan, where blasphemy against the Prophet and the desecration of the Quran have often been used against Christians.

Religious minorities in the Muslim world, who are constitutionally entitled to equality of citizenship and religious freedom, increasingly fear the erosion of those rights—and with good reason. Interreligious and intercommunal tensions and conflicts have flared up not only in Pakistan but also in Egypt, Sudan, Nigeria, Iran, Iraq, Afghanistan, Bangladesh, Malaysia, and Indonesia. Abuses range from discrimination, violence, and the destruction of villages, churches, and mosques to murder. The result in countries like Nigeria has been cycles of death and vengeance: Muslim massacre of Christians and Christian massacre of Muslims. In Pakistan and Iraq, intra-Muslim communal intolerance and violence have flared between Sunni and Shia extremist organizations and militias.

These are serious problems. Have Muslim governments and religious leaders done enough to address them? Many have not. Indeed, some governments ignore interreligious conflicts or exacerbate them to distract from their own failings. In some Muslim countries (Iraq, Pakistan, Saudi Arabia) and some Muslim communities in the West, intra-Muslim relations, in particular between Sunni and Shia, remain contentious, as do relations with Ahmadiyya, followers of Mirza Ghulam Ahmad (1835–1908), who claimed to be a "nonlegislating" prophet with a divine mandate to renew and reform Islam. Because of its founder's messianic and prophetic claims, Sunni Muslims have often condemned the Ahmadi as a non-Muslim sect, accusing it of rejecting the belief that Muhammad is the last prophet. However, there are winds of change.

Muslims today grapple with issues of religious pluralism on three fronts: the status and rights of non-Muslims in Muslim countries and of Muslims in the West as well as Sunni-Shii relations. In Muslim countries, a key issue is the status and rights of non-Muslims to worship; in the West, the swelling numbers of Muslim refugees and the migration of Muslims to Europe, America, Canada, and Australia have made Muslim minority rights and duties in the West a pressing concern. While Sunni-Shii divisions have increased in Iraq, the Gulf, and Pakistan, examples of intra-religious cooperation and intermarriage also exist. Some American Muslims take great pride in kiddingly dubbing themselves "Sushi Muslims," the products of Sunni-Shia marriages.

Muslim reformers are a vanguard, facing resistance from conservative and fundamentalist factions as they challenge long held traditions. As we saw in chapter 3, diverse Muslim reformers are laying the groundwork for a constructive response to contemporary life's challenges. American Catholics, as a religious minority, produced many of the framers of Vatican II's theology of religious pluralism. Similarly, drawing on their own experiences, American and European Muslims have provided some of the most important thinking on religious pluralism and minority rights.

Most build on but also transform notions of religious pluralism already present in the Islamic tradition. The questions of pluralism, citizenship, and political rights are not only important in modern nation-states where equality of citizenship is the accepted norm but also in self-styled Islamic states and republics in Saudi Arabia, Sudan, Iran, and the Taliban's

Afghanistan, which have often fostered intolerance of other faiths as well as diverse interpretations of Islam.

While in the past Muslims looked to the ulama and muftis in Muslim countries for their answers, today issues of the relationship of faith to politics and culture, the status and rights of minorities, pluralism, and tolerance are addressed by Muslim intellectuals as well as religious scholars in the diaspora.

From its origins, Islam developed in and Muslims responded to a pluralistic world that was multireligous and multiethnic. The Quran recognized both Jews and Christians as "People of the Book," those who have special status because God revealed his will through his prophets, including Abraham, Moses, and Jesus, which all three communities follow. The classical Islamic law that classified Jews and Christians as "protected" (*dhimmi*) people who could live and practice their faith if they paid a poll or head tax (*jizya*) may have been advanced for its time. But in today's world of modern nation-states, its application amounts to designating non-Muslims as second-class citizens.

Reformers, who redefine and broaden traditional theological notions of religious pluralism, root their interpretations in the Quran's emphasis on the equality of all humanity: God's decision to create not just a single nation or tribe but a world of different nations, ethnicities, tribes, and languages (30:22; 48:13). The purpose of these differences was not the promotion of conflict and discord, but, rather, it was a sign from God that all people should strive to understand each other and follow God's will. How do reformers frame their arguments for the Islamic roots of mutual understanding, respect and acceptance?

Temple University's Mahmoud Ayoub, born and raised in Lebanon and educated at the University of Pennsylvania and Harvard, cites two passages to argue that religious exclusivism is not in accord with the Quran's worldview and teachings: "To everyone we have appointed a way and a course to follow" (5.48) and "For each there is a direction toward which he turns; vie therefore with one another in the performance of good works. Wherever you may be, God shall bring you all together [on the Day of Judgment]. Surely God has power over all things" (2.148).

Abdulaziz Sachedina of the University of Virginia notes that during the early centuries of imperial expansion the ulama legitimated the actions of their ruler-patrons by ruling that the Quran's (2:213) message of pluralism was abrogated by other verses requiring Muslims to fight unbelievers. Sachedina, a scholar and religious leader born in Africa and educated in India, in Iran, and finally at the University of Toronto, reminds his readers that religious exclusivism has been a common phenomenon in all world religions, each of which had a tendency to act as if it held a patent on divine revelation. All, he says, espouse supremacy, not accommodation, when faced with another religious viewpoint. This lack of religious pluralism, the assertion that it alone is the one true faith, is the biggest obstacle to interreligious dialogue because each faith renders other religions false and valueless.

For Mahmoud Ayoub, religious pluralism reflects the diversity of human cultures and environments. He sees the synthesis of the dialectic between unity and diversity in the Quran's affirmation in 2:213 of the existence of "the Book which is the heavenly archetype of all divine revelations and of which all true scriptures are but earthly exemplars." In this way the Quran bridges the gap between belief in the truth of one's faith and acceptance of other faiths. Ayoub distinguishes between the Quran's teaching with respect to formal membership in an institutionalized religion (Islam) and the deeper, personal identity based upon a believer's individual faith (iman). It is "the unity of faith in one God" that leads to a genuine religious identity that is open to the acceptance of religious pluralism.[53]

For Sachedina, strict monotheism, Islam's fundamental belief in the oneness of God, unites the Muslim community with all humanity. God is the creator of all humans. The Quran teaches that on the Day of Judgment, God will judge all on their moral behavior as members of the world community, regardless of their religious affiliation. The belief "that 'the People are one community' is the foundation of a theological pluralism that presupposes the divinely ordained equivalence and equal rights of all human beings."[54]

Despite the Quran's recognition of Christians and Jews as valid faith communities, the Muslim community is still considered the "ideal" or "best." Islam and Muslims facing the future, like Christianity and Christians, are challenged to balance a sense of uniqueness or special dispensation with true respect for other faiths. For Sachedina, the "acid test of pluralism is whether a religion is willing to recognize members of other religions as potential citizens in the world to come. Is such citizenship conferred *in spite of* or *because of* the person's membership in another religion?"[55] Salvation ultimately depends not on belonging to a specific faith but more generally and importantly on ethical or moral conduct.

While reformist scholars provide theological rationales and engage in debate with more conservative colleagues, Muslim popular opinion in America reflects changing attitudes. Responses to a question on Islam and religious pluralism in a February 2008 Pew survey demonstrate the pluralistic trajectory of the community. While a minority (33 percent) of those polled responded, "My religion is the one, true faith leading to eternal life," a majority (56 percent) believed, "Many religions can lead to eternal life."

Two influential Muslim women, Ingrid Mattson and Sarah Joseph, O.B.E., exemplify contemporary reformist thinking on religious pluralism. In 2008 Geert Wilders released his controversial *Fitna*, a fifteen-minute video that juxtaposed selected Quranic verses with media clippings of acts of violence and/or hatred by Muslims to argue that Islam encourages acts of terrorism, anti-Semitism, and violence against women. Wilders, a Dutch parliamentarian and leader of the Freedom Party, has compared the Quran to Hitler's *Mein Kampf*, said that it should be banned, urged Muslims to tear out "hate-filled" verses from their scripture, and opposed Muslim immigration into Holland.

In the aftermath of the *Fitna* controversy, Ingrid Mattson reflected on the question "Now what?" Emphasizing the need for mutual respect and tolerance on the part of Muslims as well as those who would engage in racist attacks, Mattson said:

> My plea is that we also need to look at this issue more broadly so we can find better ways of living together in a world in which there will always be people whose views and beliefs we find odd or even obnoxious. We should not justify or excuse extremism of any kind, whether they are racist and hateful attacks on the Muslim community or vigilante violence by Muslims against those who make such statements. . . . The most important thing to keep in mind . . . is that we can never live together peacefully with all our differences unless we are willing to respect the different choices that others make. We do not have to agree with each other or love each other, but we have to afford respect to each other. This means that we do not deliberately try to humiliate each other. Defacing or destroying symbols of each other's most cherished beliefs violates the basic principle of respect.[56]

Sarah Joseph, executive editor of *emel: The Muslim Lifestyle Magazine*, an influential U.K.-based magazine circulated in more than thirty countries, offers another pluralistic perspective in an editorial, "Who is a muslim vs. a Muslim?" In conducting her Ph.D. research, she was struck by how "people went from being 'muslim' to being 'Muslim.'" She explains the Quranic distinction between a "muslim," that is, anyone and everyone who surrenders to God, and Muslim, as an institutionalized religious identity, as follows:

> The word Islam comes from the Arabic root aslama, meaning to surrender, to give something or someone up. In a religious context, it means to surrender one's life to God. The word Muslim is derived

from that. In Arabic when you put "mu" in front of a word it means "the one who does." So in this case mu + islam equals the one who self surrenders him or herself unto God.

However, we are in a situation [today] where Islam and Muslim are only understood in the institutionalized form. Textbooks describe the proscriptive elements of Islam as an institutionalized religion, the five pillars of Islam, the dress and practice of a Muslim, the do's and don'ts. We are told about Islam the proper noun, but we get no sense of islam the dynamic verb.

Muhammad himself spoke of how he was bringing nothing new; the Qur'an repeatedly asserts that it is a reminder of what was previously revealed. The Qur'an even describes Abraham as a muslim, that is someone who surrendered themselves to God as opposed to a member of an institutionalised religion post the 7th century.

God says in the Qur'an, "Behold, the only true religion in the sight of God is man's self-surrender unto Him" (3:19). This was the message of all the prophets from Adam onwards.[57]

Fathi Osman, an Egyptian-American scholar trained at both al-Azhar and Princeton universities, argues that Islam's religious pluralism is reflected not only in the oft-cited phrase "the children of Abraham," which joins together Jews, Christians, and Muslims, but in the Quran's use (17:70) of the phrase "children of Adam." Therefore, Muslim interreligious dialogue should include Hindus, Buddhists, Taoists, and members of other faiths on the basis of the Quran's teaching "that every human being has his or her spiritual compass, and has been granted dignity by God" (17:70). Moreover, Osman insists, Muslims are not simply to respect others but have a Quranic obligation to guarantee freedom of faith and opinion (2:256) and freedom of expression for all people (2:282). Recognition and acceptance of all humanity, all the children of Adam, provide the basis for development of universal relations and a global ethic.[58]

Muslims in the twenty-first century are also challenged to incorporate an internal pluralism, a generous space in their religious discourse and behavior for alternative opinions and dissenting voices within Islam. Regrettably, a significant minority of Muslims, like Christians who strongly affirm their faith, are less pluralistic in their attitudes toward other faiths and their co-believers. Thus some who call for greater Islamization also in practice engage in a policy of "kafirization," condemning not just followers of other faiths but Muslims with whom they disagree as unbelievers or infidels. Some practice theological exclusivism and intolerance but remain nonviolent, but others are militant extremists who threaten and commit acts of violence and terror.

THE CHALLENGE OF PLURALISM FOR WESTERN SECULAR DEMOCRACIES

The realities of globalization and immigration, and the influx of new nationalities and ethnic, and religious groups in America and Europe, challenge accepted notions of cultural pluralism in Western countries long accustomed to think of themselves as Judeo-Christian or secular. Will our understanding of pluralism be broadened to accept the new "others," to appreciate their similarities and common interests and to respect their differences? While immigrants are challenged to accept primary responsibility for making their own way, new homelands are equally challenged to provide the institutional structures and the educational and employment opportunities that immigrants need to advance and become part of the dominant culture.

Like other immigrants before them, Muslims in the West are looking for a level playing field, to have the same rights and duties and to be judged in the same way as their fellow citizens. Polling of American attitudes toward Muslims and Islam reveal the extent to which Islam often remains outside the parameters of our established pluralistic paradigm. Asked about their prejudices toward religious groups, 72 percent of Americans said they had no prejudice toward Jews, but only 34 percent could say the same about Muslims. Nineteen percent of Americans in 2007 said they had a "great deal" of prejudice against Muslims; this percentage dropped to 15 percent in 2009.[59] Americans view Islam even more negatively; 59 percent of Americans reported they have unfavorable views of the faith. Moreover, the number who said they "believed mainstream Islam encourages violence" more than doubled from 14 percent four months after 9/11 to 34 percent in 2006.[60] The percentage of Americans who believed that "Islam does not teach respect for the beliefs of non-Muslims" jumped from 22 percent in 2002 to 43 percent in 2003.[61]

Not surprisingly, there are significant differences in attitudes depending on whether a respondent has been personally acquainted with a Muslim. Only 10 percent of those who told Gallup in 2006 that they personally know a Muslim, compared to 31 percent who do not, said they would not want a Muslim as a neighbor. Similar differences are found regarding attitudes toward special security measures for Muslims and fear of sharing an airplane flight with Muslim men.[62] At a time when knowledge of Islam and Muslims is so important, little change occurred between 2002 and 2007 in the percentage of Americans who said they knew nothing at all (24 percent) or very little (41 percent) about Islam. From 2007 to 2009, the picture improved slightly, with the percentage confessing ignorance showing a slight decline from a total of 65 percent to 59 percent, still a disturbing number. Similarly, the number of Americans who said they held an unfavorable opinion of Islam decreased slightly from 59 percent in 2007 to 54 percent in 2009.[63]

Building a Global Culture of Pluralism

From Egypt and Sudan to Malaysia and Indonesia, most Muslim countries are multifaith societies. Muslim diasporas across the world live as religious minority communities. Therefore, Muslims today, like Jews, Christians, and peoples of other faiths, face a world in which robust religious pluralism has become a necessity, a matter of faith and citizenship.

Around the world, international and domestic initiatives in interreligious and intercivilizational dialogue are producing new ideas and actions. Christian and Muslim organizations in countries with long-established churches (Egypt, Lebanon, Pakistan, Malaysia, and Indonesia) increasingly turn to dialogues and exchange programs to promote mutual understanding and respect; universities in Egypt, Qatar, Lebanon, and Indonesia have newly instituted or expanded courses in comparative religions. In the Gulf, the United Arab Emirates, Qatar, Bahrain, and Kuwait are now home to Christian churches. Qatar and Saudi Arabia have joined countries like Jordan in hosting major annual interreligious dialogues with Christians and Jews. However, some Muslim countries like Saudi Arabia continue to draw criticism from religious freedom and human rights organizations for banning or severely restricting the building of Christian churches and the freedom of Christians to practice their religion.

In the United States, long-established institutions such as Georgetown University's Prince Alwaleed bin Talal Center for Muslim-Christian Understanding and Hartford Seminary's Duncan Black Macdonald Center for the Study of Islam and Christian-Muslim Relations are today joined by a seemingly endless number of new centers and international initiatives dedicated to promoting interreligious understanding.

Interest by the international community was spurred by Iran's President Mohammad Khatami. In a widely followed CNN interview with Christiane Amanpour in 1998, the then newly elected progressive Iranian president stunned many by calling for a "dialogue among civilizations" in response to Samuel P. Huntington's theory of "clash of civilizations." The United Nations subsequently adopted a resolution to name the year 2001 as the Year of Dialogue Among Civilizations.

Tracking international intercivilizational and interfaith initiatives post 9/11 is a daunting task. Sometimes, to quote the late Jimmy Durante, it looks like "everybody is trying to get into the act." While meetings and pronouncement by prominent religious and other global leaders can be impressive, the litmus test is their impact. Do they simply produce nice-sounding statements, platitudes, or reports that are archived, or do they produce initiatives to bring about real change in attitudes or behavior? Do religious leaders merely sign a statement, or do they also implement changes in their religious communities' teachings, seminary training, universities, and schools? Do global leaders invest in and implement projects that address the educational and economic needs of Muslim youth and support popular culture (media, the arts, and Internet) projects that promote greater cultural literacy and awareness, understanding, and respect? Or, absent preventive strategies, will they risk greater radicalization and then rely solely on a military response?

Among the many intercivilizational and interfaith initiatives created after 9/11 are the World Economic Forum's Council of 100 leaders (C-100), the UN Alliance of Civilizations, the archbishop of Canterbury's Building Bridges project, the Vatican–al-Azhar dialogue, the Parliament of the World's Religions, and the Organisation of the Islamic Conference (OIC).

In January 2004, the World Economic Forum (WEF) launched a West-Islamic World Dialogue designed to mobilize the international business community to promote understanding and cooperation between Western countries and those with predominantly Muslim populations. This initiative convened a council of one hundred senior political, religious, business, media, and opinion leaders. The C-100 was chaired by Lord Carey of Clifton, former archbishop of Canterbury, and H.R.H. Prince Turki Al Faisal Al Saud, a former Saudi government minister, ambassador to Great Britain and the United States, and chairman of the King Faisal Center for Research and Islamic Studies. The goal was to

> foster a culture of respect and cooperation together with mutual understanding between traditions and overcome the tensions and mistrusts of the era. Dialogues in education, media, religion and business best practice are expected to result from the initiative.... The C-100 will also establish a multifaceted intercultural

> dialogue that bridges divides through shared commitment to common values and goals, together with a programme of joint action bringing concrete practical results, transformational change and highly visible cooperation.[64]

Sponsored by the WEF, the 2007 Gallup Survey of Population Perceptions and Attitudes captured the deep divisions between Western and predominantly Muslim societies. The survey found alarmingly low levels of optimism regarding dialogue between "Islam and the West." The average score for the twenty-one countries surveyed was 37 (where 100 is the most optimistic). In all but two countries (Bangladesh and Pakistan), a majority believed the interaction between Western and Islamic communities is getting worse. The survey noted that while on average 65 percent of respondents in Muslim-majority countries say Muslims respect the West, 60 percent feel that the West does not respect Muslims. On average, 60 percent of Americans and Europeans agreed.

Islam and the West: Annual Report on the State of Dialogue, a joint venture of the WEF and Georgetown University, offers a ranking of countries based on citizen perceptions of the state of relations between the West and the Muslim world as portrayed in newspapers and television across twenty-four countries. Among religious actors presented in the media, Islam and Muslims were by far the most prominent, accounting for 56 percent of individuals and groups explicitly identified with a religion. Christianity came next, identifying approximately 28 percent of religious protagonists. Judaism accounted for approximately 4 percent of protagonists surveyed. No other religion achieved more than 1 percent visibility.

In contrast to media coverage of other religions, most reports involving Muslims depicted them engaged in political, militant, and extremist activities. While Christians, Jews, and other religious actors were most commonly portrayed as engaged in religious activities (in 75 percent of statements, on average), Muslims were only associated with religious activities in 13 percent of statements; 68 percent of journalistic coverage focused on militant or political activities. Muslims were associated with fundamentalist and extremist activities more than six times as often as other religious protagonists.[65]

The report underscored that the proliferation of dialogues has had a disappointingly limited impact. Many initiatives compete and overlap and thus miss opportunities for cooperation; they are more monologue than dialogue. The focus of media and public opinion on violence and terrorism continues to reinforce polarization and stereotypes. Not surprisingly, the report emphasizes that dialogue is no substitute for political leadership or progress on outstanding conflicts: an Israeli-Palestinian peace that combines security with self-determination; greater stability, prosperity, and democracy; equal citizenship for Muslims and non-Muslims; broad-based economic growth, upward mobility, and access to education and healthcare.[66]

However, the C-100's focus on Muslim-West relations, despite some accomplishments, failed to attract and sustain widespread interest and to generate dynamic programs within the WEF and was dissolved in a WEF reorganization in 2008.

The Alliance of Civilizations (AoC) was launched in 2005 by Kofi Annan, secretary-general of the United Nations, and co-sponsored by the prime ministers of Spain and Turkey. In its final report, the AoC's High Level Group (HLG) of twenty international leaders maintained that neither history nor religious differences were responsible for tensions and conflicts between Western and Muslim populations. Rather, their primary roots are political: the Israeli-Palestinian issue, a key symbol of the rift between Western and Muslim societies, and one of the most serious threats to international stability; Western military operations in Muslim countries and the spiraling death toll in Iraq and Afghanistan; and the perception of double standards in the application of international law and the protection of human rights.

The report also identified dangerous trends in Muslim societies that generate deep divisions and, in some cases, lead to extremism and violence: internal debates between progressive and regressive forces on social and political issues; self-proclaimed religious figures who advocate narrow, distorted interpretations of Islamic teachings and who "mis-portray certain cultural traditions, such as honor killings, corporal punishment, and suppression of women" as religious requirements; resistance to reform and political repression in many Muslim countries. It concluded that given the political rather than religious or cultural causes of current tensions, they are solvable, but only if the requisite political will can be generated and sustained to do so.

Among the report's main recommendations for action were (1) an international conference to revive the Middle East peace process, noting that absent a resolution of the Palestinian-Israeli conflict "all efforts to bridge the gap between Muslim and Western societies are likely to meet with limited success," and (2) making space for the full participation of peaceful political groups, whether religious or secular in nature, because the suppression of nonviolent political movements is an important factor in fomenting extremism.

Other recommendations included a critical review by government and religious leaders for accuracy and balance of educational materials in discussing religious beliefs; media training in intercultural understanding for journalists to encourage informed and balanced coverage; media campaigns to combat discrimination and feature the significant social, cultural, and economic contributions of immigrants and the benefits of cultural diversity; and creating youth exchange programs to increase cross-cultural understanding and developing youth-oriented Web sites linking youth to informed religious leaders who address the challenges facing young people today.[67]

The AoC continues to work for many of these goals and to develop concrete projects. Among the projects generated are Silatech, the AoC Media Fund, and Track II diplomacy initiatives. Silatech, an initiative to address young people's critical and growing need for jobs and economic opportunities, is supported by a $100 million gift from Sheikha Mozah Bint Nasser al-Missned of Qatar, a member of the HLG. One-third of the population in the Arab world is below the age of fifteen, and two-thirds are under the age of thirty. Roughly one hundred million new workers are expected to enter the labor market in the next twenty years. Silatech promotes large-scale job creation, entrepreneurship, and access to capital and markets for young people in the Arab world.

The AoC Media Fund, created in partnership with private media and global philanthropists, is launching a global Media Advocacy Campaign. Its ambitious goal is to raise people's awareness about the worldwide ramifications of negative stereotyping and to work against misconceptions. It is developing a Film Fund that will support creating and disseminating entertainment media that depicts religious and ethnic minorities with more balance. The fund's Web site states:

> Entertainment media is responsible for many of the perceptions, or misperceptions, that fuel the conflict between Western and Muslim societies. Perceived Western aggression against Muslim peoples is a significant factor contributing to Muslim radicalization around the world, according to the Gallup Poll's "Who Speaks for Islam?" (2008). Research consistently links violent and humiliating media images of ethnic and religious minorities with a rise in conflict. Therefore, how media shapes its stories about religious and ethnic minority groups has become extremely important.[68]

Less visible but important are Track II diplomacy projects on issues such as the Palestinian-Israeli conflict and American and European relations with

Islamic movements. Many governments have not been willing to officially engage leaders of Islamic movements, especially those such as Hizbollah and Hamas, which have militias involved in armed struggle. However, Track II, which is an informal nonofficial form of diplomacy, can bring together former government and military officials, policymakers, public figures, scholars, civil society leaders, religious activists, and foreign policy advisers to engage in informal discussions and dialogues that foster understanding, confidence building, and conflict resolution.

Muslim Multifaith Initiatives

Two important international Muslim initiatives are the Jordanian-sponsored Amman Message (2004–5) and "A Common Word Between Us and You" (2007). Both are examples of Muslim responses to religious extremism and global terrorism and the effort to mobilize religious leaders and others in bridge building. The limited coverage they have received in mainstream media exemplifies the media's continued lack of interest in "good news."

THE AMMAN MESSAGE

Faced with the ongoing threat of al-Qaeda and other terrorists, the inflammatory preaching of religious extremists and sectarian warfare in Iraq, and the lack of a central religious authority in Islam, many ask, "Who speaks for Islam?" In 2004 King Abdullah of Jordan sought to address religious extremism and militancy by bringing together religious leaders to develop a statement on the nature of true Islam, "to declare what Islam is and what it is not, and what actions represent it and what actions do not," emphasizing Islam's core values of compassion, mutual respect, acceptance, and freedom of religion.[69] The Amman Message intended to reject extremism as a deviation from Islamic beliefs and affirmed Islam's message of tolerance and humanity as a common ground among different faiths and peoples.

Twenty-four senior religious scholars in the Muslim world were asked to answer three key questions: (1) Who is a Muslim? (2) Is it permissible to declare someone an apostate (*takfir*)? (3) Who has the right to issue fatwas? The opinions of these scholars then became the basis in July 2005 of a major international Islamic conference of two hundred Muslim scholars from over fifty countries. Based on fatwas provided by three of the most senior Sunni and Shii religious authorities, among them Sheikh Muhammad Sayyid Tantawi of al-Azhar University, Iraq's Grand Ayatollah Ali al-Sistani, and

Yusuf Qaradawi, scholars addressed intra-Muslim conflict and violence and tried to delegitimate extremists who issue fatwas to justify their agendas. Participants issued a final declaration that

- emphasized the underlying unity and validity of the three major branches of Sunni, Shia, and Ibadi Islam and agreed upon a precise definition of a Muslim: anyone who recognizes and follows one of the eight law schools of Sunni, Shia, and Ibadi Islam (Ibadi Islam is the dominant form of Islam in Oman).
- forbade declarations of excommunication or apostasy (*takfir*) between Muslims.
- delineated the conditions for a valid fatwa: no one may issue a fatwa without the requisite personal qualifications that each school of Islamic jurisprudence determines for its adherents, and anyone issuing a fatwa must adhere to the prescribed methodology of the schools of Islamic jurisprudence.

These guidelines gained widespread support. They were unanimously adopted in December 2005 by the Organisation of the Islamic Conference, which represents the political leadership of fifty-seven Muslim-majority countries, and by six other international Islamic scholarly assemblies, including the International Islamic Fiqh (Jurisprudence) Academy of Jeddah, in July 2006. In total, over five hundred leading Muslim scholars worldwide unanimously endorsed the Amman Message. Thus for the first time in history a large number of diverse religious leaders, representatives of global Islam, joined together to issue an authoritative statement.[70]

Given the significance of these events and statements, how visible were they in Western media, major newspapers, or the writings of political commentators? They received little or no coverage in major media outlets in the United States or Europe.

"A COMMON WORD"

In September 2006, Pope Benedict XVI delivered a speech in Regensburg, Germany, which dismayed and angered Muslims all over the world. Benedict cited a fourteenth-century Byzantine emperor's remarks about the Prophet Muhammad: "Show me just what Muhammad brought that was new, and there you will find things only evil and inhuman, such as his command to spread by the sword the faith he preached." The assertion that Muhammad commanded the spread of Islam by the sword was strenuously rejected by Muslims and many non-Muslim scholars as inaccurate.

Equally controversial and offensive to Muslims was the pope's assertion that the Quranic passage "There is no compulsion in religion" (2:256) was revealed in the early years of Muhammad's prophethood in Mecca, a period "when Mohammed was still powerless and under [threat]" but was superseded by "instructions, developed later and recorded in the Koran {Quran}, concerning holy war." Both of these statements are historically incorrect. Quran 2:256 is not an early Meccan verse but is in fact from the later Medinan period. Moreover, the Quran does not equate jihad with holy war. This interpretation of jihad developed years later after Muhammad's death when it came to be used by rulers (caliphs) to justify their wars of imperial expansion and rule in the name of Islam.

A month after the Regensburg speech, thirty-eight Muslim scholars sent Pope Benedict XVI an open letter, expressing their concerns about the speech. On the first anniversary of that letter (on October 13, 2007), some 138 prominent Muslim leaders (muftis, academics, intellectuals, government ministers, authors) from across the world sent another open letter, "A Common Word Between Us and You," to the heads of the world's major Christian churches. This initiative was launched simultaneously at news conferences in Dubai, London, and Washington.

The purpose and heart of their message was this:

> Muslims and Christians together make up well over half of the world's population. Without peace and justice between these two religious communities, there can be no meaningful peace in the world. The future of the world depends on peace between Muslims and Christians.
>
> The basis for this peace and understanding already exists. It is part of the very foundational principles of both faiths: love of the One God, and love of the neighbour. These principles are found over and over again in the sacred texts of Islam and Christianity. The Unity of God, the necessity of love for Him, and the necessity of love of the neighbour is thus the common ground between Islam and Christianity.

The signers noted the importance of the Two Great Commandments, love of God and love of neighbor, and their expressions in the Torah, New Testament, and Quran. In a world in which Christianity and Islam are the two largest religions, there can be no peace if Christians and Muslims are not at peace. Thus the relationship between these two religious communities is cited as the most important factor contributing to meaningful peace around the world.

As "A Common Word" emphasizes:

> With the terrible weaponry of the modern world; with Muslims and Christians intertwined everywhere as never before, no side can unilaterally win a conflict between more than half of the world's inhabitants. Thus our common future is at stake. The very survival of the world itself is perhaps at stake.

The response to "A Common Word" from Christian leaders and scholars was immediate and global. The archbishop of Canterbury, Pope Benedict XVI, Orthodox Patriarch Alexei II of Russia, the presiding bishop of the Lutheran World Federation, and many others acknowledged its importance, as did many individuals and groups who posted their comments and criticisms on the official Web site of "A Common Word."[71] Over three hundred leading American mainline and evangelical leaders and scholars responded in an open letter endorsed a statement, "Loving God and Neighbor Together," published in the *New York Times* and elsewhere. The number of Muslim leaders and scholars who signed the initiative increased from the original 138 to over 300 with more than 460 Islamic organizations and associations also endorsing it.

As a follow-up to the letter, international conferences of religious leaders, scholars, and NGOs occurred at Yale University, Cambridge University, and Georgetown University as well as at the Vatican to explore the theological, biblical, and social implications of this initiative.

Roman Catholics account for just over half the world's two billion Christians. Islam has 1.5 billion followers. At the Vatican, to build the foundations for better understanding between Catholics and Muslims under the theme "Love of God, Love of Neighbor," some fifty papal officials, Islamic leaders, and scholars met on November 4, 2008, at a historic summit. At the end of the third day, the pope met with the delegates in a frank discussion.

The Muslim delegation was led by Grand Mufti of Bosnia-Herzegovina Mustafa Ceric and Cardinal Jean-Louis Tauran, leader of the Vatican's delegation, who called the meeting a "new chapter in a long history." The Vatican pressed on specific issues of concern: that emphasis on shared beliefs and values not gloss over real differences and issues, in particular what it terms "reciprocity"—the freedom of Christians in countries like Saudi Arabia to build churches and practice their religion freely.The three-day meeting issued a manifesto that called for a new dialogue between Muslim and Christian leaders, stressing the values shared by Islam and Christianity.

Post "A Common Word," a particularly important dialogue ensued between Muslims and evangelicals, who have tended to have a more unfavorable view of

Islam than other Americans. A March 2006 Pew poll reported that 50 percent of white evangelicals agreed with the statement "The Islamic religion is more likely than others to encourage violence."[72] A *Washington Post*–ABC poll just weeks before found that fewer than one-third of evangelical Protestants said they had a favorable view of Islam, significantly less than the 48 percent of Catholics and 42 percent of mainline Protestants and "seculars" (atheists or agnostics) who expressed positive views.[73]

An alternative group of mainstream evangelical leaders like Richard Cizik, Joel Hunter, Bob Roberts, Chris Seiple, Rick Warren, and others have reached out to Muslim leaders to explore common values (e.g., peace, justice, compassion, and mercy). These leaders initiate and participate in multifaith dialogues and projects dealing with common concerns, from social issues like poverty and the environment to security. In contrast to hard-line Christian Zionists, many evangelicals support a two-state solution that emphasizes the legitimate claims, rights, and responsibilities of both Israelis and Palestinians as affirmed in "Evangelicals for a Two-State Solution: An Open Letter to President Bush," signed by many prominent evangelical leaders and pastors.

> Historical honesty compels us to recognize that both Israelis and Palestinians have legitimate rights stretching back for millennia to the lands of Israel/Palestine. Both Israelis and Palestinians have committed violence and injustice against each other. The only way to bring the tragic cycle of violence to an end is for Israelis and Palestinians to negotiate a just, lasting agreement that guarantees both sides viable, independent, secure states.[74]

The writings and work of Chris Seiple, president of the Institute for Global Engagement, which he describes as a "think tank with legs" that "promotes sustainable environments for religious freedom worldwide," are a fine example of a mainstream evangelical approach. Seiple has written about "Ten Terms *Not* to Use with Muslims." Following is a sample of his insights, the kind that will bring Christians and Muslims together in the next century.

Seiple points out that "clash of civilizations" creates an "us as good guy and them as bad guy" scenario when in fact the only clash is between those for civilization and those against it. He demonstrates keen understanding of the feelings on both sides about the word "secular," which to Western ears represent the popular notion of separation of church and state needed for democracy and to Muslims often connote an "inconceivable" "godless society." Instead Seiple favors the word "pluralism," which, he notes, "encourages those with (and those without) a God-based worldview to have a welcomed and equal place in the public square."

When discussing Muslim minorities in the West, Seiple points out that using "integration" suggests that "all views, majority and minority, deserve equal respect as long as each is willing to be civil with one another amid the public square of a shared society." This is much more effective, he argues than "assimilation," which highlights a majority European or North American Christian culture that minority Muslims "need to look like."

Seiple also tells us that the word "tolerance," meaning "allowing for someone's existence or behavior," will not build the kind of trust and the relationships we need to face global challenges in the twenty-first century. What is needed is the true respect for each other that will enable us to honestly "name our differences and commonalities," to recognize "the inherent dignity we each have as fellow creations of God" whose different faiths call us "to walk together in peace and justice, mercy and compassion."[75]

Public Diplomacy: Building Bridges and Limiting Terrorism

Global terrorism will continue to threaten European and American policymakers as well as Muslim governments. The Bush administration quite correctly adopted a three-pronged strategy to fight global terrorism: military, economic, and public diplomacy. But although the military can kill, capture, and contain terrorists, neither military responses nor economic measures to cut off terrorists' financial support address the ideological war, the ideas as well as the conditions that radicalize mainstream Muslims and create terrorist recruits. Public diplomacy has the power to target the broader Muslim world and its mainstream majority.

A data-driven approach that reflects the realities on the ground, what Muslims really think and want, will require an agenda of educational, technological, and economic assistance on the one hand and foreign policy initiatives on the other. How much more effective it would have been if the Blair and Bush administrations had pumped in massive economic and educational aid (as they initially proposed) to rebuild the collapsed Iraqi and Afghan economies, institutions, and infrastructures and to educate and train the upcoming generation. Emphasis on job creation, education/technology, human rights and the rule of law, and change through political participation and the ballot box would respond to the desires of the mainstream and diminish the appeal of those who insist change is only possible through violence.

Under the Bush administration there was a tendency to reduce public diplomacy to a public relations campaign, an effort to prove how principled and likeable we "really" are. The strategy seemed to be based on the flawed premise that "They simply don't know or understand us," and the basic problem was reduced to religious or cultural causes or differences ("Islam is a violent religion"; "Muslims don't want democracy") and finally captured in use of the phrase "Islamofascism." However, many Muslims know America quite well; they have studied, visited, and lived here. Many do admire America's principles and values but fault Americans for not living up to them. The cause of anti-Americanism is not who we are but what we do.

Looking to the future, a new paradigm is needed, one that sees beyond the smokescreen created by neo-conservative and anti-immigrant ideologues, by Islamophobic experts and political commentators, and by autocratic rulers stressing the threat of global terrorism to repress any and all opposition. American and European policymakers have to balance their bias toward authoritarian allies with a more evenhanded response to opposition and reform movements that can combat pent-up resentment and violence. In foreign policy, as in many other areas of life, the choice often is "Pay me now or pay me later."

Too often public diplomacy has avoided recognizing the contrast between the way we talk and the way we walk. As Admiral Mike Mullen, chairman of the Joint Chiefs of Staff, stated in a critique of U.S. government "strategic communications" efforts: "To put it simply, we need to worry a lot less about how to communicate our actions and much more about what our actions communicate."[76] The marginalization and delegitimation of terrorists will require substantive reform in American foreign policy. The failures are not limited to any one political party. Under both the Democratic Clinton and Republican Bush administrations our policies have been catalysts for anti-Americanism. We have applied a double standard, officially promoting democracy and human rights in the Middle East while at the same time offering support to authoritarian regimes. We have shown a bias toward Israel in the Palestinian-Israeli conflict, in our policies, in preferential arms sales, and in our voting record in the UN. We have not paid sufficient attention to the primary causes of terrorism, the political and economic conditions feeding alienation, powerlessness, and humiliation.

While nothing should compromise America's commitment to the existence and security of the state of Israel, America's national interests and credibility not only in the Arab and Muslim world but also internationally depend on our ability to be more evenhanded. That means matching our stand on Palestinian terrorism with an equally tough stand on Israel's use of violence and terror. In Gaza, Israel went beyond trying to contain terrorism and destroyed the political, economic, and institutional infrastructure. United

Nations High Commissioner for Human Rights Navi Pillay lambasted Israel's "nearly total impunity" for its human rights violations, including arbitrary detention, torture and ill-treatment, extrajudicial execution, forced eviction and home demolition, settlement expansion and related violence, and restrictions on freedom of movement and expression: "Significant prima facie evidence indicates that serious violations of international humanitarian law as well as gross human rights violations occurred during the military operations of 27 December 2008 to 18 January 2009, which were compounded by the blockade that the population of Gaza endured in the months prior to Operation Cast Lead and which continues."[77] United States policy should make no exceptions, for Arabs or Israelis, when it comes to condemning the disproportionate use of force, indiscriminate warfare, collective punishment, or violations of human rights. In Lebanon and in Gaza, the sight of innocent civilians killed, injured, and displaced, especially women and children, led to a further erosion of America's moral leadership and credibility among its allies and provoked hatred among extremists.

Distinguishing between reform or opposition movements and extremists or terrorists has been a critical and contentious issue, historically dependent on one's political vantage point. Menachem Begin and Yitzhak Shamir, the Irgun and Stern gangs, and Nelson Mandela and the African National Congress were all regarded by their opposition as terrorist leaders. Yesterday's terrorists may be just that—terrorists; or they may be tomorrow's statesmen.

Lebanon's Hizbollah and Palestine's Hamas are regarded as resistance movements by their supporters and as terrorist movements by Israel, the United States, and the European Union. Both Hizbollah and Hamas in recent years have become major political parties, participants in democratic elections, and members of parliaments and cabinets. Hamas won a landslide electoral victory over the Fatah-led Palestinian National Authority in democratic and multiparty elections on January 25, 2006. While there must be zero tolerance for terrorists, mainstream Islamists, especially political parties, should be allowed to engage their governments and those of Western nations. If they are banned or repressed, not allowed to vote or exercise political power, further alienation and radicalization are the likely result.

The Israeli occupation of Palestine remains a major concern across the Muslim world and a stumbling block to U.S.-Muslim relations. However, the achievement of significant progress or its resolution will remain a Sisyphus-like uphill struggle. American policy will have to become less driven by domestic Israeli lobbies and their hard-line Christian Zionist allies and their influence on Congress. The president will be challenged to pursue both a short- and long-term strategy that no recent American president has been willing to pursue. These measures would entail not only support for the existence and security of the state of Israel but creation of a secure, economically supported Palestinian state. They would also include compliance with United Nations Security Council resolutions: return of Palestinian territory taken in the 1967 war, reversal of annexation of land and building of "illegal" settlements, and condemnation of illegitimate violence committed not only by Palestinians but also by the Israeli military.

Relations between America and the Muslim world began on a positive note when Morocco was the first country to recognize our fledgling republic. In recent decades, relations have been tested and strained by America's ties with authoritarian regimes, its perceived tilt toward Israel, and the impact of Muslim terrorist movements globally. Religious extremism and terrorism have clouded the lens through which Islam and Muslims, not just a small minority of terrorists, are viewed and understood. Lost have been the voices of the mainstream majority: their beliefs, hopes, and dreams for a better life. As we have seen, in contrast to those who charge, "They hate us for who we are," majorities of Muslims in fact admire America's principles and values, but they often object to America's foreign policies. Muslims' struggles for greater democratization and freedoms, economic and educational development, and religious reform are made more difficult and complex not only by the forces of modernity and globalization but also by explosive headline events, the terrorist ranting from preachers of hate, and widespread fear of a clash of civilizations. As President Obama, speaking in Cairo, has said, it is time for a "new beginning" based on the recognition that "America and Islam are not exclusive and need not be in competition."

Conclusion

Muslims in the twenty-first century stand at major crossroads, as they face a world of multiple modernities, from North Africa to Southeast Asia, from North America to Europe. Like believers of other faiths, Muslims struggle with how to live out and apply their faith in a rapidly changing world. Some want to restrict religion to private life; many others see Islam as integral to all aspects of their lives but differ significantly about how to interpret and reinterpret their faith and history. Reform-minded Muslims, religious and lay, men and women, are working to articulate a progressive, constructive Islamic framework. Informed by a deep knowledge of their religious tradition and modern educations in law, history, politics, medicine, economics, and the sciences, they are equipped to reinterpret Islamic sources and traditions to meet the challenges of modernization and development, leadership and ideology, democratization, pluralism, and foreign policy. However, reformers are still a minority facing formidable obstacles. Repressive authoritarian regimes see all reform, any real power-sharing and rule of law, as threatening to their power and privilege. Religious extremists believe they have a mandate from God to impose "their Islam" and destroy anyone who disagrees with them. Intransigent religious conservatives, well meaning but wedded to medieval paradigms, are often co-opted by governments and use their authority to delegitimate reforms as a "heresy." Thus reformers in many countries struggle in weak civil societies that do not support creative or independent thought or action.

For the foreseeable future, religion will remain a significant political and social force for reform because majorities of Muslims today stress the importance of its role for the progress of their societies. Thus it can be viewed as part of the problem if we focus on an extremist fringe or as part of the solution, sustaining Muslim majorities with their values of human rights, mutual respect, and cooperation between communities of believers intent on the same goals.

The fundamental problem for development and long-term stability in the Arab and Muslim worlds is not the religion of Islam or Islamic movements but the struggle between authoritarianism and pluralism. Hence the primary focus of American attention should be not religion but rather political, social, and economic change where Muslims live. Foreign policies have been unduly influenced by the vested interests of secular and religious dictators and extremist groups (social movements, military and security forces, and militias) who attempt to impose their will through repression, violence, and terrorism. Our efforts have not been directed first and foremost toward identifying, and then promoting, those conditions that foster and sustain viable stability. Policies should be crafted in response to events and designed to serve these interests rather than to underscore or enhance religious or cultural divides. The threat to the West will not come from civilizational differences but from the political and socioeconomic reality that breeds radicalism.

Majorities of Muslims globally clearly do not see conflict with the West as primarily religious or civilizational. Rather, they distinguish Western powers by their policies. We, in turn, need to dismiss fears of civilizational threats and disaggregate the "Muslim world" into distinct countries whose conflicts originate from the specific policies of each nation and its leaders. The solution for Washington and its European allies is not more dictatorship but institution-building and civil society. This better protects American interests and strengthens Muslim-West relations in the long run. American and many European policymakers have often been caught in a catch-22 situation. Their support for dictators to contain Islamists guarantees that Muslim governments remain institutionally weak, making Islamism a perpetual challenge. Perpetuating the culture and values of authoritarianism and repression will only contribute to instability and an anti-Americanism that empowers the terrorists.

Policies in the Muslim world require a realistic, long-term view. The transformation of political culture, values, and institutions that make for a strong civil society does not happen overnight. It is a long, drawn-out process, accompanied by battles between contending voices and factions with competing visions and interests. It entails experimentation that is necessarily accompanied by success and failure. The West's transformation from feudal monarchies to democratic nation-states took time, trial, and error. It was accompanied by political as well as intellectual revolutions, which rocked both state and church. We tend to forget that the American and French democratic experiments emerged from revolutionary experiences. The nascent American democracy, which was challenged by a horrendous civil war, functioned for decades during which equal rights remained an illusion for American blacks, Native Americans, and women. We also need to remember that in a world of multiple models of modernization, Western secular liberal democracy is "a" way (one of many possible paradigms), not "the" way, the only path for modernization and political development.

The Muslim world is not the only arena for change. One of the great ironies of history is that despite our apparent development and sophistication, too often we are bound by our own cognitive and religious ghettos. As the examples of the former Yugoslavia, Northern Ireland, India, Palestine-Israel, America, and Europe demonstrate, just because faiths exist in the same country or area, it does not mean that believers come to know much about the other's faith or respect each other. The mettle of our own democratic values and pluralism is being severely tested by globalization and immigration in an increasingly multicultural and multireligious West. As the Danish cartoon controversy underscores, pluralism and tolerance today demand mutual understanding and respect from non-Muslims and Muslims alike. Core principles and values, like freedom of speech and of religion, cannot be compromised.

However, freedoms do not exist in a vacuum; they do not function without limits. In many countries, hate speech (such as Holocaust denial, incitement to racial hatred, advocating genocide) is a criminal offense prohibited under incitement-to-hatred legislation. Our Western secular democracies represent not only freedom of expression but also freedom of religion. Belief as well as unbelief needs to be protected. Freedom of religion in a pluralistic society ought to mean that some things are sacred and treated as such. The Islamophobia that is becoming a social cancer should be as unacceptable as anti-Semitism, a threat to the very fabric of our democratic pluralistic way of life. Thus it is imperative for political and religious leaders, commentators and experts, and yes, the media, to lead in building and safeguarding our cherished values.

And what about Muslim responses? Muslim leaders are hard-pressed to take charge, asserting their faith and rights as citizens, affirming freedom of expression while rejecting those who abuse this right by using it as a cover for their religious prejudice. At the same time, a sharp line must be drawn between legitimate forms of dissent and violent demonstrations or attacks that inflame the situation and reinforce Western stereotypes. The many Muslim leaders, from America and Europe to the Muslim world, who have publicly urged restraint and strongly condemned violence play a critical role. The media is also key, not only as a vehicle for sensational stories but also, as has not often been the case, as the disseminator for Muslim leaders and organizations that denounce violence in the name of Islam.

The idea of "family" in the history of religions, as in our ordinary lives, is a source of strength, nurturing, love, and security but also of conflict and violence. Despite, or some would even argue because of, close family resemblances, relations between Judaism and Christianity, Christianity and Islam, and Judaism and Islam have often been characterized by tension, conflict, and persecution. The beliefs of each that it possesses the one true revelation and special covenant and, in the cases of Christianity and Islam, that it supersedes earlier revelations and has a universal mission have been stumbling blocks to religious pluralism and tolerance. However, there are an impressive number of initiatives by religious leaders and NGOs today that move beyond vying for who is most correct to recognizing, respecting, and cooperating with other faiths to make a positive difference in the lives of others.

The future of Islam and of Muslim-West relations remains a key political and religious issue in the twenty-first century. Understanding and appreciating shared beliefs and values has become especially critical post 9/11, no longer only in multifaith relations but also in international politics and security. Islam and Christianity are the largest and fastest-growing religions in the world. Moreover, the interaction and connection, religiously, politically, economically, and militarily, between the United States and Europe and Muslim countries globally cannot be ignored. In the twenty-first century, intercivilizational dialogue is no longer simply the preserve of religious leaders and scholars but is now a priority for policymakers and corporate leaders, a subject of domestic and foreign policy, and the agenda for international organizations.

Jews and Christians have come to affirm that beyond their distinctive beliefs and past conflicts, they have a shared Judeo-Christian heritage. Most have been raised with some appreciation of the interconnectedness of the Old and New Testaments and their faiths' common belief in God, prophets, and revelation, and moral responsibility and accountability. Few until recently have possessed the broader Abrahamic vision that recognizes the integral place of the descendants of Abraham, Hagar, and Ismail, Muslims who are coequal citizens and believers in the West.

Our next step is to acknowledge this "missing link," to recognize that the Children of Abraham are part of a rich Judeo-Christian-Islamic history and tradition. Despite the rhetoric and actions of Muslim extremists and terrorists, and religious and cultural differences, the peoples of America, Europe, and the Muslim world have many shared values, dreams and aspirations. The future of Islam and Muslims is inextricably linked to all of humanity. All of our futures will depend on working together for good governance, for freedom of religion, speech, and assembly, and for economic and educational advancement. Together we can contain and eliminate our preachers of hate and terrorists who threaten the safety, security, and prosperity of our families and societies.

Notes

Introduction

1. Fawaz Gerges, *America and Political Islam* (Cambridge: Cambridge University Press, 1999); "Is Islamism a Threat? A Debate," with Graham Fuller, Martin Kramer, and Daniel Pipes, *Middle East Quarterly* 6, no. 4 (December 1999).

Chapter 1

1. Claudia Deane and Darryl Fears, "Negative Perception of Islam Increasing: Poll Numbers in U.S. Higher than in 2001," *Washington Post*, 9 March 2006, http://www.washingtonpost.com/wp-dyn/content/article/2006/03/08/AR2006030802221_pf.html.

2. *The Great Divide: How Westerners and Muslims View Each Other*, Pew Global Attitudes Project, 22 June 2006, http://pewglobal.org/reports/display.php?ReportID=253.

3. Kofi Annan, address to the DPI Seminar, "Confronting Islamophobia," 7 December 2004, http://www.un.org/apps/sg/sgstats.asp?nid=1217.

4. Laurie Goodstein, "Poll Finds U.S. Muslims Thriving, but Not Content," *New York Times*, 2 March 2009, http://www.nytimes.com/2009/03/02/us/02muslims.html?_r=1&scp=1&sq=Dalia+Mogahed&st=nyt.

5. *Muslim Americans: A National Portrait*, Muslim West Facts Project, Gallup Organization, 2009, 25, http://www.muslimwestfacts.com/mwf/116074/Muslim-Americans-National-Portrait.aspx.

6. Ibid., 114.

7. Ibid., 23.

8. Ibid., 56–57.

9. Ibid., 75.

10. Ibid., 39–42.

11. Ibid., 131.

12. Pew Research Center, "Muslim Americans: Middle Class and Mostly Mainstream," 22 May 2007, http://pewresearch.org/pubs/483/muslim-americans?loc=interstitialskip.

13. *Muslim Americans: A National Portrait*, 33.

14. Pew Research Center, "Muslim Americans: Middle Class and Mostly Mainstream."

15. Goodstein, "Poll Finds U.S. Muslims Thriving, but Not Content."

16. *Muslim Americans: A National Portrait,* 49–50.

17. American Muslim Poll 2004, Project MAPS/Zogby International, 13, 23, http://www.zogby.com/americanmuslims2004.pdf.

18. "CNN Debunks False Report About Obama," CNN, 23 January 2007, http://www.cnn.com/2007/POLITICS/01/22/obama.madrassa.

19. Transcript, *Meet the Press*, 19 October 2008, http://www.msnbc.msn.com/id/27266223/page/2.

20. Frank Gaffney, "Obama's Islamist Problem," *Washington Times*, 19 August 2008, http://www.washingtontimes.com/news/2008/aug/19/obamas-islamist-problem.

21. Ibid.

22. Ann Coulter, "This Is War," *National Review Online*, 13 September 2001, http://nationalreview.com/coulter/coulter/091301.shtml.

23. Will Cummins, "The Tories Must Confront Islam Instead of Kowtowing to It," *Telegraph*, 18 July 2004, http://www.telegraph.co.uk/comment/personal-view/3608563/The-Tories-must-confront-Islam-instead-of-kowtowing-to-it.html.

24. "Savage: Arabs Are 'Non-humans' and 'Racist, Fascist Bigots,' " Media Matters, 14 May 2004, http://mediamatters.org/items/200405140003.

25. To hear Savage's comments on Islam and Muslims, go to http://www.cair.com/audio/savage_102907.asp.

26. "Michael Savage Lawsuit Links CAIR to 9/11 Plot," *WorldNetDaily*, 29 December 2007, http://www.worldnetdaily.com/news/article.asp?ARTICLE_ID=59440.

27. "Judge Tosses Michael Savage Copyright Suit Against CAIR," 25 July 2008, http://lawgeek.typepad.com/lawgeek/2008/07/judge-tosses-michael-savage-copyright-suit-against-cair.html.

28. Rod Parsley, *Silent No More* (Lake Mary, FL: Charisma House, 2005), 96, 90–91, 95.

29. Ibid., 95.

30. David Corn, "McCain's Spiritual Adviser: Destroy Islam," *Mother Jones*, 12 March 2008, http://www.motherjones.com/washington_dispatch/2008/03john-mccin-rod-parsley-spiritual-guide.html.

31. Ron Brown, "John Hagee Warns Against Radical Islam," *News and Advance*, 3 September 2006, http://www.religionnewsblog.com/15816/john-hagee-warns-against-radical-islam.

32. Transcript, *Meet the Press*, 19 October 2009.

33. *Muslim Americans: A National Portrait*, 96.

34. Ibid.

35. Haya El Nasser, "Poll: American Muslims Reject Extremes," *USA Today*, 23 May 2007, http://www.usatoday.com/news/nation/2007–05–22-poll-muslim-americans_N.htm.

36. *Muslim Americans: A National Portrait*, 59.

37. Ibid., 127.

38. David Machlis and Tovah Lazaroff, "Muslims 'About to Take Over Europe,'" *Jerusalem Post,* 29 January 2007, http://www.jpost.com/servlet/Satellite?cid=1167467834546&pagename=JPArticle%2FShowFull.

39. Jamie Glazov, "Interview with Bat Ye'or, Author of *Eurabia: The Euro-Arab Axis*," *FrontPage*, 21 September 2004, http://www.frontpagemag.com/readArticle.aspx?ARTID=11429.

40. Melanie Phillips, "A Friendly Warning," *National Review Online*, 8 May 2006, http://article.nationalreview.com/?q=MTAxMWIxMGFmNDExYzBhNjFkMWExNGJiODAwNDhjODU=.

41. "Bishop: 17th-century Battle Sparked Sept. 11 Attacks," *Catholic Online*, 21 September 2007, http://www.catholic.org/international/international_story.php?id=25441.

42. Jeremy Henzell-Thomas, "Language of Islamophobia," paper presented at "Exploring Islamophobia" conference, London, 29 September 2001, http://www.network54.com/Forum/257194/thread/1101174423/last-1101201260/The+Language+of+Islamophobia (posted 23 November 2004).

43. Duncan Campbell, "Abu Hamza 'Urged Followers to Bleed Enemy,'" *Guardian*, 13 January 2006, http://www.guardian.co.uk/uk/2006/jan/13/terrorism.world.

44. "In Quotes: Hamza's Preaching," BBC News, 7 February 2006, http://news.bbc.co.uk/2/hi/uk_news/4690084.stm.

45. Campbell, "Abu Hamza 'Urged Followers to Bleed Enemy.'"

46. Deborah Tannen, *The Argument Culture: Moving from Debate to Dialogue* (New York: Ballantine, 1999), 31.

47. Michael Wilson, "Evangelist Says Muslims Haven't Adequately Apologized for Sept. 11 Attacks," *New York Times*, 15 August 2002, http://www.nytimes.com/2002/08/15/national/15GRAH.html.

48. Thomas Friedman, "If It's a Muslim Problem, It Needs a Muslim Solution," *New York Times*, 8 July 2009, http://www.nytimes.com/2005/07/08/opinion/08friedman.html?_r=1&oref=slogin.

49. "Islamic World Deplores US Losses," 14 September 2001, BBC News, http://news.bbc.co.uk/2/hi/americas/1544955.stm.

50. "Islamic Statements Against Terrorism in the Wake of the September 11 Mass Murders," CAIR, http://www.cair.com/AmericanMuslims/AntiTerrorism/IslamicStatementsAgainstTerrorism.aspx; Arabic original in *al-Quds al-Arabi* (London), 14 September 2001, 2, http://www.alquds.co.uk/Alquds/2001/09Sep/14%20Sep%20Fri/Quds02.pdf.

51. The full English text of the fatwa and list of scholars who authored it can be found at www.unc.edu/%7Ekurzman/Qaradawi_et_al.htm.

52. Editorial, "The Enemy Within," *Arab News* (Jeddah, Saudi Arabia), 14 May 2003, http://www.aljazeerah.info/Opinion%20editorials/2003%20Opinion%20Editorials/May/14-b%200/The%20Enemy%20Within,%20Arab%20News.htm.

53. "US Muslims Issue Bombings Fatwa," BBC News, 19 July 2005, http://news.bbc.co.uk/2/hi/uk_news/politics/4694441.stm.

54. Masoud Sabri and Sobhy Mujahid, "Muslim Scholars, Countries Condemn London Bombings," Islam Online, 7 July 2005, http://www.islamonline.net/English/News/2005-07/07/article07.shtml.

55. See "Islamic Statements Against Terrorism," http://www.unc.edu/~kurzman/terror.htm.

56. *Muslim Americans: A National Portrait*, 40.

57. Ibid., 34.

58. Gallup World Poll 2007 and *Muslim Americans: A National Portrait*.

59. *Muslim Americans: A National Portrait*, 10.

60. Ibid., 132.

61. Brennan Linsley, "U.S. May Veto Islamic Law in Iraq," *USA Today*, 16 February 2004, http://www.mafhoum.com/press6/181P10.htm.

62. "Rumsfeld Rejects 'Cleric-Led Rule,'" BBC News, 25 April 2003, http://news.bbc.co.uk/1/hi/world/middle_east/2975333.stm.

63. John Esposito and Dalia Mogahed, *Who Speaks for Islam?* (New York: Gallup Press, 2008), 49.

64. Richard Burkholder, "The Role of Prayer in [the] Islamic World," Gallup Organization, 17 September 2002, http://www.gallup.com/poll/6814/Role-Prayer-Islamic-World.aspx.

65. Esposito and Mogahed, *Who Speaks for Islam*, 13–14.

66. Sayyid Muhammad Rizvi, "Zakãt in Shi'a Fiqh," July 2009, http://www.al-mubin.org/attachments/233_Zakat%20_revised_.pdf.

67. Malcolm X, letter from Mecca, April 1964, http://www.malcolm-x.org/docs/let_mecca.htm.

68. Jeff Stein, "Can You Tell a Sunni from a Shiite?" *New York Times*, 17 October 2006, http://www.nytimes.com/2006/10/17/opinion/17stein.html?pagewanted=print.

69. Esposito and Mogahed, *Who Speaks for Islam*, 97.

70. Lydia Saad, "Anti-Muslim Sentiments Fairly Commonplace," Gallup Organization, 10 August 2006, http://www.gallup.com/poll/24073/AntiMuslim-Sentiments-Fairly-Commonplace.aspx.

71. Gallup World Poll, 2005/06.

72. Esposito and Mogahed, *Who Speaks for Islam*, 23.

Chapter 2

1. This section is drawn from my *Unholy War: Terror in the Name of Islam* (New York: Oxford University Press, 2002), ch. 4.

2. For additional comparisons between the rhetoric of George W. Bush and Osama bin Laden, see Bruce Lincoln, *Holy Terrors: Thinking About Religion After September 11* (Chicago: University of Chicago Press, 2003).

3. Richard Mitchell, *The Society of Muslim Brothers* (New York: Oxford University Press, 1993), 229.

4. Richard Norton, *Hizbollah: A Short History* (Princeton, NJ: Princeton University Press, 2007).

5. "Shiite Parties Win Iraq Poll," *Gulf News*, 20 January 2006, http://archive.gulfnews.com/indepth/iraqelection/sub_story/10013187.html.

6. Kim Ghattas, "Conservatives 'Win Saudi Polls,' " BBC News, 23 April 2005. http://news.bbc.co.uk/2/hi/middle_east/4477315.stm.

7. "Broken Promises," *Economist*, 20 April 2006, http://www.economist.com/world/mideast-africa/displaystory.cfm?story_id=E1_GRPTJJS.

8. Sayyid Qutb, *Milestones* (Stuttgart: Ernst Klett), 221.

9. As quoted in Peter L. Bergen, *Holy War, Inc.: Inside the Secret World of Osama bin Laden* (New York: Free Press, 2002), 56.

10. Ibid.

11. Lawrence Wright, *The Looming Tower: Al-Qaeda and the Road to 9/11* (New York: Knopf, 2006), 122.

12. Youssef M. Ibrahim, "Saudi Strips Citizenship from Backer of Militants," *New York Times*, 10 April 1994, http://partners.nytimes.com/library/world/africa/041094 binladen.html?scp=1&sq=Saudi%20Strips%20Citizenship&st=cse.

13. For a global perspective, see Mark Juergensmeyer, *Terror in the Mind of God: The Global Rise of Religious Violence*, 3rd ed. (Berkeley: University of California Press, 2003), and Robert Pape, *Dying to Win: The Strategic Logic of Suicide Terrorism* (New York: Random House, 2006).

14. Saad Eddin Ibrahim, "Egypt's Islamic Militants," *MERIP Reports* 103 (February 1982): 11.

15. Vali Nasr, "Regional Implications of Shi'a Revival in Iraq," *Washington Quarterly* 27, no. 3 (Summer 2004): 8. See also Nasr's *The Shia Revival: How Conflicts Within Islam Will Shape the Future* (New York: Norton, 2006).

16. Joyce N. Wiley, *The Islamic Movement of Iraqi Shi'as* (Boulder, CO: Lynne Rienner, 1992).

17. "Guide: Armed Groups in Iraq," BBC News, 15 August 2006, http://news.bbc.co.uk/2/hi/middle_east/4268904.stm#mehdi.

18. Juan Cole, "Everday Apocalypse in Iraq," *Informed Comment: Thoughts on the Middle East, History, and Religion*, 20 June 2007, http://www.juancole.com/2007/06/everyday-apocolypse-in-iraq-war-of.html.

19. Ibid.

20. Valentinas Mite, "Doubts over Young Pretender," *Asia Times Online*, 5 August 2003, http://www.atimes.com/atimes/Middle_East/EH05Ak03.html; Christopher Blanchard et al., *Iraq: Regional Perspectives and U.S. Policy,* Congressional Research Service Report RL33793, updated 4 April 2008, 12–13, htpp://fpc.state.gov/documents/organization/104282.pdf.

21. Tom Lasseter, "Mahdi Army Gains Strength Through Unwitting Aid of US," McClatchy Newspapers, 2 February 2007, http://www.commondreams.org/headlines07/0202–06.htm.

22. John L. Esposito and Dalia Mogahed, *Who Speaks for Islam? What a Billion Muslims Really Think* (New York: Gallup Press, 2008), 62.

23. Ibid., 83.

24. Richard Haass, "Towards Greater Democracy in the Muslim World," speech before the Council on Foreign Relations, 4 December 2002, http://www.state.gov/s/p/rem/15686.htm.

25. Esposito and Mogahed, *Who Speaks for Islam*, 126.

26. Richard Curtis, "In Sixth Arab-Israeli War, Hizbollah Survives, Israel Loses, Bush Missing in Action," *Washington Report on Middle East Affairs* 25, no. 8 (November 2006): 12.

27. David Fickling, "Amnesty Report Accuses Israel of War Crimes," *Guardian*, 23 August 2006, http://www.guardian.co.uk/world/2006/aug/23/israelandthepalestinians.syria.

28. Avi Shlaim, "How Israel Brought Gaza to the Brink of Humanitarian Catastrophe," *Guardian*, 7 January 2009, http://www.guardian.co.uk/world/2009/jan/07/gaza-israel-palestine.

29. Carol Glatz, "Gaza Strip Resembles a Concentration Camp, Says Top Vatican Official," Catholic News Service, 9 January 2009, http://www.catholicnews.com/data/stories/cns/0900084.htm.

Chapter 3

1. John O. Voll, "Renewal and Reform in Islamic History," in *Voices of Resurgent Islam,* ed. John L. Esposito (New York: Oxford University, 1983), ch. 2.

2. Tariq Ramadan, "The Way of Islam," in *The New Voices of Islam,* ed. Mehran Khamrava (London: I. B. Tauris, 2006), 70.

3. Ibid.

4. Ibid., 72–73.

5. Ann Kull, "Modern Interpretion of Islamic History in the Indonesian Context: The Case of Nurcholish Madjid," 4, http://www.smi.uib.no/pal/kull.pdf.

6. Ibid.

7. David Waters, "Fatwas and Modernity," *Washington Post*, 8 June 2007, http://newsweek.washingtonpost.com/onfaith/guestvoices/2007/06/fatwas_and_modernity.html.

8. Ali Gomaa, 14 January 2008, written response to series of questions I posed to him.

9. Yusuf Qaradawi, *Islamic Awakening Between Rejection and Extremism*, new ed., ed. Nancy Roberts (Herndon, VA: International Institute of Islamic Thought, 2006), 39.

10. Tariq Ramadan, *Western Muslims and the Future of Islam* (New York: Oxford University Press, 2004), 35.

11. Yusuf Qaradawi, *The Lawful and Prohibited in Islam* (Indianapolis, IN: American Trust Publications, 1980), 14.

12. Ibid.

13. Ali Gomaa, 14 January 2008, written response to series of questions I posed to him.

14. Shaikh Abdal-Hakim Murad, "Bombing Without Moonlight: The Origins of Suicide Terrorism," October 2004, http://www.masud.co.uk/ISLAM/ahm/moonlight.htm.

15. Tim Winter (aka Dr. Abdul Hakim Murad), "Bin Laden's Violence Is a Heresy Against Islam," http://groups.colgate.edu/aarislam/abdulhak.htm.

16. Yusuf Qaradawi, *Priorities of the Islamic Movement,* (Swansea, U.K.: Awakening Publications, 2000), 137.

17. Ibid., 138.

18. Barbara Stowasser, "Regarding Shaykh Yusuf al-Qaradawi on Women's Political Rights in Islam," *CCAS News*, March 2007, 1–2, http://ccas.georgetown.edu/files/Newsletter%203.07.pdf.

19. "Sheikh Yusuf Al-Qaradawi Condemns Attacks Against Civilians: Forbidden in Islam," Islam Online, 13 September 2001, http://www.islamonline.net/English/News/2001–09/13/article25.shtml.

20. Ibid.

21. Murad, "Bombing Without Moonlight."

22. Transcript, *Analysis: The Search for Certainty*, BBC Radio 4 documentary, 23 December 2004, http://news.bbc.co.uk/nol/shared/spl/hi/programmes/analysis/transcripts/23_12_04.txt.

23. Winter, "Bin Laden's Violence Is a Heresy Against Islam."

24. Ibid.

25. Murad, "Bombing Without Moonlight."

26. Ibid.

27. Ibid.

28. Qaradawi, *Islamic Awakening,* 45.

29. Ibid., 43–44.

30. "Saudi Grand Mufti Condemns Terrorist Acts in U.S.," Royal Embassy of Saudi Arabia, Washington, DC, 15 September 2001, http://www.saudiembassy.net/archive/2001/news/page180.aspx.

31. *Public Statements by Senior Saudi Officials and Religious Scholars Condemning Extremism and Promoting Moderation*, Royal Embassy of Saudi Arabia, Washington, DC, May 2008, 13, www.saudiembassy.net/files/PDF/.../Extremism_Report_May08.pdf.

32. "Muslim Reactions to September 11," http://www.crescentlife.com/heal%20the%20world/muslim_reactions_to_sept_11.htm.

33. "Qatari Sheikh Slams Top Islamic Authority for Condemning Civilian Attacks," *Agence France Presse—English*, 4 December 2001.

34. "Makkah Imam Condemns Terrorism, Attacks on Innocent People," 4 December 2001, http://www.saudiembassy.net/2001News/News/IslDetail.asp?cIndex=3318.

35. *Ar-Rayah* (Doha), 26 October 2002. See also Haim Malka, "Must Innocents Die? The Islamic Debate over Suicide Attacks," *Middle East Quarterly* (Spring 2003): 19–28.

36. *Ash-Sharq al-Awsat* (London), 12 December 2001.

37. Transcript, *Analysis: The Search for Certainty*, BBC Radio 4.

38. Yusuf Qaradawi, "Muslim Duty to Resist Invastion of Iraq," http://www.islamfortoday.com/qaradawi03.htm.

39. Winter, "Bin Laden's Voice Is a Heresy Against Islam."

40. "Feature Interview: Tim Winter (aka Abdul Hakim Murad)," *Sunday Nights*, 18 April 2004, http://www.abc.net.au/sundaynights/stories/s1237986.htm.

41. Ibid.

42. Communication with author.

43. Nadeem Azam, "A Conversation with Dr. Mustafa Ceric," n.d. 2005, http://www.angelfire.com/hi/nazam/Aceric.html.

44. Erich Rathfelder, "Interview with Mustafa Ceric: 'The West Does Not Want to Share Its Values,'" *Qantara.de: Dialogue with the Islamic World*, 6 May 2004, http://www.qantara.de/webcom/show_article.php/_c-478/_nr-105/i.html.

45. Mustafa Ceric, "State of the State of Bosnia-Herzegovina," lecture delivered at the Muslim Community Association in San Jose, CA, 3 November 1997, http://www.sunnah.org/events/ceric/dr.htm.

46. Ibid.

47. Jajang Jahroni, "Islam and Democratization in Indonesia," *Jakarta Post*, 18 February 2001, http://www.thejakartapost.com/news/2001/02/18/islam-and-democratization-indonesia.html?1.

48. Yoginder Sikand, review of *The True Face of Islam: Essays on Islam and Modernity in Indonesia*, by Nurcholish Madjid, http://www.renaissance.com.pk/SeptBore2y5.htm.

49. Andi Faisal Bakti, "Nurcholish Madjid and the Paramadina Foundation," *IIAS Newsletter* 34 (July 2004), http://www.iias.nl/nl/34/IIAS_NL34_22.pdf.

50. Greg Barton, "Peaceful Islam and Nurcholish's Lasting Legacy," *Jakarta Post*, 6 September 2005, http://www.thejakartapost.com/news/2005/09/06/peaceful-islam-and-nurcholish039s-lasting-legacy.html.

51. Sikand, review of *The True Face of Islam.*

52. Kull, "Modern Interpretation," 5.

53. Sikand, review of *The True Face of Islam.*

54. Devi Asmarani, "No Glitch to My Inter-faith Union," *Straits Times* (Singapore), 15 August 2004.

55. Ibid.

56. Ibid.

57. See Robert W. Heffner, *Civil Islam: Muslims and Democratization in Indonesia* (Princeton, NJ: Princeton University Press, 2002).

58. Mujiburrahman, "Islam and Politics in Indonesia: The Political Thought of Abdurrahman Wahid," *Islam and Christian-Muslim Relations* 10, no. 3 (October 1999): 342.

59. Ibid.

60. Patrick Buchanan, "Rising Islam May Overwhelm the West," *New Hampshire Sunday News*, 20 August 1989.

61. Rathfelder, "Interview (with) Mustafa Ceric."

62. Dominic Casciani, "Islamic Encounters of the Third Kind," BBC News, 21 February 2005, http://news.bbc.co.uk/2/hi/uk_news/magazine/4283717.stm.

63. Rathfelder, "Interview (with) Mustafa Ceric."

64. Tariq Ramadan, "Europe's Muslims Show the Way," *New Perspectives Quarterly* (Winter 2005), http://www.digitalnpq.org/archive/2005_winter/05_ramadan.html.

65. Tariq Ramadan, "What the West Can Learn from Islam," *Chronicle of Higher Education* 53, no. 24 (16 February 2007), http://chronicle.com/weekly/v53/i24/24b00601.htm.

66. Tariq Ramadan, "Muslim Minorities in Western Europe," lecture at Georgetown University via satellite, Gaston Hall, 11 April 2007.

67. Ibid.

68. Ibid.

69. Ramadan, "Europe's Muslims Show the Way."

70. Casciani, "Islamic Encounters of the Third Kind."

71. Ibid.

72. Ibid.

73. Abdal Hakim Murad, "Tradition or Extradition: The Threat to Muslim Americans," http://www.masud.co.uk/ISLAM/ahm/AHM-TradorExtradNew.htm.

74. Ibid.

75. Ibid.

76. Ibid.

77. Ibid.

78. Azam, "Conversation with Dr. Mustafa Ceric."

79. Ibid.

80. Tariq Ramadan, "The Global Ideology of Fear," *New Perspectives Quarterly* (Spring 2006), http://www.digitalnpq.org/archive/2006_winter/ramadan.html.

81. Ibid.

82. Ibid.

83. Ibid.

84. Heba Raouf, "Muslim Women at the Cross Roads: Cultural and Traditional Values vs. Religious Imperatives," paper presented at "Muslim Women in the Midst of Change" conference, 1–2 September 2007, 3.

85. Mohamed Shuman, *Working Women Leaders: Current Situation and Future Horizons* (Arabic; Cairo: Group for Democratic Development, 1999).

86. In this context, see an account of the situation of women in Kuwait: Haya al-Mughni, *Women in Kuwait: The Politics of Gender* (London: Saqi Books, 2001) 11, 153–66, 178.

87. Gerald Gaus, *Political Concepts and Political Theories* (Boulder, CO: Westview Press, 2000), 241–42.

88. Salwa S. Gomaa, ed., *Governance* (Cairo: Public Administration Research and Consultation Center, 2001),14. See also the shift in political theory from talking about state versus society in a vertical power relation to the study of state-society relation as a complex horizontal relation, and rather as intersecting circles, or as Joel Migdal describes it, seeing "the state in society." Joel Migdal, *State in Society: Studying How States and Societies Transform and Constitute One Another* (Cambridge: Cambridge University Press, 2001).

89. Heba Raouf, "On the Future of Women and Politics in the Arab World," in *Islam in Transition*, ed. John J. Donohue and John L. Esposito, 2nd ed. (New York: Oxford University Press, 2007), 190. On rising interest in engaging people on the local level and empowering the masses of poor men and women, see Deepa Narayan et al., *Voices of the Poor: Crying out for Change* (Oxford: Oxford University Press for the World Bank, 2000), 27, 86–87, 105, http://www.wds.worldbank.org/external/default/WDSContentServer/WDSP/IB/2001/04/07/000094946_01032805491162/Rendered/PDF/multiopage.pdf.

90. For a substantial contribution to a reformist approach from an Islamic perspective, see Yusuf Al Qaradawi, "Introduction," in *Abdul Halim Abou Shukka, Tahrir Al Maraa Fi Aasr Al Risala*, vol. 1 (Cairo: Dar Al-Qalam, 1990), 9–14; Yusuf Qaradawi, *Muslimat Al Ghadd* (Cairo: Dar Al Wafaa, 1992); Yusuf Qaradawi, *Awlaweyyat Al Haraka Al Islameyya Fi Al Marala Al Kadema* (Beirut: Dar Al Resalah, 1991). Al-Azhar issued a fatwa in 1952 denying women the right to be elected to Parliament. See the formal magazine of al-Azhar, *Resalat Al Islam* no. 3, year 4 (July 1952). And note the change in the book published in 1995—just before Beijing: *Al Azhar and Higher Islamic Academy, Ma' Houkouk Al Maraa Fi Al Islam* (Cairo: Al Azhar, 1995).

91. Amina Wadud, *Gender Jihad* (Oxford: Oneworld Publications, 2006), 17.

92. Timothy Winter, "Islam, Irigaray, and the Retrieval of Gender," April 1999, http://www.masud.co.uk/ISLAM/ahm/gender.htm.

93. Dr. Muzammil H. Siddiqi, "Are Women Too Inferior to Lead Men in Prayer?" 21 March 2005, http://www.islamonline.net/servlet/Satellite?pagename=IslamOnline-English-Ask_Scholar/FatwaE/FatwaE&cid=1119503549600.

94. Sahar Ali, "Pakistan Women Socialites Embrace Islam," BBC News, 6 November 2003, http://news.bbc.co.uk/go/pr/fr/-/2/hi/south_asia/3211131.stm.

95. Sharmeen Obaid-Chinoy, "Islamic School for Women: Faithful or Fundamental?" *Globe and Mail*, 29 October 2005; "Al-Huda at a Glance," *Al-Huda International* 2005, http://www.alhudapk.com//home/about-us.

96. Abiya Ahmed, "Bringing About *Change*, Without Causing Much *Rage*," interview with Farhat Hashmi, 21 November 2002, http://jaihoon.com/pearls2/farhathashmi.htm.

97. Ali, "Pakistan Women Socialites Embrace Islam."

98. To download lectures, see "Farhat Hashmi," *Aswat al-Islam: The Sounds of Islam*, http://www.aswatalislam.net/DisplayFilesP.aspx?TitleID=2023.

99. "[Tariqas] Samina Ibrahim's Interview of Dr. Farhat Hashmi," *Newsline*, February 2001, http://stderr.org/pipermail/tariqas/2001-May/000581.html.

100. Ibid.

101. Ibid.

102. Ibid.

103. Ibid.

104. Ahmed, "Bringing About *Change*, Without Causing Much *Rage*."

105. Obaid-Chinoy, "Islamic School for Women."

106. "[Tariqas] Samina Ibrahim's Interview of Dr. Farhat Hashmi."

107. Obaid-Chinoy, "Islamic School for Women."

108. Syed A. Edmonton Rahman, "Islamophobic Sentiments," *Maclean's*, 7 August 2006, 4.

109. Greater London Authority, "Why the Mayor of London will maintain dialogues with all of London's faiths and communities: A reply to the dossier against the Mayor's meeting with Dr Yusuf al-Qaradawi," January 2005, 9, http://www.london.gov.uk/news/docs/qaradawi_dossier.pdf.

110. "Reading in Qaradawism: Part 2, Arts and Entertainment," http://www.allaahuakbar.net/jamaat-e-islaami/qaradawism/arts_and_entertainment.htm.

111. "Egypt's Mufti Gomaa Declares Muslim Woman Can Be President," Islam Today, 5 February 2007, http://www.islamtoday.com/showme2.cfm?cat_id=29&sub_cat_id=892.

112. Ibid.

113. Ali Gomaa, *Al-Bayan Lima Yushgil al-Adhhan* (Cairo: Al-Muqtam lil nashr wal tawzee', 2005), 46.

114. Ibid., 45–46.

115. "[Tariqas] Samina Ibrahim's Interview of Dr. Farhat Hashmi."

116. David Hardacker, "Amr Khaled: Islam's Billy Graham," *Independent*, 4 January 2006, http://news.independent.co.uk/world/middle_east/article336386.ece.

117. "*Life Makers*: Episode 1–Introduction Part 1," Amr Khaled's official Web site, http://www.amrkhaled.net/articles/articles62.html.

118. Ibid.

119. Ibid.

120. "*Life Makers:* Episode 4: Proactiveness—Part 1," Amr Khaled's official Web site, http://www.amrkhaled.net/articles/articles65.html.

121. "Now Danes Respect Muslims," *Al-Ahram Weekly*, 23–29 March 2006, http://weekly.ahram.org.eg/print/2006/787/cg11.htm.

122. Lindsay Wise, "Amr Khaled: Broadcasting the Nahda," *TBS* 13 (Fall 2004), http://www.tbsjournal.com/Archives/Fall04/wiseamrkhaled.html.

123. "Now Danes Respect Muslims."

124. Ibid.

125. Simon Elegant and Jason Tedjasukmana/Bandung, "Holy Man," *Time*, 4 November 2002, http://www.time.com/time/magazine/article/0,9171,386977,00.html.

126. C. W. Watson, "A Popular Indonesian Preacher: The Significance of Aa Gymnastiar," *Journal of the Royal Anthropological Institute*, N.S. 11, no. 4 (December 2005: 778).

127. Alan Sipress, "Indonesian Cleric's Media Empire," *Washington Post*, 2 June 2004.

128. Elegant and Tedjasukmana/Bandung, "Holy Man."

129. Shahed Amanullah, "Post–Feng Shui: Muslim Scholar Now a Management Guru," 7 April 2002, http://www.altmuslim.com/perm.php?id=262_0_26_30_C28.

130. Ibid.

131. Elegant and Tedjasukmana/Bandung, "Holy Man."

132. Greg Sheridan, "Muslim Televangelist Points the Way to Moderation," *Australian*, 1 February 2007.

133. Sipress, "Indonesian Cleric's Media Empire."

134. Devi Asmarani, "Jakarta May Extend Ban on Polygamy After Cleric Takes 2nd Wife," *Straits Times* (Singapore), 7 December 2006.

135. Ibid.

136. Ibid.

Chapter 4

1. Barack Obama, "President Barack Obama's Inaugural Address," White House Blog, 21 January 2009, http://www.whitehouse.gov/blog/inaugural-address.

2. John L. Esposito and Dalia Mogahed, *Who Speaks for Islam? What a Billion Muslims Really Think* (New York: Gallup Press, 2008), 157.

3. Dalia Mogahed and John Esposito, "What a Billion Muslims Think," press statement, 7 April 2008, 2, http://www.radicalmiddleway.co.uk/articles.php?&id=5&art=49&page_49=2.

4. Esposito and Mogahed, *Who Speaks for Islam,* 84.

5. Ibid., 126.

6. Mogahed and Esposito, "What a Billion Muslims Think," 2.

7. Esposito and Mogahed, *Who Speaks for Islam,* 47.

8. Ibid., 48–50.

9. Human Rights Watch, "Egypt: Call for Reform Met with Brutality," 25 May 2005, http://www.hrw.org/en/news/2005/05/25/egypt-calls-reform-met-brutality.

10. Esposito and Mogahed, *Who Speaks for Islam*, 101.

11. Karin Gwinn Wilkins, "Middle Eastern Women in Western Eyes: A Study of U.S. Press Photographs of Middle Eastern Women," in *The U.S. Media and the Middle East: Images and Perception*, ed. Yahya Kamalipour (Westport, CT: Greenwood, 1997), 56.

12. Dalia Mogahed, *Perspectives of Women in the Muslim World*, Gallup Organization, 2006, 1, http://www.gallup.com/press/109699/Perspectives-Women-Muslim-World.aspx.

13. Esposito and Mogahed, *Who Speaks for Islam*, ch. 2.

14. Zainah Anwar, "Bearers of Change," *New York Times*, 5 March 2009, http://www.nytimes.com/2009/03/05/opinion/05iht-edanwar.1.20613399.html?scp=1&sq=%22Bearers%20of%20Change%22&st=cse.

15. Ibid.

16. Esposito and Mogahed, *Who Speaks for Islam*, 51.

17. Mogahed, *Perspectives of Women in the Muslim World*.

18. Esposito and Mogahed, *Who Speaks for Islam*, 48.

19. Azizah al-Hibri, "Who Defines Women's Rights? A Third World Woman's Response," *Human Rights Brief*, 1994, http://www.wcl.american.edu/hrbrief/v2i1/alhibr21.htm.

20. Esposito and Mogahed, *Who Speaks for Islam*, 70.

21. Ibid.

22. Ibid., 81.

23. Ibid., 80.

24. Mogahed and Esposito, "What a Billion Muslims Think," 2.

25. Esposito and Mogahed, *Who Speaks for Islam*, 62.

26. World Economic Forum, *Islam and the West: Annual Report on the State of Dialogue*, January 2008, 26, http://www.weforum.org/pdf/C100/Islam_West.pdf.

27. Zsolt Nyiri, "Muslims in Europe: Basis for Greater Understanding Already Exists," Muslim West Facts Project, Gallup Organization, http://www.muslimwestfacts.com/mwf/105928/Muslims-Europe-Basis-Greater-Understanding-Already-Exists.aspx.

28. *The Great Divide: How Westerners and Muslims View Each Other*, Pew Global Attitudes Project, 22 June 2006, http://pewglobal.org/reports/display.php?ReportID=253.

29. *Muslim Americans: A National Portrait*, Muslim West Facts Project, Gallup Organization, 2009, 50, http://www.muslimwestfacts.com/mwf/116074/Muslim-Americans-National-Portrait.aspx.

30. Kate Connolly, "Germans to Put Muslims through loyalty test," *Telegraph*, 31 December 2005. http://www.telegraph.co.uk/news/worldnews/europe/germany/1506712/Germans-to-put-Muslims-through-loyalty-test.html.

31. Daniel Pipes, "The Danger Within: Militant Islam in America," November 2001, http://www.danielpipes.org/77/the-danger-within-militant-islam-in-america.

32. David Cole, "Are We Safer?" *New York Review of Books*, 9 March 2006, http://www.nybooks.com/articles/18752.

33. Center for American Progress, Center for Democracy and Technology, and Center for National Security Studies, "Strengthening America by Defending Our Liberties: An Agenda for Reform," 31 October 2003, http://www.cnss.org/Defending%20our%20Liberties%20report.pdf.

34. David Cole and Jules Lobel, *Less Safe, Less Free: Why America Is Losing the War on Terror* (New York: New Press, 2007), 3.

35. TRAC Reports, "Criminal Terrorism Enforcement in the United States During the Five Years Since the 9/11/01 Attacks," http://trac.syr.edu/tracreports/terrorism/169.

36. See, for example, Haviv Retting, "Expert: Saudis Have Radicalized 80% of US Mosques," *Jerusalem Post*, 5 December 2005, http://www.jpost.com/servlet/Satellite?cid=1132475689987&pagename=JPost%2FJPArticle%2FShowFull, and Discover the Networks, "Islamic Society of North America (ISNA)," 14 February 2005, http://www.discoverthenetworks.org/groupProfile.asp?grpid=6178.

37. "Secret FBI Report Questions Al Qaeda Capabilities," ABC News, 9 March 2005, http://abcnews.go.com/WNT/Investigation/story?id=566425&page=1.

38. Center for Constitutional Rights, *Restore. Protect. Expand: The Right to Dissent*, 2009, 4, http://ccrjustice.org/files/CCR_100days_dissent_1.pdf.

39. "Franklin Graham: Islam Still Evil," *Water Cooler*, 16 March 2006, http://cbs11tv.com/watercooler/Franklin.Graham.Islam.2.265296.html.

40. Ontario Consultants on Religious Tolerance, "Attacks on Muslims by Conservative Protestants: Graham, Finn, Falwell, Robertson, Swaggart, and Baldwin," 13 May 2003, http://www.religioustolerance.org/reac_ter18b.htm.

41. Mary Jayne McKay, "Zion's Christian Soldiers," *60 Minutes*, 8 June 2003, http://www.cbsnews.com/stories/2002/10/03/60minutes/main524268.shtml.

42. Ontario Consultants on Religious Tolerance, "Attacks on Muslims by Conservative Protestants."

43. Statement by the Patriarch and Local Heads of Church in Jerusalem, "The Jerusalem Declaration on Christian Zionism," 22 August 2006, posted with response on the International Christian Embassy Jerusalem Web site 29 August 2006, http://www.icejusa.org/site/News2?page=NewsArticle&id=5429.

44. Reformed Church in America, "Position on Christian Zionism," 2004, http://www.rca.org/Page.aspx?pid=3839.

45. McKay, "Zion's Christian Soldiers."

46. Ibid.

47. "Root Out the Preachers of Hate," 5 January 2007, http://www.shahidmalikmp.org/News/Root-out-the-preachers-of.

48. Martin Marty, "Fundamentalism in Europe," *Ekklesia: A New Way of Thinking*, 29 August 2008, http://www.ekklesia.co.uk/node/7618.

49. Gallup World Poll, 2007. See also Lydia Saad, "Anti-Muslim Sentiments Fairly Commonplace," Gallup Organization, 10 August 2006, http://www.gallup.com/poll/24073/AntiMuslim-Sentiments-Fairly-Commonplace.aspx.

50. El Nasser, "American Muslims Reject Extremes."

51. Quoted in *Muslim Americans: A National Portrait*, 48.

52. Quoted ibid., 80.

53. Mahmoud Ayoub, "Islam and the Challenge of Religious Pluralism," *Global Dialogue* 2, no. 1 (Winter 2000): 57.

54. Abdulaziz Sachedina, *The Islamic Roots of Democratic Pluralism* (New York: Oxford University Press, 2001), 28.

55. Ibid., 38.

56. Ingrid Mattson, "Respecting the Qur'an," Islamic Society of North America, http://www.isna.net/articles/News/RESPECTING-THE-QURAN.aspx.

57. Sarah Joseph, "Text Book Islam," *emel,* July 2008, 7.

58. Ibid.

59. Gallup Poll 2007 and 2009.

60. Gallup World Poll 2007. See also Saad, "Anti-Muslim Sentiments Fairly Commonplace."

61. David Morris, "Unease over Islam Poll: Critical Views of Muslim Faith Growing Among Americans," ABC News, http://abcnews.go.com/sections/us/World/sept11_islampoll_030911.html.

62. Gallup World Poll 2007.

63. Gallup Poll 2007 and 2009.

64. "World Economic Forum Initiatives Bridge Divides," *Global Giving Matters*, May–June 2005, http://www.synergos.org/globalgivingmatters/features/0506wefinitiatives.htm.

65. World Economic Forum, *Islam and the West*, 105–6.

66. The report is available at http://www.weforum.org/pdf/C100/Islam_West.pdf.

67. United Nations Alliance of Civilizations, *Report of the High-Level Group*, 13 November 2006, http://www.unaoc.org/repository/HLG_Report.pdf.

68. Alliance of Civilizations Media Fund, "About Us," http://www.aocmediafund.org/about_us.php.

69. "Summary," Amman Message official Web site, http://www.ammanmessage.com.

70. "Amman Message," 1 March 2007, ibid.

71. "A Common Word Between Us and You," 10 October 2007, "A Common Word" official Web site, http://www.acommonword.com/index.php?lang=en&page=option1.

72. Pew Forum on Religion and Public Life, *Prospects for Inter-religious Understanding: Will Views Toward Muslims and Islam Follow Historical Trends?* Prepared for delivery at the International Conference on Faith and Service, Washington, DC, 22 March 2006, http://pewforum.org/publications/surveys/Inter-Religious-Understanding.pdf.

73. Jim Lobe, "Evangelical Christians Most Distrustful of Muslims," Inter Press Service, 23 March 2006, http://www.commondreams.org/headlines06/0323-08.htm.

74. "Evangelicals for a Two-State Solution: An Open Letter to President Bush," *Review of Faith and International Affairs*, December 2007, http://www.rfiaonline.org/archives/issues/5-4/179-open-letter-to-president.

75. Chris Seiple, "Ten Terms *Not* to Use with Muslims," *Christian Science Monitor*, 28 March 2009, http://www.csmonitor.com/2009/0328/p09s01-coop.html.

76. Thom Shanker, "Message to Muslim World Gets a Critique," *New York Times*, 28 August 2009.

77. "U.N. Rights Chief Slams Israel over Gaza Violations," Reuters, 14 August 2009, http://news.yahoo.com/s/nm/20090814/wl_nm/us_pelestinians_israel_rights_1.

Selected Bibliography

Reference Works

Cesari, Jocelyne. *Encyclopedia of Islam in the United States*. Westport, CT: Greenwood Press, 2007.

Esposito, John L., ed. *The Oxford Dictionary of Islam*. New York: Oxford University Press, 2003.

——. *The Oxford Encyclopedia of the Islamic World*. New York: Oxford University Press, 2009.

——. *The Oxford Encyclopedia of the Modern Islamic World*. New York: Oxford University Press, 1995.

Introductions to Islam

Aslan, Reza. *No God but God: The Origins, Evolution, and Future of Islam*. New York: Random House, 2005.

Bloom, Jonathan, and Sheila Blair. *Islam: A Thousand Years of Faith and Power*. New Haven, CT: Yale University Press, 2002.

Esposito, John L. *Islam: The Straight Path*. 3rd rev. ed. New York: Oxford University Press, 2005.

——. *What Everyone Needs to Know About Islam*. New York: Oxford University Press, 2002.

Nasr, Sayyed Hossein. *The Heart of Islam: Enduring Values for Humanity*. San Francisco: Harper SanFrancisco, 2002.

——. *Ideals and Realities of Islam*. New rev. ed. Chicago: Kazi Publications, 2000.

Peters, F. E. *Muhammad and the Origins of Islam*. Albany: State University of New York Press, 1994.

History of Islam

Afsaruddin, Asma. *The First Muslims: History and Memory*. Oxford, U.K.: Oneworld, 2008.

Armstrong, Karen. *Islam: A Short History.* New York: Modern Library, 2002.
Donner, Fred McGraw. *The Early Islamic Conquests*. Princeton, NJ: Princeton University Press, 1981.
——. *The Expansion of the Early Islamic State*. Burlington, VT: Ashgate, 2008.
Esposito, John L., ed. *The Oxford History of Islam*. New York: Oxford University Press, 1999.
Lapidus, Ira. *A History of Islamic Societies*. 2nd ed. New York: Cambridge University Press, 2002.
Lowney, Chris. *A Vanished World: Medieval Spain's Golden Age of Enlightenment*. New York: Free Press, 2005.
Sonn, Tamara. *Islam: A Brief History.* 2nd ed. Malden, MA: Blackwell, 2010.
Voll, John Obert. *Islam: Continuity and Change in the Modern World*. 2nd ed. Syracuse, NY: Syracuse University Press, 1994.

Law and Society

Abou El Fadl, Khaled. *Islam and the Challenge of Democracy.* Ed. Joshua Cohen, and Deborah Chasman. Princeton, NJ: Princeton University Press, 2004.
——. *Speaking in God's Name: Islamic Law, Authority and Women*. Oxford, U.K.: Oneworld, 2001.
Afsaruddin, Asma, ed. *Hermeneutics and Honor: Negotiating Female "Public" Space in Islamic/ate Societies*. Cambridge, MA: Distributed for the Center for Middle Eastern Studies at Harvard University by Harvard University Press, 1999.
Ahmed, Leila. *Women and Gender in Islam*. New Haven, CT: Yale University Press, 1993.
Esposito, John L., and Natana J. Delong-Bas. *Women in Muslim Family Law.* 2nd ed. Syracuse, NY: Syracuse University Press, 2001.
Esposito, John L., and Dalia Mogahed. *Who Speaks for Islam? What a Billion Muslims Really Think*. New York: Gallup Press, 2008.
Haddad, Yvonne Yazbeck, and John L. Esposito, eds. *Islam, Gender, and Social Change.* New York: Oxford University Press, 1998.
Mernissi, Fatima. *The Veil and the Male Elite: A Feminist Interpretation of Women's Rights in Islam*. Trans. Mary Jo Lakeland. New York: Addison-Wesley, 1991.
Qaradawi, Yusuf al-. *The Lawful and Prohibited in Islam*. Qum, Iran: Islamic Culture and Relations Organization, 1998.
Ramadan, Tariq. *Radical Reform: Islamic Ethics and Liberation*. New York: Oxford University Press, 2008.

Islam in the West

Cesari, Jocelyne. *Muslims in the West After 9/11: Religions, Politics and Law.* London: Routledge, 2008.
Daniel, Norman. *Islam and the West: The Making of an Image.* Rev. ed. Oxford, U.K.: Oneworld, 1993.
Esposito, John L., Yvonne Haddad, and Jane Smith. *Immigrant Faiths: Christians, Jews, and Muslims Becoming Americans*. Walnut Creek, CA: Alta Mira Press, 2002.
Haddad, Yvonne Yazbeck, ed. *Muslims in the West: From Sojourners to Citizens*. New York: Oxford University Press, 2002.

Haddad, Yvonne Yazbeck, and John L. Esposito, eds. *Muslims on the Americanization Path.* New York: Oxford University Press, 2000.
Haddad, Yvonne Yazbeck, Jane I. Smith, and Kathleen M. Moore. *Muslim Women in America: The Challenge of Islamic Identity.* New York: Oxford University Press, 2006.
Hunter, Shireen. *Islam, Europe's Second Religion.* Westport, CT: Praeger, 2002.
Klausen, Jytte. *The Islamic Challenge: Politics and Religion in Western Europe.* New York: Oxford University Press, 2005.
Lewis, Philip. *Islamic Britain: Religion, Politics and Identity Among British Muslims.* London: I. B. Tauris, 1994.
Nielsen, Jorgen. *Muslims in Western Europe.* 3rd ed. Edinburgh: Edinburgh University Press, 2005.
Ramadan, Tariq. *To Be a European Muslim.* Leicester, U.K.: Islamic Foundation, 2003.
——. *Western Muslims and the Future of Islam.* New York: Oxford University Press, 2004.
Smith, Jane I. *Islam in America.* New York: Columbia University Press, 1999.

Politics, Violence, and Terrorism

Abou El Fadl, Khaled. *The Great Theft: Wrestling Islam from the Extremists.* New York: HarperSanFranscico, 2005.
——. *The Place of Tolerance in Islam.* Ed. Joshua Cohen and Ian Lague. Boston: Beacon Press, 2002.
Ahmed, Akbar S. *Islam Under Siege: Living Dangerously in a Post-Honor World.* Malden, MA: Polity Press, 2003.
Ahmed, Akbar S., and Brian Forst, eds. *After Terror: Promoting Dialogue Among Civilizations.* Malden, MA: Polity Press, 2005.
Bunt, Gary R. *iMuslims: Rewiring the House of Islam.* Chapel Hill: University of North Carolina Press, 2009.
——. *Islam in the Digital Age: E-Jihad, Online Fatwas and Cyber Islamic Environments.* London: Pluto Press, 2003.
Esposito, John L. *The Islamic Threat: Myth or Reality?* Rev. ed. New York: Oxford University Press, 1999.
——. *Unholy War: Terror in the Name of Islam.* New York, New York: Oxford University Press, 2002.,
——, ed. *Voices of Resurgent Islam.* New York, New York: Oxford University Press, 1983.
Esposito, John L., and John O. Voll. *Islam and Democracy.* New York: Oxford University Press, 1996.
——. *Makers of Contemporary Islam.* New York: Oxford University Press, 2001.
Esposito, John L., John O. Voll, and Osman Bakar, eds. *Asian Islam in the 21st Century.* New York: Oxford University Press, 2007.
Hroub, Khaled. *Hamas: Political Thought and Practice.* Washington, DC: Institute for Palestine Studies, 2000.
Jansen, Johannes J. G. *The Neglected Duty: The Creed of Sadat's Assassins and Islamic Resurgence in the Middle East.* New York: Free Press, 1988.
Kepel, Gilles, and Jean-Pierre Milelli, eds. *Al Qaeda in Its Own Words.* Trans. Pascal Ghazaleh. Annotated ed. Cambridge, MA: Belknap Press of Harvard University Press, 2008.
Kimball, Charles. *When Religion Becomes Evil.* New York: HarperCollins, 2002.

Laden, Osama bin. *Messages to the World: The Statements of Osama bin Laden*. Ed. Bruce Lawrence. Annotated ed. New York: Verso, 2005.
Lewis, Bernard. *The Crisis of Islam: Holy War and Unholy Terror.* New York: Modern Library, 2003.
——. *What Went Wrong? Western Impact and Middle Eastern Response.* 4th ed. New York: Oxford University Press, 2002.
Mamdani, Mahmood. *Good Muslim, Bad Muslim: America, the Cold War, and the Roots of Terror.* New York: Three Rivers, 2005.
Mandaville, Peter. *Global Political Islam: International Relations of the Muslim World.* London: Routledge, 2007.
Nasr, Vali. *The Shia Revival: How Conflicts Within Islam Will Shape the Future*. New York: Norton, 2006.
Peters, Rudolph. *Jihad in Classical and Modern Islam*. Princeton, NJ: Markus Wiener, 1996.
Qutb, Sayyid. *Milestones.* Rev. ed. Boll Ridge, IN: American Trust Publications, 1991.
——. This Religion of Islam. Chicago: Kazi Publications, 1996.
Rashid, Ahmed. *Taliban: Militant Islam, Oil, and Fundamentalism in Central Asia*. New Haven, CT: Yale University Press, 2000.
Roy, Olivier. *Globalized Islam: The Search for a New Ummah*. New York: Columbia University Press, 2004.
Saad-Ghorayeb, Amal. *Hizbu'llah: Politics and Religion*. London: Pluto Press, 2002.
Sachedina, Abdulaziz Abdulhussein. *The Islamic Roots of Democratic Pluralism*. New York: Oxford University Press, 2001.

Muslim-Christian Relations

Armour, Rollin. *Islam, Christianity, and the West: A Troubled History.* Maryknoll, NY: Orbis, 2002.
Armstrong, Karen. *The Battle for God: Fundamentalism in Judaism, Christianity, and Islam*. New York: Alfred A. Knopf, 2000.
——. *Holy War: The Crusades and Their Impact on Today's World*. 2nd ed. New York: Anchor Books, 2001.
Ayoub, Mahmoud. *A Muslim View of Christianity: Essays on Dialogue.* Ed. Irfan A. Omar. Maryknoll, NY: Orbis Books, 2007.
Bill, James A., and John Alden Williams. *Roman Catholics and Shi'i Muslims*. Chapel Hill: University of North Carolina Press, 2002.
Bulliet, Richard W. *The Case for Islamo-Christian Civilization*. New York: Columbia University Press, 2004.
Cragg, Kenneth. *The Call of the Minaret*. Oxford, U.K.: Oneworld, 2000.
——. *Islam Among the Spires: An Oxford Reverie*. London: Melisende, 2000.
——. *Muhammad and the Christian: A Question of Response*. Oxford: Oneworld, 1999.
Daniel, Norman. *The Arabs and Mediaeval Europe*. London: Longman, 1975.
——. *Islam and the West: The Making of an Image*. London: Oneworld, 2000.
Dardess, George. *Meeting Islam: A Guide for Christians*. Brewster, MA: Paraclete Press, 2005.
Faruqi, Isma'il R al-. *Islam and Other Faiths*. Ed. Ataullah Siddiqui. Leicester, U.K.: Islamic Foundation and International Institute of Islamic Thought, 1998.

Fitzgerald, Michael L., and John Borelli. *Interfaith Dialogue: A Catholic View.* Maryknoll, NY: Orbis, 2006.

Griffith, Sidney. *The Beginnings of Christian Theology in Arabic: Muslim-Christian Encounters in the Early Islamic Period.* Burlington, VT: Ashgate, 2002.

——. *The Church in the Shadow of the Mosque.* Princeton, NJ: Princeton University Press, 2008.

Goddard, Hugh. *A History of Christian-Muslim Relations.* Chicago: New Amsterdam Books, 2001.

Haddad, Yvonne Yazbeck, and Wadi Z. Haddad, eds. *Christian-Muslim Encounters.* Gainesville: University Press of Florida, 1995.

Kimball, Charles. *Striving Together: A Way Forward in Christian-Muslim Relations.* Maryknoll, NY: Orbis, 1991.

Menocal, Maria Rosa. *The Ornament of the World: How Muslims, Jews, and Christians Created a Culture of Tolerance in Medieval Spain.* New York: Little, Brown, 2002.

Peters, F. E. *Children of Abraham.* Princeton, NJ: Princeton University Press, 2006.

Smith, Jane I. *Muslims, Christians, and the Challenge of Interfaith Dialogue.* New York: Oxford University Press, 2007.

Southern, R. W. *Western Views of Islam in the Middle Ages.* Cambridge, MA: Harvard University Press, 1978.

Watt, W. Montgomery. *Muslim-Christian Encounters: Perceptions and Misperceptions.* London: Routledge, 1991.

Index